Controller-Based Wireless LAN Fundamentals

Jeff Smith, Jake Woodhams, Robert Marg

Cisco Press

800 East 96th Street

Indianapolis, IN 46240

Controller-Based Wireless LAN Fundamentals

Jeff Smith, Jake Woodhams, Robert Marg

Copyright© 2011 Cisco Systems, Inc.

Published by:
Cisco Press
800 East 96th Street
Indianapolis, IN 46240 USA

Printed in the United States of America

First Printing November 2010

Library of Congress Cataloging-in-Publication data is on file.

ISBN-13: 978-1-58705-825-7

ISBN-10: 1-58705-825-1

Warning and Disclaimer

This book is designed to provide information about controller-based wireless local-area networks. Every effort has been made to make this book as complete and as accurate as possible, but no warranty or fitness is implied.

The information is provided on an "as is" basis. The authors, Cisco Press, and Cisco Systems, Inc. shall have neither liability nor responsibility to any person or entity with respect to any loss or damages arising from the information contained in this book or from the use of the discs or programs that may accompany it.

The opinions expressed in this book belong to the author and are not necessarily those of Cisco Systems, Inc.

Trademark Acknowledgments

All terms mentioned in this book that are known to be trademarks or service marks have been appropriately capitalized. Cisco Press or Cisco Systems, Inc., cannot attest to the accuracy of this information. Use of a term in this book should not be regarded as affecting the validity of any trademark or service mark.

Corporate and Government Sales

The publisher offers excellent discounts on this book when ordered in quantity for bulk purchases or special sales, which may include electronic versions and/or custom covers and content particular to your business, training goals, marketing focus, and branding interests. For more information, please contact: **U.S. Corporate and Government Sales**   1-800-382-3419   corpsales@pearsontechgroup.com

For sales outside the United States, please contact: **International Sales**   international@pearsoned.com

Feedback Information

At Cisco Press, our goal is to create in-depth technical books of the highest quality and value. Each book is crafted with care and precision, undergoing rigorous development that involves the unique expertise of members from the professional technical community.

Readers' feedback is a natural continuation of this process. If you have any comments regarding how we could improve the quality of this book, or otherwise alter it to better suit your needs, you can contact us through email at feedback@ciscopress.com. Please make sure to include the book title and ISBN in your message.

We greatly appreciate your assistance.

Publisher: Paul Boger

Associate Publisher: Dave Dusthimer

Executive Editor: Mary Beth Ray

Managing Editor: Sandra Schroeder

Senior Development Editor: Christopher Cleveland

Senior Project Editor: Tonya Simpson

Copy Editor: John Edwards

Editorial Assistant: Vanessa Evans

Indexer: Tim Wright

Manager, Global Certification: Erik Ullanderson

Business Operation Manager, Cisco Press: Anand Sundaram

Technical Editors: Saurabh Bhasin, Sujit Ghosh

Proofreader: Sheri Cain

Book Designer: Louisa Adair

Cover Designer: Sandra Schroeder

Composition: Mark Shirar

Americas Headquarters
Cisco Systems, Inc.
San Jose, CA

Asia Pacific Headquarters
Cisco Systems (USA) Pte. Ltd.
Singapore

Europe Headquarters
Cisco Systems International BV
Amsterdam, The Netherlands

Cisco has more than 200 offices worldwide. Addresses, phone numbers, and fax numbers are listed on the Cisco Website at **www.cisco.com/go/offices**.

CCDE, CCENT, Cisco Eos, Cisco HealthPresence, the Cisco logo, Cisco Lumin, Cisco Nexus, Cisco StadiumVision, Cisco TelePresence, Cisco WebEx, DCE, and Welcome to the Human Network are trademarks; Changing the Way We Work, Live, Play, and Learn and Cisco Store are service marks; and Access Registrar, Aironet, AsyncOS, Bringing the Meeting To You, Catalyst, CCDA, CCDP, CCIE, CCIP, CCNA, CCNP, CCSP, CCVP, Cisco, the Cisco Certified Internetwork Expert logo, Cisco IOS, Cisco Press, Cisco Systems, Cisco Systems Capital, the Cisco Systems logo, Cisco Unity, Collaboration Without Limitation, EtherFast, EtherSwitch, Event Center, Fast Step, Follow Me Browsing, FormShare, GigaDrive, HomeLink, Internet Quotient, IOS, iPhone, iQuick Study, IronPort, the IronPort logo, LightStream, Linksys, MediaTone, MeetingPlace, MeetingPlace Chime Sound, MGX, Networkers, Networking Academy, Network Registrar, PCNow, PIX, PowerPanels, ProConnect, ScriptShare, SenderBase, SMARTnet, Spectrum Expert, StackWise, The Fastest Way to Increase Your Internet Quotient, TransPath, WebEx, and the WebEx logo are registered trademarks of Cisco Systems, Inc. and/or its affiliates in the United States and certain other countries.

All other trademarks mentioned in this document or website are the property of their respective owners. The use of the word partner does not imply a partnership relationship between Cisco and any other company. (0812R)

About the Authors

Jeff Smith is a wireless consulting systems engineer in the Cisco Systems Borderless Networking Organization. His 25 years of experience include the planning, analysis, design, implementation, installation, and support of numerous wireless network-based solutions for enterprises, municipalities, hospitals, universities, airports, warehouses, mines, and product manufacturers worldwide. He has developed and instructed dozens of training courses on wireless networking topics. Prior to joining Cisco Systems, Jeff was an early employee at several wireless and security startup companies. Jeff's education includes a bachelor's degree in electrical engineering and a master's degree in telecommunications with emphasis on wireless communications. Jeff's certifications include CWNE (Certified Wireless Network Expert), IEEE WCET (Wireless Communications Engineering Technology Certification), and CISSP (Certified Information Systems Security Professional).

Jake Woodhams is a senior manager of technical marketing in the Cisco Wireless Networking Business Unit. In this role, he is responsible for technical product definition and systems architecture, focusing on Cisco Unified Wireless LAN architecture. He hass been working with wireless technology at Cisco for seven years and has an intimate knowledge of the protocols and products in the Cisco wireless portfolio. As a writer, he's the author of numerous white papers and design and deployment guides as well as several contributed articles.

Robert Marg is a wireless consulting systems engineer in the Cisco Systems Borderless Networks Organization. As a technical leader in wireless, Robert is responsible for planning, designing, and supporting numerous wireless network–based solutions for enterprises, hospitals, universities, manufacturers, and K–12 customers. Prior to his role as a wireless consulting systems engineer, Robert spent time as a member of the federal, public sector, enterprise, and commercial sales organizations as a systems engineer, helping customers solve business challenges with technical solutions. Mr. Marg holds a bachelor's degree in bacteriology from the University of Wisconsin–Madison. As a writer, Robert has been the author of numerous white papers and a technical editor for the Cisco Press *CCNA Exam Certification Guide*.

About the Contributing Author

Jeff DiMaio is a consulting systems engineer in the Cisco Systems Unified Communications Organization. Jeff specializes in unified communications and wireless and security technologies. Prior to joining Cisco, Jeff worked for the leading provider of Voice over WLAN solutions. Jeff has been active in the Wi-Fi Alliance and other industry organizations and has helped develop the Wi-Fi Multimedia (WMM) specification. Jeff recently finished his graduate work at the University of Colorado, where he earned a master's degree in interdisciplinary telecommunications.

About the Technical Reviewers

Saurabh Bhasin has been involved with various wireless technologies over the years, since the first days of 802.11 becoming a standard and, more recently, with the evolution of the wireless industry to 802.11n. Mr. Bhasin has been with the Cisco Wireless Networking Business Unit for more than four years, and in this role, he has worked closely with Cisco technology partners (enabling advanced services over wireless networks), leading key architectural features and training various members of the Cisco and partner community in person or through the numerous papers he has authored.

In his past, Mr. Bhasin has authored numerous articles for reputable industry publications. He has also worked with a packet analysis company, thus completely understanding the inner workings of a network.

Sujit Ghosh, CCIE No. 7204, is a manager of the technical marketing team in the Wireless Networking Business Unit of Cisco and has 16 years of experience in the networking industry. Sujit has extensive customer contact and is responsible for developing and marketing enterprise networking solutions using the Cisco Unified Wireless Network. He has focused on the areas of wireless LAN security and wireless/wired LAN integration.

Prior to joining the Wireless Business Unit, Sujit worked as a TAC engineer at Cisco for five years on the Security/VPN team working on security, wireless, and VPN products. Sujit actively speaks at the Networkers Conference on the subjects of deploying secure wireless LANs, troubleshooting wireless LANs, designing and deploying 802.11 wireless LANs with centralized controllers and guest access design, and deploying wired and 802.11 wireless LANs.

Dedications

We dedicate this book to our families, who put up with many nights and weekends spent on rewrites.

Acknowledgments

We would like to thank the Pearson production team for their time and effort in creating this book:

- Thanks to Mary Beth Ray for getting this book contracted and managing the process from several restarts and changes in authors.

- Thanks to Christopher Cleveland, Tonya Simpson, and John Edwards for their editing of the book and perseverance in dealing with the authors' crazy schedules and missing of deadlines.

- Thanks to the many others at Pearson who were part of developing and producing this book.

- Thanks to our colleagues at Cisco who have been supportive in this project.

We would like to thank Tom Carpenter for providing technical feedback on the many topics this book covers.

Contents at a Glance

Contents

Icons Used in This Book

Access Point   Dual-Mode Access Point   Mesh Access Point   Lightweight Single Radio Access Point   Lightweight Double Radio Access Point   WiSM   WLAN Controller   Wi-Fi Tag   Wireless Bridge

Router   Route Switch Processor   Multilayer Switch   Ethernet Switch   Mobile Services Engine   Cisco 7505   Service Router   Data Center Switch   IntelliSwitch Stack   Voice-Enabled Switch

IP Telephony Router   Management Engine   Cisco ASA   Network Management Appliance   PC   Laptop   Printer   Server   Web Server

Cell Phone   PDA   Mobile Access Phone   Network Cloud   Wireless Connectivity

Command Syntax Conventions

The conventions used to present command syntax in this book are the same conventions used in the IOS Command Reference. The Command Reference describes these conventions as follows:

- **Boldface** indicates commands and keywords that are entered literally as shown. In actual configuration examples and output (not general command syntax), boldface indicates commands that are manually input by the user (such as a **show** command).

- *Italic* indicates arguments for which you supply actual values.

- Vertical bars (|) separate alternative, mutually exclusive elements.

- Square brackets ([ ]) indicate an optional element.

- Braces ({ }) indicate a required choice.

- Braces within brackets ([{ }]) indicate a required choice within an optional element.

Introduction

Since the first Cisco Press book on the fundamentals of 802.11 networks, much has changed. Wireless local-area networks (WLAN) have grown dramatically in size and scope, creating changes for traditional wireless deployment architectures. Many of the challenges with prior generations of wireless networking designs have been greatly reduced with development of the Cisco Wireless Unified Network (CUWN) architecture. The Cisco Unified approach has allowed wireless networks to efficiently scale to meet new requirements and business needs. WLAN controllers rapidly became the dominant wireless architecture and have been standardized through the IETF Control and Provisioning of Wireless Access Points (CAPWAP) protocol. CAPWAP defines an industry-standard protocol for how controllers manage wireless access points. The other foundational change to wireless has been the increased performance supported by the 802.11n amendment to the IEEE 802.11 wireless LAN standard. While the controller removed the management and scaling constraints, 802.11n is removing many of the performance constraints with wireless networking. The results have been a shift from wireless networks being a convenience to becoming mission-critical for most organizations.

This book focuses on introducing the concepts and reasoning behind controller-based wireless and higher-performance wireless networks. The elements of wireless LAN controller (WLC)–based WLANs are introduced, and the goal is to provide an update on many of the fundamentals that have been introduced since the publication of the Cisco Press 802.11 fundamentals book. This book is targeted toward IT engineers who are new to wireless controllers, 802.11n, Wireless Control System (WCS), wireless multicast, and mission-critical wireless networks. This book should be viewed as an introduction to wireless controllers and the knowledge needed to support life cycle design and support of controller-based architectures. Organizations new to wireless controllers and those migrating from legacy wireless networks to controller-based and 802.11n wireless networks will find this book to be a valuable guide.

This book also has a wealth of knowledge gleaned from the authors' experiences in terms of guidelines, deployments, and configuration of wireless LAN architectures.

Goals and Methods

The goal of this book is to introduce you to the concepts and principles of mission-critical, high-performance, controller-based wireless LAN deployments. To accomplish this, the book includes the following elements:

- **Drivers for the migration to controller architecture:** The book covers the evolution, challenges, and reasoning about why WLAN controllers have become essential in modern WLAN deployments.

- **Elements of the controller-based wireless architecture:** The book introduces each of the elements in the end-to-end controller-based wireless architecture.

- **Wireless controller WLAN design and implementation:** The book includes details on how to design and implement WLANs with wireless controllers.

■ **Wireless security with a wireless LAN controller:** This book covers the key principles of security WLANs with a wireless LAN controller.

■ **Wireless multicast design and implementation:** This book covers the key principles of both wired and wireless multicast implementations within the wireless LAN controller.

Who Should Read This Book

This book is planned and written for network engineers who design, configure, implement, and maintain wireless networks, with an emphasis on WLAN controller basics, 802.11n principles, wireless architecture designs, and wireless network management. This book also focuses on the "newbie" to wireless networking in the hopes of clarifying the alphabet soup commonly known as IEEE 802.11 and introducing the key principles to designing and managing a wireless architecture.

How This Book Is Organized

Although this book can be read from cover to cover, it is designed to be flexible and allow you to easily move between chapters and sections of chapters to learn just the information that you need.

The book covers the following topics:

■ **Chapter 1, "The Need for Controller-Based Wireless Networks":** This chapter describes the evolution of WLANs and the principles that drove the development of the wireless LAN controller.

■ **Chapter 2, "Wireless LAN Protocols":** This chapter explains radio wave fundamentals so that you have the basis for understanding the complexities of deploying wireless LANs.

■ **Chapter 3, "802.11n":** This chapter describes the key features provided by 802.11n. 802.11n increases the performance and reliability of WLAN through protocol improvements and the support for multiple input, multiple output (MIMO) radio systems. The concepts on how MIMO improves performance are presented.

■ **Chapter 4, "Cisco Unified Wireless LAN Security Fundamentals":** This chapter explains the key elements of wireless security in the unified wireless networks.

■ **Chapter 5, "Design Considerations":** This chapter provides a background and consideration for designing unified wireless networks.

■ **Chapter 6, "Cisco Unified Wireless LAN Architectures":** This chapter explains the details of the unified wireless LAN architecture.

■ **Chapter 7, "Troubleshooting":** This chapter focuses on how to troubleshoot client issues using the unified wireless networks.

- **Chapter 8, "Introduction to WCS":** This chapter provides an overview of the key features and principles and configuration steps that you should complete when deploying a wireless LAN management solution. This chapter also navigates you through the key menus within the WCS management platform, highlighting the key elements in planning, designing, and configuring the Cisco Unified Wireless Network architecture.

- **Chapter 9, "Next-Generation Advanced Topics: Multicast":** This chapter focuses on both the wired and wireless design and implementation phases of multicast. This chapter takes a deep approach to multicast, with a detailed emphasis of controller-based multicast design best practices and principles.

Chapter 1

The Need for Controller-Based Wireless Networks

Wireless local-area networks (WLAN) have evolved as the quantity and types of mobile devices have increased. The number of devices that support Wi-Fi continues to expand. The term *Wi-Fi* is an industry acronym meaning wireless fidelity for devices with support for the IEEE 802.11 wireless standard. This means the device has been certified to meet interoperability standards established by the Wi-Fi Alliance. The type of devices that include Wi-Fi support continues to expand from laptops to many other devices, such as cameras, phones, automobiles, and other consumer devices. The uses of Wi-Fi have expanded beyond just data usage, often including voice, video, and innovative contextual applications. Contextual usage is a combination of application data, voice, and video services with information provided by the data network, such as device location, security posture, or access media type information. Contextual applications increase the value or relevance of data service by using the additional metadata provided by the wireless network. An example of a contextual data application would be a repair dispatch system generating work orders, using the WLAN's location information to dispatch the closest technician to repair a failed device.

Many organizations use wireless networks with applications specifically created for the mobile environment, which requires the WLAN to provide secure communications anyplace the user might wander. An example would be a hospital where paper records are no longer utilized. This requires access to the patient's electronic medical record that is available at all locations to provide health services. With pervasive WLAN coverage, further optimization to healthcare quality and costs can be achieved utilizing the WLAN. For example, many diagnostic and monitor systems utilize devices that load patient data through the WLAN directly into the patient's medical record. It is practical today to enable more devices to always be on the network because there is no longer wired network cable encumbering device usage. Regardless of the industry or application, everywhere you turn, people and devices are leveraging an always-on network through WLANs. This has driven more pervasive WLANs to be deployed, with increased size and scope of use. The reliance on WLANs has changed from being a convenience to being a critical edge access method.

WLANs have become an essential component for most organizations and are mission critical for many. The increased reliance on WLANs has increased the coverage, security, performance, and reliability requirements. Numerous impairments to usage of WLANs have been identified as the usage and scale of WLANs have increased. Originally, WLANs were deployed with the use of a relatively simple architecture of standalone enterprise access points (AP). The early WLAN APs were built to simply translate between the radio frequency (RF) media and Ethernet media, as shown in Figure 1-1.

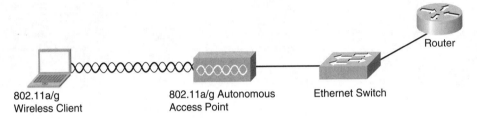

802.11a/g
Wireless Client

802.11a/g Autonomous
Access Point

Ethernet Switch

Router

Figure 1-1   *Early WLANs Simply Extended the Wired LAN to Wireless Using Standalone Autonomous Access Points*

With increased adoption, additional functions are needed beyond simply translating the traffic between media types. Examples of the additional functions needed include increased wireless security, wireless intrusion prevention, Layer 3 roaming, centralized management, application services, and operational support and reporting capabilities. As with all technology evolutions, numerous approaches were considered and tested for increasing the functionality of WLANs. Without going through all the trials and tribulations of what worked and failed along the way, the concept of a wireless switch emerged to address the shortcomings of WLANs being built using the autonomous or IOS AP architecture. Wireless switches later became referred to as *wireless LAN controllers (WLC)*, and this architecture is also referred to as lightweight APs, Cisco Unified Wireless Network (CUWN), controller-based architecture, and WLC-based architecture. With lightweight APs, part of the functionality moved from the AP to the wireless controller. The key concept is to centralize some functions of the WLAN to optimize the overall system's operation, where the system's operation is a combination of the network elements and the human element needed to install, maintain, and operate the WLAN. Centralizing some functionality created a WLAN system versus a system of disparate network elements, with numerous access points, switches, wireless clients, and the RF media working together in a more ad hoc manner. The centralized approach implements a control and management plane across the many functions in the end-to-end WLAN system.

The main drivers for changing from an autonomous to a centralized WLAN are operational costs, wireless expertise, and risk management. Pervasive WLANs and the inherent requirement for a large number of access points put pressure on the staff's abilities and in-house expertise. A simpler means to manage the WLAN was needed. More RF-specific functions needed to be automated in the infrastructure, reducing the amount of RF expertise and workload required to design, implement, and operate a large WLAN. Operational expenses often limit the capabilities of WLANs. The initial deployment and ongoing support costs for autonomous APs were prohibitive because of the continuous requirement to tune and optimize the autonomous AP WLAN. This is because of the nature of the RF environment constantly changing. Everything from new sources of interference to new walls, machines, and additional people cause the Wi-Fi environment to change. This requires frequent tuning to maintain consistent operations. Autonomous AP tuning is the changing of each AP's channel (frequency) and transmit power level to restore or optimize wireless communications. The centralized AP architecture automates the AP RF tuning with Radio Resource Management (RRM), which is discussed in more detail throughout the book. RRM essentially automates the RF tuning, with the centralized controller providing built-in automated RF expertise in the infrastructure instead of relying on technicians to constantly take measurements and make manual adjustments. A comparable wired network analogy is building a network with static routes versus building a network using a routing protocol such as Enhanced IGRP (EIGRP) to automate route distribution.

The WLAN controller architecture has prevailed in the marketplace as the best architecture to address the needs for the next generation of business-class WLANs. This architecture is also referred to as the *Cisco Unified Wireless Network (CUWN) architecture*. The prior Cisco WLAN architecture is referred to as the *autonomous AP architecture*. The autonomous AP architecture did not go away with the introduction of the controller-based architecture; it became an additional architecture solution for the WLAN designer to consider based on an organization's requirements. The majority of Cisco WLANs have transitioned to a controller-based architecture because it addresses a wide array of issues identified through the evolution of 802.11 WLAN usages. The tipping point for the shift from WLAN architectures using standalone APs to WLC-based WLAN architectures occurred around 2006. In 2004, Airespace published the Lightweight Access Point Protocol (LWAPP) standard as an RFC based on the Internet Engineering Task Force (IETF) Control and Provisioning of Wireless Access Points (CAPWAP) standard. In 2005, Cisco acquired Airespace and started shipping wireless LAN controllers. By 2006, the majority of large new Cisco-based WLANs were deployed using wireless LAN controllers. In fact, many WLANs are already at the state where they are used as the primary access network access method for many users. With this paradigm shift, the user expectations have changed to demand that WLANs have the same reliability and resiliency characteristics that wired Ethernet provides today for the access layer.

To gain a better understanding of controller-based WLAN fundamentals and the other enhancements created to solve WLAN issues, this chapter takes a closer look at some of the issues that drove the architecture for next-generation WLAN technologies to use WLAN controllers and other WLAN technologies. This book will not scrutinize each minute change that brought about the evolution of WLANs; rather, the focus is on the more practical and relevant issues to the WLAN practitioner who needs an operational and design-level understanding of the WLAN controller (WLC) architecture and other newer technologies.

This chapter begins with a discussion of some of the problems that WLCs were created to alleviate. Next, the chapter reviews additional issues that needed to be resolved because the initial 802.11a/b/g standards were created and the first Cisco Press book on

WLAN fundamentals was published. The intent is to transition your knowledge from WLAN fundamentals to understanding the fundamentals of controller-based WLANs.

Why Wireless LAN Controllers Were Created

WLCs were created to solve numerous issues in the deployment and operation of WLANs. WLANs can obviously be implemented without the use of a WLC as is evident by all the WLANs that were deployed for many years before the invention of the WLC.

The importance of WLCs to implementing WLANs today is analogous to the importance routers have to interconnecting networks. Consider that Ethernet-based IP networks did not originally have routers. The router was invented, along with router protocols, through an evolution of necessity. The router was invented to address the problems in scaling the size of LANs and the issues limiting the numbers of internetwork connections that could be established. Routers provided enhanced functionality and reduced the management costs that would have been incurred from trying to manage a business-class network environment. Can you imagine what it would be like today if we did not have routing protocols running on routers? You would have to create thousands of static routes or routing table entries for each network and device manually. Without the use of routers, networks would be difficult to manage, and they would not be able to scale to provide large intranets as well as have the enormous numbers of Internet connections we have today. Similar to the role that the routers running routing protocols played for wired Ethernet-based IP networks, the WLC and its associated protocols solve analogous issues for WLANs.

The WLC was invented from an evolution of needs. The needs for the WLAN changed because of more pervasive deployments with heavy reliance by the business, organizational, and user communities. WLANs started as a convenience for most organizations, a nice-to-have feature, with small or hotspot-style deployments that extended the LAN through wireless to a few devices. The size and coverage of WLANs quickly grew to be a mainstream access requirement for many organizations. More and more applications continue to be written specifically to take advantage of wireless communications, driving WLANs to become a mainstream access method. As the size and criticality of WLANs increase, many realized that scaling, reliability, security, and operating costs would limit the ability to deploy business-class WLANs. The WLC was invented to address these issues. The transition to WLC-based WLANs allows scalability and does not require hundreds or thousands of man-hours to be consumed with labor-intensive installation, configuration, and maintenance tasks as the size of the WLAN increases.

To understand controller-based WLAN network fundamentals, you must first understand the problems that WLCs were created to solve. This knowledge will help you understand when, where, and how to apply the WLCs. This knowledge will also provide valuable insight into why the WLC solution differs in operation compared to prior noncontroller-based WLANs. While WLCs address the majority of WLAN needs, they might not always be the most practical solution for all situations. As with any technology solution and architecture, the individuals responsible for designing the WLC architecture made design decisions for optimizing the architecture and to solve specific issues. Where practical, the implication of these design decisions or trade-offs will be highlighted to help increase your understanding of how WLCs work. To further relate how controller-based wireless fundamentals apply to solving business application requirements and enabling next-generation solutions, specific examples will also be provided later in this book.

Why You Need to Use a Wireless LAN Controller

Numerous issues are driving the need for WLCs. The need for an organization to deploy the WLAN to multiple locations or deploy large numbers of APs will often be the initial driver for the need of a WLC-based network implementation. A WLC-based network implementation might not make sense, however, for a business with a single location that has a WLAN with only one or a few APs.

For many organizations, the greatest number of network infrastructure devices will be wireless APs. This is true for most educational institutions, hospitals, warehouses, retail environments, and enterprises networks. It is not uncommon to hear of organizations with wireless LAN deployments consisting of 1000 APs or more. Some schools have as many as one AP per classroom. Some organizations have over 30,000 access points installed using WLCs. Can you imagine the management challenges and potential operating expense if you had to manage that many APs independently?

A network with a few hundred wireless components has the same challenges and relative operating expenses as a wired network—from configuring, monitoring, and maintaining hundreds of devices. The operational expenses for managing so many devices drive the need for a centralized methodology using WLCs. Some of the concepts that controller-based wireless networks use for dealing with the issues of managing and scaling the wireless LANs were learned from cellular phone deployments. The cellular phone industry learned a valuable lesson many years before Wi-Fi on how to build large, reliable wireless networks without breaking the bank on operating costs. They learned that the access, control, and traffic-forwarding (transport) functions must be separated to scale and control operating costs. This similar concept applies to WLAN controllers. Figure 1-2 illustrates the major functions needed for a wireless LAN.

Figure 1-2   *Functional Elements in a WLAN*

Controller-Based WLAN Functional and Elemental Architecture

This section examines the functions within the WLC architecture, also referred to as the CUWN architecture. There are a few mandatory elements in the CUWN architecture and various optional elements. LWAPP APs or CAPWAP APs require a WLC, which acts as the brains and manages the coordination efforts between the managed APs. Figure 1-3 shows the elements of the CUWN architecture. Figure 1-4 shows how those elements map to the functional elements in a controller-based architecture implementation. The controller-based architecture enables security across all the functional areas. Compare the controller-based architecture to how the functional elements are implemented in an autonomous AP architecture (also referred to as a standalone or fat AP architecture), as shown in Figure 1-5. In the autonomous architecture, each AP operates independently, with all of its functionality self-contained. Centralization provides consistency in configuration of the WLAN infrastructure. This ensures that the WLAN is secure and is operating correctly with the wireless clients. For example, inconsistent WLAN configurations will cause voice devices to drop calls, data devices to be disconnected, or any device to have degraded performance.

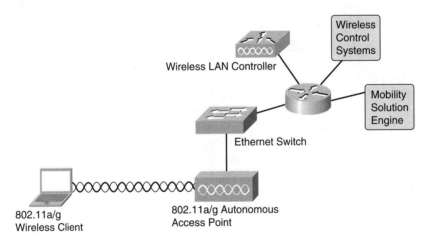

Figure 1-3   *Elements for Controller-Based WLAN*

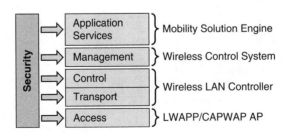

Figure 1-4   *Functional Implementation in a Controller-Based Wireless Network (CUWN)*

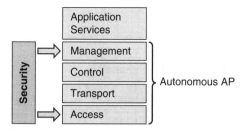

Figure 1-5 *Functional Implementation for an Autonomous WLAN*

The functional elements of a WLC architecture, as compared to the autonomous architecture, provide separation of functions to allow centralized management, control and transport functions, increased security, as well as scalability. Separating the functional elements reduces operating costs while increasing functionality. This is analogous to how a PC separates computing tasks from graphics tasks by using a CPU for computing tasks and a graphics processing unit (GPU) for graphics tasks, which results in greater overall performance at lower costs. The controller architecture enables the separation of the functional layers, which in turn helps in optimization by delegating each function to the most appropriate element. Some functions are centralized, such as RF management and authentication, whereas other functions are distributed to the AP, such as client association and encryption. This is often referred to as a *split MAC architecture*, where each function is performed where it provides the most operational management efficiency. This reduces the complexity and automation of WLAN management functions.

To understand how centralization optimizes configuration tasks for a WLAN, consider the task of configuring a WLAN. Autonomous APs have several hundred configuration parameters that need to each be set discretely. Yet when you analyze each discrete setting, the majority of parameters are configured to the exact same value. This makes sense because in most WLAN deployments, the security settings and service set identifier (SSID) names are typically the same from AP to AP across an organization. Typically, the number of unique parameter settings used in each AP in a WLAN is only a few percent of all the possible AP configuration parameters, which means that the large percentage of configuration parameters will typically be the same from AP to AP in the WLAN.

The designers of the WLC architecture created a means to simplify this laborious task by using a centralized approach to globally manage values to optimize the WLAN system to control these settings and to mitigate costly mistakes. Some settings will require a unique value (most likely RF settings such as transmit power and channel), which a controller-based WLAN solution was designed to automatically manage, using proven algorithms that are continuously monitoring to ensure a healthy WLAN. Setting the configuration values on a global basis for the WLAN optimized the system architecture, but more importantly, saved operating costs associated with configuring and maintaining the WLAN. The trade-off is that while the WLC architecture can allow setting unique values per AP, it is not optimized for a large number of unique configuration values per AP. Of course, autonomous APs are standalone, so every configuration value is uniquely created and managed; thus, global WLAN configurations using a standalone AP approach offer no architectural benefits.

An additional benefit of the WLC architecture is that security can be applied across all functional layers. Security was a great focus during the design of controller-based architecture because this was done at the time that WLANs had a black eye from all the security issues associated with Wired Equivalent Privacy (WEP). The controller-based architecture took a holistic view to implement security benefits embedded in each of the functional layers, thus laying a solid security foundation for deployment of secure end-to-end WLAN solutions.

The mandatory elements of the controller-based architecture are an AP and a WLC. Cisco APs support the capability to operate as either a standalone AP for the autonomous mode or as a lightweight or CAPWAP AP for the controller-based mode. CAPWAP is an IETF standards-based version of LWAPP for communications between the lightweight AP and the WLC. Think of CAPWAP as a superset of LWAPP, which was the original Cisco controller-to-AP protocol and is the foundation for CAPWAP. CAPWAP is discussed in more detail in later chapters in this book, and the full CAPWAP RFC specifications can be found at the ietf.org website. This functional architecture might need a few additional items that are strictly optional; however, depending on the WLAN deployment, they might be necessary to provide additional key services or to simply keep operating expenses down.

The Wireless Control System (WCS) is a network and services management entity that sits above the WLC, as shown previously in Figure 1-3. WCS eases the task of managing a number of controllers and provides additional management services beyond what is provided in the WLC. WCS also provides advanced reporting and monitoring capabilities that are essential for your network operations center to manage the WLAN as well as for quick trouble ticket resolutions. WCS has many other capabilities, such as help desk client troubleshooting tools and security reporting tools. WCS is also used to manage other devices that are part of the Cisco controller-based WLAN architecture, such as the mobility services engine (MSE).

Figure 1-3 (shown previously) illustrates the WLC architecture with an MSE. The MSE provides the application service platform for mobility-enabled applications. This is where the mobility application can access the contextual information about the wireless network and devices to provide additional value-added services on top of an existing wireless deployment. Application service architectures are used to separate the application resources from the data transport operations on the WLCs. This way, the applications cannot interfere with the time-sensitive operations that the WLC must perform. Related to the MSE is the location appliance that is an applications services engine used only for location applications. The MSE is a general-purpose application service environment that can run location as well as many other network and mobility services.

For very large WLANs with potentially multiple administrative domains, the WCS Navigator element, as shown in Figure 1-6, acts as a manager of managers for multiple wireless controller systems. Navigator provides centralized monitoring for distributed WCS deployments. Chapter 8, "Introduction to WCS," covers WCS in greater detail.

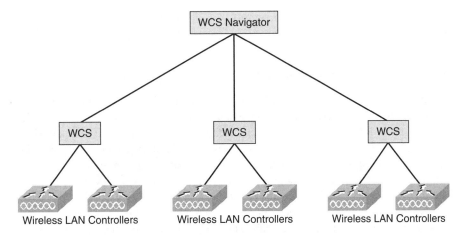

Figure 1-6 *Management Architecture for Multiple WCS Deployments with WCS Navigator*

Autonomous AP Issues and the WLC Remedy

The following sections review many of the issues with the autonomous AP architecture that drove the creation of the WLC architecture. You will learn how the WLC remedies many of the problems in deploying and operating an autonomous AP solution.

Problem: WLAN APs Are Difficult to Deploy

Deploying WLANs using autonomous APs is labor intensive because each device must be individually configured and managed—both in a day-zero scenario and also on an ongoing basis. The introduction of WLCs removed this burden by making the APs "plug and play," thereby making a wireless deployment a real "zero-touch deployment." APs no longer need to be individually configured. Lightweight APs self-configure, self-optimize, and self-heal with the advent of WLCs. WLCs also remove the requirement to configure virtual LANs (trunk ports) to each AP for segregated traffic as was required with autonomous APs; the lightweight architecture brings the VLAN termination directly to the WLC in most deployment models. WLCs also remove the requirement of assigning static IP address to each AP. Static IP addressing can be used, but is not required with lightweight APs in order to be managed. The lightweight APs can simply use DHCP services for IP address assignment, and CAPWAP will take care of management without the need to use a static IP address, thereby further building on the zero-touch approach to deploying wireless networks.

RF channels and power settings do not need to be manually configured with the controller-based architecture. A WLC solution works as a system, across multiple controllers, to automate the detection of RF conditions in real-time to automatically configure each AP for the proper RF channel and power setting for optimal performance. This Radio Resource Management (RRM) process dramatically reduces the load on RF expertise for operating the WLAN. The RRM functionality also continuously tunes the RF settings to optimize the WLAN's performance by mitigating coverage holes.

Problem: WLANs Are Not Secure

Security issues also drove the need for WLC deployments. Individually configured autonomous AP architectures invariably result in some misconfigured APs that could result in poor performance or something much worse such as a security breach. The autonomous AP architecture also does not provide assurances that all APs are running the same version of software with all the latest security patch levels. Autonomous APs also do not provide security across all function layers, as shown previously in Figure 1-6. Often, when security updates are needed with autonomous APs, whether it is a software update or a security configuration change, there is not a quick or consistent way to do this for large numbers of deployed APs. The WLC architecture provides a quick way to change security settings globally as well as efficiently update the WLAN because it is only the WLC that needs to be updated versus each individual AP. Each autonomous AP is operating independently, and there is no easy way to provide a synergistic view of how the WLAN is working. The list that follows describes additional security elements that autonomous APs could not provide but are addressed with the WLC architecture:

- No central reporting or correlation of events to monitor for security attacks.

- No seamless integration of common wired security requirements with wireless.

- No control of data transport traffic ingress and egress point nor the capability to specify based on traffic types.

- No capability to force data encryption.

- Difficult to configure a WLAN for security such as Extensible Authentication Protocol (EAP) authentication because each AP has to be configured to talk to the radius server versus one WLC. Also, each AP must be added to the RADIUS server client database.

- No centralized user policy and authentication.

- No authentication of APs to the infrastructure.

- Complex and error-prone configuration can result in APs being misconfigured with weak security.

Problem: Infrastructure Device Configuration and Scaling

Cisco APs that are used without WLCs are referred to as autonomous or IOS-based APs. An autonomous or IOS-based AP (abbreviated as *aIOS*) is the most accurate term to use because different versions of IOS code are used on the APs for either controller- or autonomous-based architectures. The term *autonomous AP* is used to describe access points that do not use a WLC. The word *autonomous* is used because autonomous wireless access points can function as a complete standalone system. It has its own software image and its own configuration stored on the AP's flash drive. To update software or to change the configuration requires accessing each AP individually. This can be done manually or through tools that contact each AP discretely to update software images or perform configuration changes. The WLC architecture addresses this problem by reducing the operating costs as a result of simplifying the configuration and management of wireless LAN deployments.

Problem: Autonomous AP Costs for Configuring Each AP

Autonomous APs have hundreds of configuration parameters; however, for a typical WLAN deployment, all but a few configuration parameters are set to the same value on all APs in the WLAN. By recognizing that the majority of configuration values will be globally set to the same values across the WLAN, the WLC creates a centralized architecture that optimizes this desired state. It is extremely simple and fast to set or change a configuration value for an entire WLAN with a large number of APs using the WLC architecture. It takes literally seconds to accomplish versus the hours or days required for WLAN deployments of autonomous APs. When an AP is added to the WLAN in a controller-based deployment, the AP will self-configure based on the defined parameters in the controller.

Problem: Autonomous AP Costs for Keeping Each AP's Software Up to Date

With a large number of autonomous APs, it is challenging to keep all APs upgraded to the desired version of software. Each autonomous AP stores and runs its own copy of an operating system. WLAN operators of autonomous APs need to individually update their APs to the current version of software for security updates, defect fixes, or new features enabled by the updated versions. Often, autonomous AP WLAN administrators will find that they rarely have all the APs running on the same software version. The WLC uses its centralized management paradigm to ensure that each AP that joins the WLC is running the same software image. The WLC is the device that gets the software updates, and the WLC automatically updates the AP's software. This ensures that all the APs in the WLAN are current and saves operating costs doing so. In an aIOS environment, the administrator has to update hundreds or thousands of APs individually. However, with the controller-based solution, only the WLCs themselves need to be updated. This, in turn, pushes configuration or firmware down to connected APs.

The WLC also addresses security issues of trust for the software image being updated. With software updates, you are always concerned about the possibility that a particular software update has been compromised in some malicious way. To prevent this, the WLC architecture digitally signs software updates to prevent the loading of malicious code. LWAPP or CAPWAP APs get their software from the WLC over a secure, encrypted, and authenticated communications mechanism. All management communications with a CAPWAP AP are carried in an Advanced Encryption Standard (AES) encrypted control channel. This ensures protection of infrastructure information and secure management and monitoring of the APs.

Problem: RF Expertise and Configuration Challenges

Before the invention of the WLC, the RF settings for each aIOS AP had to be uniquely configured. This was accomplished by performing a wireless site survey to determine the number of APs, their placement based on a transmit power level, plus a channel plan created by the WLAN designer. After each AP was installed, the transmit power and channel assignment had to be configured for each AP. Over time, things inevitably change in the RF environment, resulting in reduced performance of the WLAN. To resolve this, a tuning survey must be done periodically to understand the changes to the RF environment, and a new transmit power and channel plan has to be created and deployed for each access point.

The changes to the RF environment can be anything from the introduction of new walls in the building or additional equipment or furniture, to changing the density of people in the building, as well as simply adding additional APs for increased performance or coverage requirements. Interference and noise from other devices operating at the same frequency will cause performance issues and must be managed. The definition for *interference* that is used in this book and the Cisco WLAN products is spectrum usage by 802.11 devices using the 802.11 in the same RF ranges as your APs; for example, this could be your neighbor's WLAN. The definition of *noise* is non-802.11 devices operating in the same RF range as your APs, such as Bluetooth devices, microwave ovens, video devices, and so on.

Interference is a common source of major performance problems requiring changes to the RF environment. The RF environment is very dynamic, and many quickly learned that it is essential to have a central means to monitor the RF settings with the ability to automatically optimize the channel and power levels for the APs based on the current environment. A series of algorithms were created; these are referred to as Radio Resource Management (RRM) and also known as Auto-RF. The suite of algorithms in RRM constantly monitors and analyzes the data from the APs' radios and then methodically optimizes the performance of the WLAN. The ancillary benefit is that this reduces the demand for having an RF expert and analysis equipment to routinely analyze and then manually adjusting RF settings for the WLAN.

Mobility Applications Enabled by Controller-Based WLANs

Many of the mobility applications that run on wireless networks require additional services to enable seamless functionality. These functions range from quality of service (QoS) support and fast secure roaming to contextual information identifying the wireless device's identification, signal quality, security level, and physical location. Autonomous AP architectures require redundant overlay infrastructures and management solutions to be deployed to provide these services. The WLC architecture was specifically designed to provide these services without requiring the repetition of similar functionality in the network. This is accomplished by providing a services-oriented architecture that allows the service layer to efficiently receive the required information from the lower functional layers, as shown previously in Figure 1-5.

WLANs Do Not Provide the Performance and Robustness Needed for Use as a Primary Access Network

The WLC architecture, when used with additional 802.11 enhancements, allows the capacity and performance of the WLAN to meet the requirements necessary to use the WLAN as the primary access network. In some instances, they might even be used as a complete substitute for wired Ethernet access methods. The enhancements inherent in 802.11n, 802.11h, 802.11i, 802.11k, and 802.11r provide additional security and capacity to the WLAN. For example, by allowing more channels to be used through 802.11h, the WLC optimizes the use of the RF spectrum to provide increased capacity. Similarly, 802.11n adds greater wireless link speed support and additional reliability to allow network operations at the same performance levels as 100-Mbps Ethernet.

Summary

As many network administrators start dealing with the realities of managing large wireless networks that contain hundreds of wireless access points, the idea of a wireless switch started bubbling up as a way to deal with the need to centrally manage all those access points. Through various revisions of products, the concept of the wireless switch transformed to what we now refer to as wireless LAN controllers. Satisfying the need to centrally manage large wireless LAN deployments, the wireless LAN controller architecture has become the desired solution for network administrators. The WLC simplifies management and provides centralization of functions to address many deficiencies of deploying an autonomous AP architecture by splitting the functional requirements among the APs, WLCs, and services engines to address the overall business needs. The WLC architecture address the following issues:

- Reducing WLAN operating expenses through centralized management and control.

- Improving security through an integrated security architectural design that spans all functional layers in the WLAN.

- Mitigating slow roaming time by enabling Fast Secure Roaming through the centralization of control.

- Reducing the expertise and man-hours required to optimize the RF configuration by providing continuous Auto-RF management.

- Removing the inability for granular control of data traffic, which is addressed by providing a centralized mechanism for data transport and control options.

- Providing support for contextual mobility applications by providing an applications services layer in the WLAN architecture.

- Addressing the limited resiliency by increasing the reliability through failover and self-healing mechanisms inherent in the controller architecture and RF management functions.

- Dramatically improving performance and capacity utilizing the built-in spectrum intelligence and support of 802.11 standards.

- Configuration consistency, pushing the same WLAN and security policies to all the APs managed by the WLC.

- Zero-touch deployment, providing automated authentication and provision for every new AP added to the WLAN.

- Scaling for large WLANs with simplified and automated management functions. This includes auto-tuning of RF configuration.

The controller-based architecture addresses the security, operation, and application requirements for the mobility and wireless applications that business networks have been waiting for. Controller-based wireless networks have allowed WLANs to move from being a convenience to being a primary access method that can be relied on to run mission-critical applications. Chapter 2, "Wireless LAN Protocols," provides detailed information on the protocols that were developed to support the WLC architecture.

Wireless LAN Protocols

Chapter 1, "The Need for Controller-Based Wireless Networks," discussed the need for a controller-based architecture to support scalable wireless LANs (WLAN). This chapter reviews the relevant industry standards and the bodies that generate them, and introduces the critical protocols that make WLANs work so well.

Because this is an overview chapter in an introductory book, this chapter covers only the critical components of the protocols. This chapter does not provide an in-depth, bit-and-byte walk-through of all the protocol details. The focus of this chapter is on the most important components of the protocols. After you understand the fundamentals and are ready for the gory details, there are some excellent references at the end of the chapter, including books you should have on your shelves or papers that you should refer to regularly.

Understanding the Relevant Standards

The 802.11 family of standards from the Institute of Electrical and Electronics Engineers (IEEE) defines the basic behavior of WLANs. The IEEE is an international, nonprofit organization with members from industry and academia. Part of the charter of the IEEE is to create standards documents that advance aspects of the communications industry through an arm called the IEEE Standards Association.

The IEEE first settled on the base 802.11 standard in 1997 and subsequently revised that standard in 1999. The original 1997 version of the 802.11 standards described a WLAN media access control (MAC), MAC management and control, and three physical layers (PHY). These PHYs included an infrared baseband and two modulation schemes for the 2.4-GHz industrial, scientific, and medical (ISM) radio band. These two 2.4-GHz PHYs were based on frequency-hopping spread spectrum (FHSS) and dynamic sequence spread spectrum (DSSS) radio modulation schemes, delivering at both 1- and 2-Mbps data rates.

The 1999 version of the 802.11 standard added two new PHYs:

- A PHY based on orthogonal frequency-division multiplexing (OFDM) modulation in the higher-frequency UNI-II radio band (5 GHz)

- An extension to the original 2.4-GHz DSSS PHY that enhanced its capabilities up to an 11-Mbps data rate

The 5-GHz-based PHY is defined by the 802.11a addendum and offers up to 54-Mbps data rates. The 2.4-GHz PHY extension is defined by the 802.11b add-on. 802.11b is further enhanced with OFDM, offering potential data rates as high as 54 Mbps in the 2.4-GHz band by the 2002 802.11g document.

In 2007, the IEEE rolled up all ratified amendments and the previous, base standard into an omnibus 802.11 document. This new document includes the original 802.11 standards plus the a, b, g, e, g, h, and i amendments.

In 2009, the IEEE ratified another addendum, 802.11n, which enhances both the MAC and PHY functionality, offering potential data rates as high as 600 Mbps. Chapter 3, "802.11n," covers 802.11n in detail.

The IEEE has continued to grow and evolve the 802.11 protocols in response to industry demand. Table 2-1 lists some of the most important and relevant developments at press time.

Of course, there might be developments between the time this chapter was written and the time you are reading it, so there might be new protocol amendments to address industry problems in the works. If you're interested, check with the IEEE at http://ieee.org.

As it turns out, there has never been much industry uptake for the IR- or FHSS-based PHYs in 802.11-based WLANs, but the 802.11a, b, g, and now n PHYs have seen extremely wide adoption. Chapter 3 covers 802.11n in detail, which is probably the most significant new development in WLAN technology since the original 802.11 definition. Chapter 4, "Cisco Unified Wireless LAN Security Fundamentals," covers 802.11i and WLAN security in detail. For even greater detail, consult the references at the end of the chapter.

Wi-Fi Alliance

While the IEEE defines the basic operations of WLANs through the 802.11 family of protocols, an organization called the Wi-Fi Alliance (WFA) drives industry adoption of WLAN technology and certifies intervendor interoperability. The Wi-Fi Alliance is an industry consortium with more than 300 member companies at press time. These member companies include infrastructure vendors such as Cisco Systems, silicon companies such as Intel and Atheros, and end-device vendors and software companies such as Apple and Microsoft.

The WFA owns the trademark "Wi-Fi" and applies this trademarked term to its industry interoperability certifications. The term *Wi-Fi* has become synonymous with 802.11-based

WLAN technologies in the common vernacular over time. You'll find the term used this way throughout this book and in industry literature.

Table 2-1 *IEEE 802.11 Standards*

Standards Document	Description	Ratification
802.11	Base definition of MAC; IR, FHSS, and DSSS in 2.4-GHz-band PHYs with 1- and 2-Mbps data rates	1997; amended 1999, 2007
802.11a	OFDM PHY in 5.8-GHz UNI-II spectrum, data rates up to 54 Mbps	1999
802.11b	DSSS PHY extension in 2.4-GHz band for data rates up to 11 Mbps	1999
802.11e	QoS enhancements and modifications to 802.11 MAC	2005
802.11h	Spectrum and transmit power management for interference avoidance in the 5-GHz spectrum	2003
802.11i	Security enhancements to 802.11	2004
802.11k	Radio Resource Measurement enhancements	Targeted for 2011 at press time
802.11n	Higher-throughput 802.11 WLANs	2009
802.11r	Fast BSS transitions	2008
802.11s	Mesh networking	Targeted for 2011 at press time
802.11u	Improved interworking with other wireless technologies	Targeted for Dec. 2010 at press time
802.11v	Wireless network management	Targeted for Dec. 2010 at press time
802.11w	Protected management frames	2008
802.11aa	Robust media streaming	Targeted for 2012 at press time
802.11ac	Very high throughput	Targeted for 2012 at press time

The WFA was originally formed in 1999 with the goal of "driving adoption of a single worldwide standard for high-speed wireless local-area networking." Though this sounds similar to the charter of the IEEE, the IEEE works on creating standards while the WFA focuses on making IEEE and other relevant standards commercially applicable and viable through interoperability testing and industry certification programs.

The WFA began its "Wi-Fi CERTIFIED" program in 2000, testing vendor interoperability based on the IEEE 802.11 protocols. Over time, the WFA has evolved and expanded its interoperability testing to cover more than just basic access. The Wi-Fi Protected Access (WPA) tests define table-stakes security for authentication and encryption. WPA certifications are based on the IEEE 802.11i addendum. The Wi-Fi Multimedia (WMM) program certifies quality of service (QoS) based on elements of the IEEE 802.11e document.

The WFA's role in the growth of the WLAN industry cannot be understated. Wi-Fi is the first and really only global industry standard, and this is largely the reason it has been adopted so widely; the WFA is what made it the global industry standard.

The WFA also creates certification programs based on drafts of IEEE standards. An unfortunate reality of large industry standards organizations such as the IEEE is that arriving at a consensus among a diverse membership, often with competing interests and agendas, takes a long time—sometimes too long for the good of the industry. By creating early certification programs based on IEEE drafts, vendors can implement industry-validated and -blessed solutions to critical customer problems.

Cisco Compatible Extensions

The Cisco Compatible Extensions (CCX) program first began in 2002 as a way for Cisco to collaborate with Wi-Fi client silicon and device vendors in developing and implementing Cisco innovations royalty-free. The CCX program evolved to also create incentives for Cisco partners to also adopt WFA certifications in addition to implementing Cisco innovations.

CCX features try to address problems not yet being solved by current standards. Many CCX features ultimately end up as standards. Figure 2-1 illustrates the CCX cycle of innovation.

As you can see from Figure 2-1, the Cisco strategy with CCX is to create some innovative features to solve a customer problem, join with CCX partners in implementing the feature, take the feature to the standards organizations, and ultimately achieve wide industry adoption through WFA certification programs.

This book covers different CCX features in context.

IETF

The Internet Engineering Task Force (IETF) is an open standards organization that develops and promotes Internet standards, cooperating closely with other standards bodies and dealing in particular with standards of the TCP/IP and Internet protocol suite. IETF standards are articulated in Request For Comment (RFC) documents that are developed through a working group process defined by "rough consensus and running code."

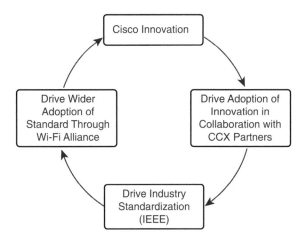

Figure 2-1 *Cycle of CCX Innovation*

When it comes to Wi-Fi technology, the relevant standard is defined in IETF RFC 5415, the "Control and Provisioning of Wireless Access Points," or CAPWAP, standard. You will see additional coverage of CAPWAP in greater detail later in this chapter, and indeed, throughout the rest of this book.

The Physical Layer

To really understand 802.11-based WLANs, you have to understand both the physical and the link-layer technologies. As previously noted, the IEEE 802.11 specifications call out both the physical, or PHY, layer and the link layer, or MAC. There's already plenty of literature out there describing these layers in detail, so the focus here will be only on the most important concepts that are necessary for a fundamental understanding of WLANs. For the nitty-gritty details, see the references listed at the end of the chapter.

Physical Layer Concepts

As shown in Figure 2-2, the physical layer is divided into two sublayers:

- **The Physical Medium Dependent (PMD) sublayer:** An intermediary layer between the MAC and radio transmissions

- **The Physical Layer Convergence Procedure (PLCP) sublayer:** Where bits are transferred on and off the air

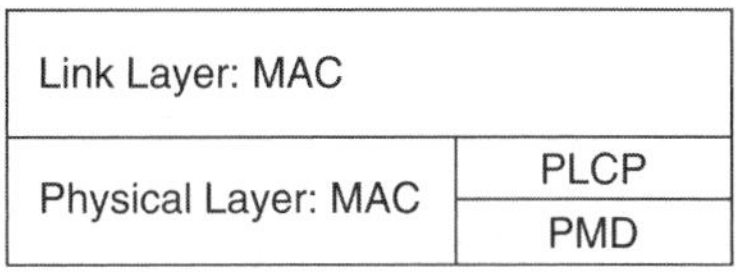

Link Layer: MAC		
Physical Layer: MAC	PLCP	
	PMD	

Figure 2-2 *Logical View of the Physical Layer*

There's an additional, very important function performed at the physical layer—the *Clear Channel Assessment (CCA)*. The CCA tells the MAC layer whether the air is free for transmission, which is absolutely critical for appropriate arbitration of the transmission medium. You learn more about this in the MAC layer section, later in the chapter.

Recall from earlier in this chapter that the IEEE 802.11 protocol and its addendum specify several physical layers, or PHYs. The first revision of the 802.11 specification defined a frequency-hopping spread spectrum (FHSS), a dynamic sequence spread spectrum (DSSS), and an infrared PHY. The 1999 revision of the 802.11 standard added OFDM in the 50-GHz spectrum and an extension to the previous version of DSSS, something often called High-Rate Direct Sequence Spread Spectrum. The details of how these modulation schemes work is outside the scope of this book, but for the sake of discussion, it's important to understand the terms.

What is, perhaps, most important to understand about the PHY, however, is that the physical layer's transmission medium is unlicensed and shared radio frequency (RF). The paragraphs that follow review these concepts.

Many wireless networks, including Wi-Fi, use radio communications technologies as the physical transmission medium. The transmitter and receiver use a radio frequency, defined in some unit of hertz (such as kHz or MHz), to exchange signals between each other, with the signal carrying a data transmission. The range of frequencies allowed for a specific radio technology is called the *band*. The band is divided into independent *channels*, each of which is a certain number of hertz (Hz) wide. *Channel bandwidth* then refers to the carrying capacity of a channel. *Spectrum bandwidth* refers to the total capacity of the allocated spectrum.

Now, just to be sure that you understand these concepts, consider the radio in your car as an example. The FM radio broadcast band ranges in frequency from 87.5 to 108.0 kHz in the Americas. This band is divided into channels that are 200 kHz wide, with 75 kHz of allowed deviation on both sides of the channel to allow potential adjacent channel interference. When you tune your radio to the center frequency of a channel, you can pick up a broadcast.

But what happens when multiple broadcasters try to use the same channel? Interference. Your radio is confused and probably picks up nothing but junk and noise, which is a radio term for distortions in the frequency band. To make sure that this doesn't happen, governments have set up regulatory bodies that control and allocate broadcast licenses and regulate the amount of power a transmitter is allowed to use.

There are, however, some unlicensed frequency bands allowed by the regulatory bodies; the logic behind unlicensed bands is to allow low-cost innovation typically for consumer markets. Between 2.4 and 2.5 GHz, this band is called the Industrial, Scientific, and Medical (ISM) band. Additional unlicensed spectrum is available in the 5.15–5.25-GHz, 5.25–5.35-GHz, and 5.725–5.825-GHz bands. The ISM band and these frequencies in the 5-GHz spectrum are the bands used by Wi-Fi.

Just think of the implications of Wi-Fi using the unlicensed spectrum:

■   Because there is limited channel bandwidth available that can be freely used, regulatory agencies limit the allowed output power.

■   The spectrum is shared with other radio technologies, which can and do compete with Wi-Fi for radio spectrum.

■   Adjacent Wi-Fi networks can interfere with each other when on the same channel—an important concept called *cochannel interference (CCI)*.

■   Radio spectrum is finite—there's a carrying capacity to the WLAN that is fixed, not by engineering or radio design, but by the laws of physics.

Remember these key points because they govern much of what Wi-Fi networks can do and many of the design and deployment decisions you need to make.

CAPWAP

One thing that should be apparent from the previous section is that 802.11, as defined by the IEEE, is designed from a per-access point and radio link perspective. To scale the architecture to a systems level for more scalable, enterprise-class deployments, the IETF created RFC 5415, which defines the *Control and Provisioning of Wireless Access Points (CAPWAP)* protocol. CAPWAP extends the functionality of Wi-Fi to a much more scalable level. Consider Figure 2-3.

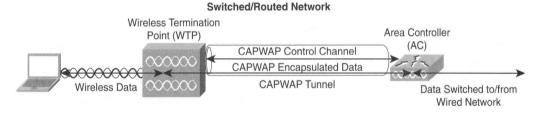

Figure 2-3   *CAPWAP Architecture*

CAPWAP centralizes WLAN configuration and control into a device called an access controller (AC). In the Cisco Unified Wireless Network (CUWN), the wireless LAN controller (WLC) serves as the area controller. This allows the entire WLAN to operate as an intelligent information network that uses wireless as the access medium to support advanced services. The CUWN simplifies operational management by collapsing large numbers of managed endpoints (autonomous access points) into a single managed system comprised of the WLAN controller(s) and its corresponding, joined access points.

In the CUWN architecture, APs are *lightweight*, meaning that they cannot act independently of a WLC. APs are typically "zero-touch" deployed, and no individual configuration of APs is required. The APs learn the IP address of one or more WLC through a controller discovery algorithm and then establish a trust relationship with a controller through a "join" process. After the trust relationship is established, the WLC pushes firmware to the AP, if necessary, and a runtime configuration. APs do not store a configuration locally.

After they are joined to a controller, the APs are also lightweight in the sense that they handle only a subset of 802.11 MAC functionality. Typically, this subset includes only real-time 802.11 MAC functionality, with the controller handling all non-real-time 802.11 MAC processing. This division of 802.11 labor is called *Split MAC* and enables the architecture to provide seamless mobility and a number of advanced features in an elegant and scalable way.

As you can see from Figure 2-3, APs interact with the WLC through the CAPWAP protocol. CAPWAP defines both a control-messaging protocol and format and a data path component. CAPWAP supports both a distributed and centralized data path.

CAPWAP control messages are exchanged between the WLC and AP for a variety of reasons, including the controller discovery and join process, AP configuration and firmware push from the controller, and statistics gathering and wireless security enforcement. WLC control messages are also used to support wireless station access, authentication, and mobility. CAPWAP control messages are secured in a Datagram Transport Layer Security (DTLS) tunnel.

In a centralized data path, the WLAN client data packets are encapsulated in CAPWAP between the AP and WLC. When a WLAN client sends a packet, it is received by the AP and encapsulated with a CAPWAP header and forwarded to the controller. At the controller, the CAPWAP header is stripped off and the frame switched from the controller onto a VLAN in the switching infrastructure. When a client on the wired network sends a packet to a WLAN client, the packet first goes into the WLC, where it is encapsulated with a CAPWAP header and then forwarded to the appropriate AP. The AP strips off the CAPWAP header and then bridges the frame onto the RF medium. The CAPWAP data path between controller and AP can be secured through DTLS.

Certain network architectures require some level of "hybrid" deployment, or distributed data plane. CAPWAP supports bridging data frames onto the wired network at the AP, too. The CUWN implementation of this distributed data path architecture is called *Hybrid Remote Edge Access Point (HREAP)*. The secured version of this implementation is called *Office Extend AP (OEAP)*. In this configuration, more of 802.11 MAC processing is pushed to the network edge at the AP, and some data traffic might be bridged onto the Ethernet LAN at the AP instead of being encapsulated in CAPWAP and carried to the controller.

CAPWAP Versus LWAPP

Cisco transitioned to the CUWN architecture from a standalone AP architecture for WLANs after acquiring a company called Airespace Networks. Airespace's lightweight architecture was based on a protocol called Lightweight Access Point Protocol (LWAPP). For a number of years, the CUWN was then based on LWAPP.

Recognizing the need for an industry standard, Airespace and then Cisco after the acquisition submitted LWAPP to the IETF for standardization. The IETF chartered the CAPWAP working group, which selected LWAPP as a basis for its work and ultimately released RFC 5415 and several other CAPWAP RFCs. CAPWAP is heavily based on LWAPP, though there are some important differences like the use of Datagram Transport Layer Security (DTLS).

Cisco transitioned from LWAPP to CAPWAP with the 5.2 WLC software release, and all subsequent developments have been CAPWAP based.

CAPWAP Protocol Fundamentals

The following sections review the fundamentals of CAPWAP. As defined in the RFC draft, CAPWAP is a generic mobility protocol with a binding definition for the IEEE 802.11 WLAN protocol. Because this is a book about Wi-Fi technologies, the discussion assumes the 802.11 binding. CAPWAP, in simple terms, defines how access point(s) communicate with WLAN controller(s). The CAPWAP RFC defines the following:

■ Control protocol and message format

■ Data encapsulation

■ Transport modes for CAPWAP messages

■ System-level operational state machine

■ Split and local MAC processing modes

The following sections examine these CAPWAP definitions in greater detail.

CAPWAP Terminology

Some key terms need to be defined before delving into the details of the CAPWAP protocol. These definitions come directly from RFC 5415, Section 1.4:

■ **Access Controller (AC):** The network entity that provides WTP access to the network infrastructure in the data plane, control plane, and management plane, or a combination therein.

■ **Wireless Termination Point (WTP):** The physical or network entity that contains an RF antenna and wireless Physical Layer (PHY) to transmit and receive station traffic for wireless access networks.

■ **CAPWAP control channel:** A bidirectional glow defined by the AC IP address, WTP IP address, AC control port, WTP control port, and the transport layer protocol (UDP or UDP-Lite) over which CAPWAP data packets are sent and received.

■ **CAPWAP data channel:** A bidirectional flow defined by the AC IP address, WTP IP address, AC data port, WTP data port, and the transport layer protocol (UDP or UDP-Lite) over which CAPWAP data packets are sent and received.

Mapping these terms to implementation in the CUWN, the WLC assumes all functions of the access controller, and the AP takes the role of the WTP.

CAPWAP Control Messages

CAPWAP defines how WTPs and ACs communicate with each other. CAPWAP defines both control messages and a data encapsulation mechanism.

The CAPWAP protocol defines a control protocol and message format. The CAPWAP control protocol is used for the following purposes:

- AC discovery by WTPs

- Establishing a trust relationship between WTPs and the AC

- Downloading firmware to the WTPs

- Downloading configurations to the WTPs

- Statistics collection from the WTP by the AC

- Mobility-related tasks

- Event notifications from the WTP to the AC

- Other tasks

CAPWAP control messages are marked with a Control Bit (C-bit) in the CAPWAP encapsulation header that when set to 1, indicates that the CAPWAP message is a control message. You will see many of these CAPWAP control messages in functional context throughout this document. CAPWAP control communications between the AC and WTP follow the standard User Datagram Protocol (UDP) client/server model.

CAPWAP Data Messages

A CAPWAP data message is a forwarded data frame, encapsulated inside a CAPWAP transport header. The C-bit in the CAPWAP header of CAPWAP data packets is set to 0.

When the data frame is forwarded from the WTP to the AC, the entire 802.11 frame received by the WTP is encapsulated with the CAPWAP header and then transported to the AC using the appropriate CAPWAP transport technology. When the data frame is forwarded from a host on the wired network through the AC to the WTP, the AC receives an Ethernet-encapsulated frame. The AC strips off the Ethernet header and builds an 802.11 frame. This frame is then encapsulated with a CAPWAP header and transported to the AC using the appropriate transport technology.

CAPWAP State Machine

The CAPWAP RFC defines a state machine. The state machine explains how infrastructure devices (specifically WTPs and ACs) interact with each other from startup through operations. The CAPWAP RFC explains the CAPWAP state machine in detail; this section explains only some of the key states in the CAPWAP state machine for the sake of simplicity.

Figure 2-4 shows the simplified CAPWAP state machine.

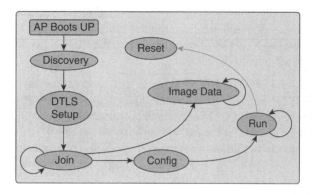

Figure 2-4   *CAPWAP State Machine*

As you can see from Figure 2-4, the key states considered in this document are as follows:

- Discovery

- DTLS setup

- Join

- Image data

- Config

- Run

- Reset

During the AC discovery phase, the WTP locates available and eligible ACs and selects the best AC with which to establish a CAPWAP relationship.

RFC 5415 actually states that the discovery state is optional if a preconfigured AC exists for the WTP. But, the WTP must discover the AC through a CAPWAP Discovery Request message sent to a limited IP broadcast address (255.255.255.255), a well-known CAPWAP multicast address (224.0.1.140), or a unique AC IP address. DHCP vendor-specific options and Domain Name System (DNS) resolution of a well-known IP address are also allowed.

The WTP anticipates receiving one or more CAPWAP Discovery Response messages from the AC(s) to which it sent CAPWAP Discovery messages. The WTP will select an AC from the ACs that have responded to the CAPWAP Discovery Request with a CAP-WAP Discovery Response.

After the AC is selected, the WTP and AC establish a trust relationship through a DTLS handshake. Datagram Transport Layer Security (DTLS) is a protocol defined by RFC

4347. DTLS is a well-defined and -used protocol for securing datagram protocols and applications that run over them. It allows client/server applications and protocols like CAPWAP to securely establish a trust relationship and exchange messages privately.

A CAPWAP DTLS session is established through a handshake protocol between the WTP and AC. CAPWAP allows an exchange of nonces based on pre-shared keys (PSK) or an exchange of public-key-based certificates in this handshake process. The CUWN contains factory-installed X.509 certificates by default; the CUWN has no PSK-based option because it is cryptographically inferior.

After an initial successful DTLS handshake, the WTP and AC transition to the CAPWAP join state. The WTP sends the AC a CAPWAP Join Request, which if successfully received, is answered with a CAPWAP Join Response, establishing a join relationship between the WTP and AC. In the CUWN implementation, the WTP and AC exchange cryptographic nonces in this join transaction to establish cryptographic keys that are used to secure subsequent CAPWAP control messages using industry-standard Advanced Encryption Standard (AES)–based encryption.

The WTP and AC then transition into either the image data or config state. In the CUWN implementation, the WTP checks for the code version on the AC, and if there is a mismatch, the WTP downloads code from the AC. If there is no mismatch, the WTP downloads its configuration from the AC, including all security, QoS, and other settings. CAPWAP then transitions into the run state, and data service for stations starts.

CUWN Implementation of the CAPWAP Discovery

At this point, it's worth describing a few more details about the CUWN implementation of the CAPWAP discovery process and state. In this section, the term *AP* is substituted for *WTP* and *WLC* for the AC to reflect the real-world implementation in the CUWN.

As previously discussed, the AP enters the CAPWAP discovery state after booting up. In the discovery state, two important CAPWAP control messages are used—the CAPWAP Discovery Request and the CAPWAP Discovery Response. The AP sends CAPWAP Discovery Request messages to one or more WLCs, expecting a CAPWAP Discovery Response message from the WLC.

The AP puts each WLC that responds to the CAPWAP Discovery Request with a CAPWAP Discovery Response into a candidate WLC list. The AP will select the WLC to join from the candidate WLC list. But how does the AP determine where to send the CAPWAP Discovery Request messages?

Cisco CAPWAP APs implement a WLC hunting and discovery algorithm that is defined as follows:

1. The AP attempts to acquire an IP address, typically through the DHCP process, unless of course it has previously been configured with a static IP address.

2. The AP broadcasts a CAPWAP Discovery Request on the local IP subnet. Any WLC that is connected on the local IP subnet will receive the Layer 3 CAPWAP Discovery

Request. Each of the WLCs receiving the CAPWAP Discovery Request replies with a unicast CAPWAP Discovery Response message to the AP.

3. The AP sends a unicast CAPWAP Discovery Request to a locally stored list of WLC IP addresses, if this list exists. The AP will have this WLC IP address list stored in its NVRAM if it has previously joined a WLC. The list is provisioned on the AP by a joined WLC during the Config phase of the CAPWAP state machine, when the AP downloads the first 32 entries of the joined WLC's Mobility List. The concept of the Mobility List is discussed in Chapter 6.

4. DHCP servers can be programmed to return WLC IP addresses in vendor-specific Option 43 in the DHCP offer to lightweight Cisco APs. When the AP gets an IP address through DHCP, it will look for WLC IP addresses in the Option 43 field in the DHCP offer. The AP will send a unicast CAPWAP Discovery Request to each of the WLCs listed in the DHCP Option 43. WLCs receiving the CAPWAP Discovery Request messages unicast a CAPWAP Discovery Response to the AP.

5. The AP will attempt to resolve the DNS name *CISCO-CAPWAP-CONTROLLER.localdomain*. When the AP is able to resolve this name to one or more IP addresses, the AP sends a unicast CAPWAP Discovery Request to the resolved IP address(es). Each WLC receiving the CAPWAP Discovery Request will reply with a unicast CAPWAP Discovery Response to the AP.

6. If, after Steps 2 through 5, no CAPWAP Discovery Response is received, the AP resets and restarts the hunting algorithm.

The controller hunting process repeats ad infinitum until at least one WLC is found and joined.

It is important to understand that during the CAPWAP WLC discovery, the AP will always complete Steps 2 through 5 to build a list of candidate WLCs. After the AP has completed the CAPWAP WLC discovery steps, it selects a WLC from the candidate WLC list and attempts to join that WLC.

But how does the AP select a WLC from the candidate WLC list? WLCs embed important information in the CAPWAP Discovery Response, including

■ The controller's sysName

■ The controller type

■ The controller AP capacity and its current AP load (how many APs are joined to the WLC)

■ Something called the *Master Controller* status

The AP uses this information to make a controller selection, using the following precedence rules:

1. If the AP has previously been configured with a primary, secondary, and/or tertiary controller, the AP will select these controllers based on precedence. If the AP finds a

match, it then sends a CAPWAP join to the secondary controller. If the secondary WLC cannot be found or the CAPWAP join fails, the AP repeats the process for its tertiary controller.

2. When no primary, secondary, and/or tertiary controllers have been configured for an AP, or when these controllers cannot be found in the candidate list, or if the CAP-WAP Join Requests to those controllers have failed, the AP then looks at the Master Controller status field in the CAPWAP Discovery Responses from the candidate WLCs. If a WLC is configured as a Master Controller, the AP will select that WLC and send it a CAPWAP Join Request.

3. If the AP is unsuccessful at joining a WLC based on the criteria in (1) and (2), it will attempt to join the WLC with the greatest excess capacity. The greatest excess capacity is defined as the ratio of currently joined APs to the total controller capacity expressed as a percentage.

After a WLC is selected, the AP transitions to the DTLS setup and then CAPWAP join states.

CAPWAP Transport

Figure 2-5 illustrates CAPWAP transport with CAPWAP control and data packets encapsulated in UDP datagrams.

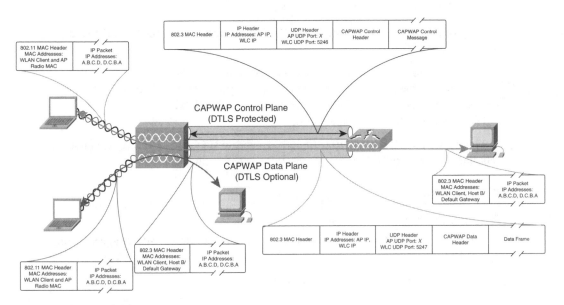

Figure 2-5   *CAPWAP Transport*

The CAPWAP control and data messages are encapsulated in UDP packets that are carried over the IP network. The only requirement is established IP connectivity between the

WTPs and the AC. On the WTP side, both CAPWAP control and data messages use an ephemeral port that is derived from a hash of the WTP Ethernet MAC address as the UDP port. On the AC side, CAPWAP Data messages always use UDP port 5246. On the AC side, CAPWAP control messages always use UDP port 5247. Figure 2-5 shows how CAPWAP control messages, including the CAPWAP header with the C-Bit set to 1 and the CAPWAP control message elements, are transported in UDP packets encapsulated in IP. Figure 2-5 also shows how CAPWAP data messages are also transported in UDP packets, with the C-Bit in the CAPWAP header set to 0.

RFC 5415 notes that the CAPWAP protocol supports both UDP and UDP-Lite (RFC 3828). When CAPWAP runs over IPv4, UDP is mandatory for both control and data channels. When CAPWAP runs natively over IPv6, RFC 5415 states that the control channel must use UDP, but the data channel can use either UDP or UDP-Lite. Because, at press time, the CUWN supports native IPv4 only, the UDP-based implementation is assumed in the rest of this book.

Because the AC is the point of ingress/egress for WLAN traffic, the IP address of WLAN clients like Host A comes from the pool of addresses on the network upstream of the AC.

CAPWAP provides fragmentation and reassembly services. The task group defining RFC 5415 added these capabilities to the CAPWAP protocol, instead of just relying on IP layer fragmentation and reassembly services, so that CAPWAP would be flexible enough to traverse Network Address Translation (NAT) and firewall boundaries, where IP fragments are often dropped.

The sender of the CAPWAP packet (either the WTP or the AC) is responsible for fragmenting the frame when the encapsulated frame exceeds the transport layer MTU. Reassembly of the original fragmented frame is handled by the receiver (either the WTP or the AC) before the frame is processed further. There is a Fragment ID field defined in the CAPWAP header used to assist in reassembly.

To assist in selecting an optimal fragmentation boundary, RFC 5415 says that the WTP and AC should perform a Path MTU discovery of some kind and periodically update the Path MTU during operations. The CAPWAP RFC suggests using well-known methods of Path MTU discovery, as defined in RFC 1191, RFC 1981, and RFC 4821.

CAPWAP MAC Modes

The CAPWAP RFC defines two modes for handling 802.11 MAC functionality—Split MAC mode and Local MAC mode. The sections that follow describe these modes.

Split MAC Mode

The default CAPWAP mode of operation is called *Split MAC* mode. The term *Split MAC* derives from the fact that responsibility for processing the 802.11 MAC is divided between the WTP and the AC. Figure 2-6 illustrates CAPWAP Split MAC mode.

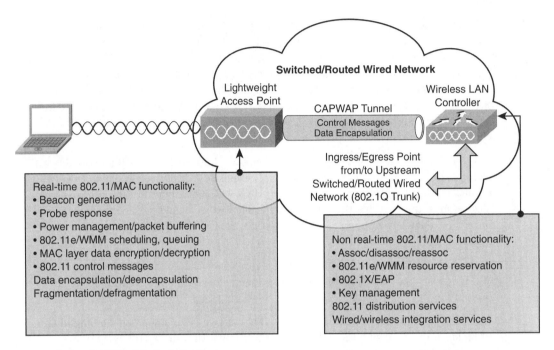

Figure 2-6   *CAPWAP Split Mac Mode*

Conceptually, the division of labor is between real-time and non-real-time 802.11 MAC functionality. 802.11 MAC functionality that requires direct, real-time access to the RF medium (for example, 802.11 control frames) is processed directly at the WTP. 802.11 MAC functionality requiring non-real-time access to the RF medium (for example, 802.11 association requests) is processed at the AC.

When the system is operating in Split MAC mode, all wireless station data must traverse the network through the AC. Wireless data coming off the RF medium is encapsulated in CAPWAP data messages and forwarded to the controller. Data intended for any wireless client device is routed/switched to the AC, where it is encapsulated in CAPWAP and forwarded to the appropriate WTP.

CAPWAP Split MAC mode allows the CUWN to support scalable, secure client mobility as well as other interesting advanced services. It is the default mode of operation in the CUWN. Unless otherwise explicitly specified, CAPWAP Split MAC mode is the assumed mode of operation in this document.

Local MAC Mode

The CAPWAP RFC also defines an operational mode called *Local MAC*, as illustrated in Figure 2-7.

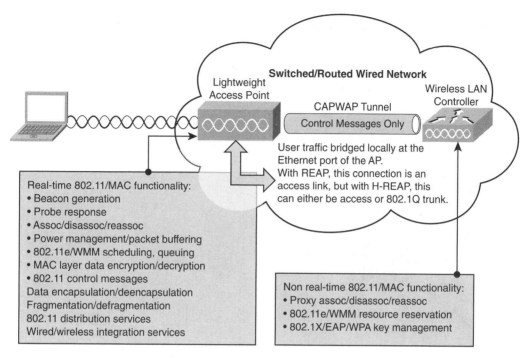

Figure 2-7 *CAPWAP Local Mac Mode*

The Local MAC implementation pushes some of the non-real-time MAC functionality back to the WTP. Additionally, the Local MAC implementation allows the WTP to bridge data traffic onto a local network instead of encapsulating and forwarding it to the AC.

Local MAC mode provides some advantages over Split MAC mode when the network between the WTP and AC is bandwidth and latency constrained. But it also has big disadvantages in that key non-real-time functionality related to managing mobility is distributed instead of centralized. This means that in Local MAC mode, support for roaming and other advanced features related to mobility is more challenging and has some limitations. Chapter 6, "Cisco Unified Wireless LAN Architectures," describes the implementations of these MAC modes in an architectural context.

Summary of CAPWAP

An understanding of CAPWAP fundamentals is essential to designing and deploying the CUWN. CAPWAP is the underlying fabric of the CUWN. CAPWAP defines the control protocol and data encapsulation mechanisms used by the CUWN. CAPWAP is transported in UDP datagrams across the network. The CAPWAP state machine describes the lifetime of WTPs in the CUWN. The key states are discovery, join, image data, config, and run. CAPWAP has two MAC processing modes—Split MAC and Local MAC.

Packet Flow in the Cisco Unified Wireless Network

The following sections look at how packets flow in the CUWN. The sections begin by looking at CAPWAP control messages and then move on to CAPWAP data messages.

For these sections, refer to Figure 2-8.

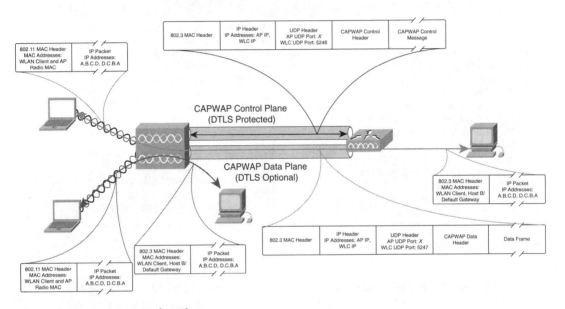

Figure 2-8 *CAPWAP Packet Flow*

CAPWAP Control

As shown in Figure 2-8, CAPWAP control messages flow between the WTP and AC in UDP datagrams. The WTP uses a UDP port number that is derived from a hash of the WTP's Ethernet MAC address. This port number is always greater than 1024 and will be unique for each WTP. The AC will always use UDP port number 5247 for CAPWAP control messages.

Naturally, the UDP datagrams are transported over the network in IP packets. The IP addresses used are the WTP's IP address and the AC's WTP manager IP address.

CAPWAP Data Path: Centrally Bridged Traffic

Figure 2-8 also illustrates the data path when the system is centrally switching CAPWAP data traffic, which is typical with Split MAC operation and the default with the CUWN. In Figure 2-8, wireless station Host A is associated to WTP-1 and is communicating with the wired device Host B. When Host A transmits a data frame, it is received by WTP-1, encapsulated into a CAPWAP data packet, and transmitted to the AC. As Figure 2-8 illustrates, the entire 802.11 data frame is encapsulated with a CAPWAP header and then encapsulated into a UDP datagram, which of course is carried as an IP packet. The IP packet uses the WTP's IP address as the source IP address and the AC's WTP manager IP address as the destination address. After the IP packet arrives at the AC, the AC extracts the CAPWAP header for processing. The AC extracts the 802.11 data frame, strips off the 802.11 MAC header, and then places the payload into an 802.3 Ethernet frame that is bridged onto an appropriate VLAN on the wired network. The wired, switched/routed network delivers the data frame to Host B.

When Host B transmits a data packet to Host A, the process essentially works in reverse. The wired, switched/routed network delivers an Ethernet-encapsulated IP packet to the AC. The AC extracts the IP packet from the Ethernet frame and builds an 802.11 data frame. The controller adds a CAPWAP header and builds a UDP datagram with the CAPWAP-encapsulated 802.11 data frame as the protocol data unit (PDU). Of course, the UDP datagram is carried in an IP packet, with the AC WTP manager IP address as the source IP address and the WTP's IP address as the destination. After the CAPWAP packet arrives at the WTP, the WTP processes the CAPWAP header and extracts the 802.11 data frame. The 802.11 data frame is bridged onto the wireless network to deliver it to Host A.

As shown in Figure 2-8, the WTP uses a UDP port number that is derived from a hash of the WTP's Ethernet MAC address. This port number is always greater than 1024 and will be unique for each WTP. The AC will always use UDP port number 5246 for CAPWAP data messages.

CAPWAP Data Path: Locally Bridged Traffic

Data traffic can be locally bridged on a per-WLAN basis.

As shown in Figure 2-8, when the WTP is locally bridged traffic, data frames are bridged directly onto or off of the wired network at the WTP instead of being passed through the AC. So, when the wireless station Host A sends a data frame destined for wired Host B, the WTP receives the 802.11 data frame off the air, strips off the 802.11 header, and replaces it with an 802.3 Ethernet header. The Ethernet frame is then bridged directly onto the wired network by the WTP. The wired switched/routed network delivers the data frame to Host B.

When wired Host B sends a data frame destined for wireless Host B, the switched/routed network delivers the data frame to the WTP as an Ethernet frame. The WTP strips off the Ethernet header and replaces it with an 802.11 header to make an 802.11 data frame. This 802.11 data frame is subsequently sent out over the air by the WTP to wireless station Host A.

Summary of Packet Flow

Understanding how packets flow is important for successfully designing and deploying the CUWN. CAPWAP control messages traverse the network between the WTP and AC as UDP datagrams. The AC always uses UDP port 5247 for CAPWAP control messages while the WTP uses a port number that is greater than 1024 and is based on a hash of the WTP's Ethernet MAC address.

Data packets will traverse the network differently, depending on the CAPWAP MAC mode. With CAPWAP Split MAC mode, all data frames flow through the AC on and off the network. The data packets are carried between the AC and WTP in CAPWAP-encapsulated packets. The AC will always use UDP port 5246 for CAPWAP data packets, while the WTP uses a port number that is greater than 1024 and is based on a hash of the WTP's Ethernet MAC address. With CAPWAP Local MAC mode, data frames are bridged on and off the wired network at the WTP instead of at the AC.

Summary

This chapter reviewed the relevant physical, MAC, and network layer protocols for deploying controller-based WLANs. These included the IEEE 802.11 family of protocols and the IETF's CAPWAP protocol. With this background, you can now move on to more advanced topics, starting with 802.11n. Later chapters discuss wireless security.

References

Books on WLAN Technology

1. Roshan, P. and Leary, J. *802.11 Wireless LAN Fundamentals*. Indianapolis, Indiana: Cisco Press; 2003.

2. O'Hara, B. and Petrick, A. *IEEE 802.11 Handbook*. New York, New York: IEEE Press; 2005.

3. Gast, M.S. *802.11 Wireless Networks, The Definitive Guide*. Sebastopol, California: O'Reilly & Associates, Inc; 2002.

4. Perahia, E. and Stacey, R. *Next Generation Wireless LANs, Throughput, Robustness, and Reliability in 802.11n*. New York, New York: Cambridge University Press; 2008.

Relevant RFCs and Standards Documentation

1. **RFC 4564**, "Objectives for Control and Provisioning of Wireless Access Points (CAPWAP)," S. Govindan, H. Cheng, ZH Yao, WH Zhou, and L. Yang, IETF, www.rfc-editor. org/rfc/rfc4564.txt, July 2006.

2. **RFC 5415**, "Control and Provisioning of Wireless Access Points (CAPWAP) Protocol Specification," P. Calhoun, M. Montemurro, and D. Stanley, IETF, www.rfc-editor.org/ rfc/rfc5415.txt, March 2009.

3. RFC 5416, "Control and Provisioning of Wireless Access Points (CAPWAP) Protocol Binding for IEEE 802.11," P. Calhoun, M. Montemurro, and D. Stanley, IETF, www.rfc-editor.org/rfc/rfc5416.txt, March 2009.

4. RFC 5417, "Control and Provisioning of Wireless Access Points (CAPWAP) Access Controller DHCP Option," P. Calhoun, IETF, www.rfc-editor.org/rfc/rfc5417.txt, March 2009.

5. RFC 5418, "Control and Provisioning of Wireless Access Points (CAPWAP) Threat Analysis for IEEE 802.11 Deployments," S. Kelly and T. Clancy, IETF, www.rfc-editor.org/rfc/rfc5418.txt, March 2009.

6. RFC 4347, "Datagram Transport Layer Security," E. Rescorla and N. Modadugu, IETF, www.rfc-editor.org/rfc/rfc4347.txt, April 2006.

7. IEEE 802.11-2007, "Wireless LAN Medium Access Control (MAC) and Physical Layer (PHY) Specifications," http://standards.ieee.org/getieee802/download/802.11-2007.pdf, IEEE, June 12, 2007.

Chapter 3

802.11n

The demand for higher-performance wireless LANs (WLAN) drove the development of the IEEE 802.11n standard. IEEE 802.11a and IEEE 802.11g WLANs support a maximum physical layer data rate of 54 Mbps and approximate application level data rates of 30 Mbps. Many wired applications using higher data rates, such as high-definition video and system backup applications, are slowly migrating to WLANs. The IEEE created the 802.11n standard to provide increased WLAN capacity to meet the requirements for many applications on wired Ethernet networks. The goal of 802.11n was to provide performance parity with 100-Mbps Fast Ethernet over a wireless media. This goal was driven by the state of most wired Ethernet devices supporting 100-Mbps Fast Ethernet at the time the 802.11n working group started on the development of 802.11n. To migrate the majority of LAN clients to the WLAN requires providing performance parity with the wired LAN, which for many devices until recently was 100-Mbps Fast Ethernet. Achieving this performance goal with 802.11n would allow many more devices and applications to migrate to the WLAN. Gigabit Ethernet was not common in client devices at the time the work started on 802.11n. With the proper design and deployment, the 802.11n standard provides the potential to meet the performance requirements for the many client devices and applications that require at least 100-Mbps Ethernet connections.

The 802.11n standard supports up to a physical layer data-link rate of 600 Mbps. 802.11n is backward compatible with 802.11a/b/g, and 802.11n devices can coexist with 802.11a/b/g devices. 802.11n dual-band devices can support communications using any of the 802.11a/b/g protocols, where dual-band support means providing support for both 2.4-GHz and 5-GHz 802.11 frequency bands at the same time. Legacy devices communicating with 802.11n devices might experience the benefits of performance improvement when communicating with 802.11n devices. The term *legacy device* refers to any device that does not have 802.11n support and uses 802.11a/b/g. Many of the 802.11n technology improvements provide increased signal-to-noise ratio (SNR) improvements for legacy device communications. This chapter presents an overview of the changes introduced with 802.11n and explains the fundamentals driving improved performance.

IEEE 802.11n Standard

The 802/11n standard was ratified in September 2009 and can be obtained from www.ieee.org. It took the IEEE working group, task group N (TGN) approximately five years to produce the ratified version of the 802.11n standard. Numerous draft revisions of the 802.11n standard were created to produce the final product of the IEEE-ratified 802.11n standard that consists of over 500 pages of specifications. 802.11n is similar to many of the other standards in the 802.11 family. It builds upon and adds to many prior 802.11 standards. 802.11n should be viewed as an addition to the current baseline 802.11 standards until a roll-up standard emerges that encompasses 802.11n and the other foundation 802.11 standards it is built upon. The 802.11n specification draws into use many additional radio technologies such as multiple input, multiple output (MIMO) and antenna arrays that provide major performance improvements; however, the details of use are left to the radio developers and not specified by the 802.11n standard. For example, the radio designer might choose to use MIMO to provide increased downlink signal strength using a beam-forming technique such as Cisco Client Link, which is unique to Cisco radio implementation and not specified by the 802.11n standards. But it should be noted that some MIMO techniques, such as Cisco Client Link, can interoperate with any Wi-Fi client, whereas some MIMO techniques require specific support on both sides of the radio link.

Three commercial phases of products developed over the span of 802.11n's development. The need for higher-capacity WLAN products produced several phases of commercial 11n products. The first were the pre-802.11n-like products. The early pre-802.11n-like products provided some performance improvement, but were not interoperable with other vendors or the standards-based 802.11n products that appeared in the second and third phases of the market.

The second phase of the 802.11n market occurred when 802.11n products took a form that the industry standardized on to ensure interoperability. The second phase built products to the 802.11n Draft 2 (D2) mandatory features. 802.11n D2 was used by the Wi-Fi Alliance to set a foundation for interoperability testing. Any 802.11n vendors could build their products to the Draft 2 specification and submit to the Wi-Fi Alliance for testing of interoperability and compliance to the minimum set of features required for 802.11n interoperability. The device that achieves this certification is branded as Draft n certification, with the logo shown in Figure 3-1.

The third phase of the 802.11n market is based on the ratified 802.11n standard. The 802.11n standard consists of mandatory features and optional features. A very large part of the standard has optional features that no product is required to support to be considered compliant to the standard. The ratified standard added no additional mandatory features since the release of the Draft 2 specification. This means that all products produced to the Draft 2 specification and certified by the Wi-Fi Alliance are interoperable and compliant with the final ratified 802.11n standard. The Wi-Fi Alliance updated its certification testing to reflect the ratification of the 802.11n standard with a new logo, as show in Figure 3-2. The result is that all Draft n– and n-certified 802.11n products are interoperable.

Figure 3-1   *Wi-Fi Alliance Draft n Interoperability Certification Logo*

Figure 3-2 *Wi-Fi Alliance 802.11n Interoperability Certification Logo for Ratified Version of IEEE 802.11n*

The capabilities and performance of 802.11n products can vary depending upon which 802.11n optional features are implemented. Prior 802.11 standards did not have different data rates based upon the options implemented in the device, as is the case for 802.11n. For example, all 802.11a adapters talking to an 802.11a access point provide a maximum physical data rate connection of 54 Mbps with adequate signal strength. With 802.11n devices, the maximum physical data rate could be anywhere from 802.11a or 802.11g rates of 54 Mbps to a maximum of 600 Mbps. The maximum data rate is dependent on which 802.11n features are supported between the 802.11n devices and what the environment will support.

Tip   Evaluate the 802.11n options support by the wireless clients to ensure the capability to achieve the desired throughput. Support of 802.11n is not enough to ensure achieving desired performance because the various 802.11n implementation options can produce differing levels of performance.

802.11n MAC

The 802.11n MAC layer adds the high-throughput (HT) elements to the 802.11 MAC layer. All additional 802.11n capabilities are signaled through the HT elements in 802.11 management frames. Any 802.11 devices that associate with a data rate greater than 54 Mbps obviously support 802.11n. When uncertain whether a device supports 802.11n, an easy method to verify 802.11n capabilities is to look for the presence of the HT elements in the device's transmission of 802.11 management frames, which contain device capabilities. The HT fields should be present in beacons and association request frames for devices with 802.11n support enabled. Figure 3-3 shows the HT capabilities section that appears in an 802.11n management frame such as a beacon or association request. The HT capabilities information contains several subsections describing the various 802.11n options. Throughout this chapter, you find overview coverage of the HT fields as a means to identify what specific 802.11n features are supported. 802.11n defines numerous optional features that might require a wireless packet capture to determine the features supported. Understanding the HT fields also provides insight into the capabilities that 802.11n devices might support in the future. The HT capabilities fields that you might encounter are as follows:

- **HT capabilities:** Defines whether 802.11n HT capabilities are supported

- **HT operations:** Signaling of HT operations

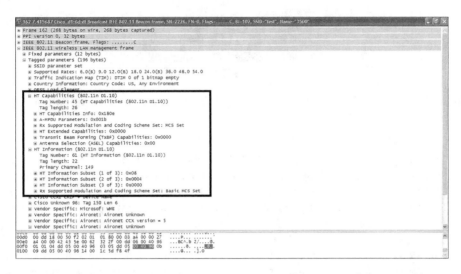

Figure 3-3 *802.11n Protocol Analyzer Trace Showing the HT Capabilities Fields*

- **MPDU:** Message Protocol Data Unit (MPDU) packet aggregation operations

- **MSDU:** MAC Service Data Unit (MSDU) packet aggregation options

- **BACK:** Block transfer and acknowledge operations

- **Protection:** Protection for using HT PHY with legacy devices

- **L-SIG TXOP:** Setting Network Allocation Vector (NAV) for non-HT devices

- **RD:** Reverse direction protocol

- **Link adoption:** HT-specific link adoption and feedback

- **Transmit beam forming:** HT transit beam-forming operations

- **ASEL:** Transmit antenna selection operation

- **NDP:** Null data packet support

- **STBC:** Space time block coding transmit diversity

- **SMPS:** Spatial multiplexing power save operations

- **20/40-Mhz channels:** 20- and 40-MHz channel operations

- **PCO:** Phased coexistence of 20- and 40-channel operations

Tip Determine the 802.11n capabilities of a device using an 802.11n protocol analyzer such as Wireshark (www.wireshark.com) or OmniPeek (www.wildpackets.com). The contents of the HT capabilities fields will indicate which optional 802.11n capabilities are supported. Some devices allow 802.11n support to be enabled or disabled in the device driver configuration, which might need to be configured to enable all 802.11n capabilities the device supports.

Other 802.11 Standards Used with 802.11n

Many of the capabilities in 802.11n build upon the functionality specified in other 802.11 standards. The 802.11n standard is additive to 802.11-2007 as a foundation. 802.11-2007 is a roll-up standard of the original 802.11 standard plus 802.11a, b, d, e, g, h, j, and i. 802.11n also utilizes capabilities in 802.11r, 802.11k, and 802.11w. The 802.11n standard is also used by the 802.11y standard. Table 3-1 lists the various standards related to 802.11n and their key features.

Table 3-1 *IEEE 802.11 Standards Used with 802.11n*

IEEE Standard	Main Feature
802.11	1 and 2 Mbps (2.4 GHz)
802.11a	54 Mbps in 5-GHz band
802.11b	5.5 and 11 Mbps (2.4 GHz)
802.11d	International (country to country)
802.11e	Quality of service
802.11g	54 Mbps (2.4 GHz)
802.11h	Spectrum management (5 GHz)
802.11i	Enhanced security (AES)
802.11j	Japan extension
802.11k	Radio Resource Management
802.11r	Fast roaming
802.11w	Management frame protection
802.11y	Point to point (3.6 GHz)
802.11-2007	Roll-up of 802.11 plus 802.11a, b, d, e, g, h, i, and j

Frequency Bands Supported by 802.11n

802.11n specifies support for increased data rates for both the 2.4-GHz and 5-Ghz frequency bands, unlike prior 802.11 standards such as 802.11a, 802.11b, and 802.11g, which were designed for a specific frequency band (2.4 GHz or 5 GHz). 802.11n can be utilized in both frequency bands. This means you can have devices that support 802.11a and 802.11n in the 5-GHz band as well as devices will that support 802.11b, 802.11g, and 802.11n in the 2.4-GHz band. Most devices will likely support 802.11n in both frequency bands but there is no mandate saying an 802.11n-compliant device *must* support both frequency bands. The dual-frequency band support is an optional feature.

The 5-GHz band is allowed in certain countries, thus allowing a larger spectrum for 802.11n. The channels in the 5-GHz range are nonoverlapping unlike in the 2.4-GHz range. The greatest amount of WLAN capacity will be achieved utilizing 802.11n in both the 5-GHz and 2.4-GHz channels.

Tip   Using dual-band 802.11n adapters provides greater performance and capacity. Enable 802.11n for both 2.4-GHz and 5-GHz bands to maximize efficient use of the spectrum to provide greater capacity.

Antenna Arrays

Antenna arrays are used with 802.11n access points and clients to improve performance. An *antenna array* is an antenna system that employs multiple antenna elements. The use of an antenna array enables increased signal gain and performance over a single-element antenna configuration. Single antenna elements will produce a specific propagation pattern. When several antenna elements are combined into an antenna array, the overall propagation pattern and signal-to-noise levels are improved because of the array effect. The actual performance improvements achieved are dependent on the signal-processing techniques used with the antenna array. Signal-processing techniques are methods that use microprocessors to manipulate the RF signal to or from each antenna in a manner that increases the performance of the radio link.

A common use of antenna arrays before 802.11n was to enable receiver diversity. *Receiver diversity* is an RF technique to increase the performance of the radio link. Receiver diversity is discussed in more detail later in this chapter. An example of antenna diversity is with 802.11a/b/g devices using two antennas with one radio to provide branch selection diversity, also referred to as *switched diversity*. With 802.11n, the antenna arrays are used to enable additional receiver diversity techniques. More than two antennas can be used with the advanced receiver diversity techniques supported by 802.11n devices.

The antenna array can also be used for techniques that employ multiple simultaneous transmitters with 802.11n devices. Examples of multiple simultaneous transmission techniques are techniques such as beam forming, spatial multiplexing, and space-time block coding (STBC). Note that some techniques that use simultaneous transmitter techniques might not be used at the same time in a communication for a single communication event. Each technique uses the antenna and signal processor in a different manner, producing different results. Some simultaneous transmit techniques are mutually exclusive, with only one type of transmit technique used at a time. The radio sends each transmission using a specific transmission array technique. For example, the radio might send a transmission to one client with a beam-forming signal and send the next packet transmission to a different client using a spatial multiplexed signal. The receivers might use both receive antenna diversity techniques.

Transmit Beam Forming (TxBF)

Transmit beam forming (TxBF) is the use of an antenna array with multiple transmitters to increase the signal gain to a specific client or propagation area. This is achieved by electronically changing the propagation characteristics of the wireless signal. This can be accomplished through different combinations of antennas and modification of the transmit signal applied to each individual antenna element within the antenna array. The result is an improvement of the signal quality between the sender and receiver. Figure 3-4 shows an example of beam forming. The top picture depicts propagation without beam forming, where the client might be out of range, and the bottom picture depicts using multiple transmitters to change the propagation area to communicate with a client that would otherwise be out of range. Beam forming can be used to either extend the coverage area or to increase the data rate by increasing the SNR.

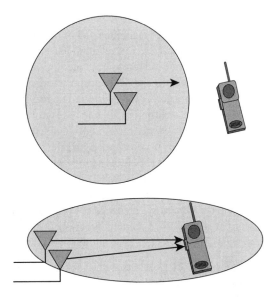

Figure 3-4 *Comparison of Beam Forming Providing Improved Coverage (Bottom) Compared to Non-Beam-Forming Coverage (Top)*

Proper signal processing causes multiple simultaneous transmitters to create regions where the signal arrives, creating constructive interference and increasing the signal strength and quality. In this case, the multipath produces a good effect by increasing the signal's strength. The multiple transmissions will also arrive in some regions with destructive interference, reducing the quality of the signal. To create constructive interference, the signal needs to arrive at the destination in phases. This is commonly referred to as *cophase* such that the signal can be combined into a stronger signal at the reception point for that specific client.

Figure 3-5 shows an example of beam forming with constructive and destructive interference areas. The top picture depicts the propagation areas with no beam forming, and the bottom picture depicts the propagation with beam forming. Notice that beam forming might produce multiple formed lobes and not just a single lobe for the desired client, where a lobe is the direction of propagation with stronger signal strength. Several additional lobes can be generated away from the intended direction of the target client, as shown in the bottom example of Figure 3-5. The radio's signal processor makes adjustments to the transmitter to control the direction of the beams. Two types of beam forming exist, legacy and 802.11n, the key difference being how the beam is created and the feedback mechanisms used to control the direction of the beam. The result of beam forming is that the propagation lobe produced will have a reduced beam width, providing increased signal strength or range for each receiver.

Beam Steering

Beam steering is another beam-forming technique used to direct the propagation pattern in a specific direction or to a specific area. Several methods exist for beam-form steering. One method is to use an electronically adaptive array method, where a set of adjustments, referred to as *array weight*, are used to change the propagation pattern. An analogy of array weight is surround-sound processing on a surround-sound stereo system, which results in specific sounds radiating at different volume levels from specific speakers. With a stereo system, you can adjust the volume front to back and left to right, but you can also make the vocal louder than the drums if you choose, and the surround-sound encoding tells the sound processor which sounds should be sent to what speaker and at what volume. The wireless device's digital signal processor (DSP) uses array weights with the antenna array to achieve an analogous control over the direction and strength of wireless signal propagation. This results in the capability to change the propagation pattern of an antenna array. Even if the antenna area consists of an omnidirectional antenna, the antenna can electronically be made to produce effective propagation like a directional antenna.

Other methods of beam steering are possible, such as mechanically steering a directional antenna in the antenna array or using multiple types of antennas in the antenna array with different propagation patterns and switching between antennas to steer the propagation direction of the antenna array. The use of mechanical and switched antenna methods is often referred to as a *smart antenna*. A smart antenna can be employed with adaptive array methods. The result of all beam-steering approaches is to increase the SNR to each receiver.

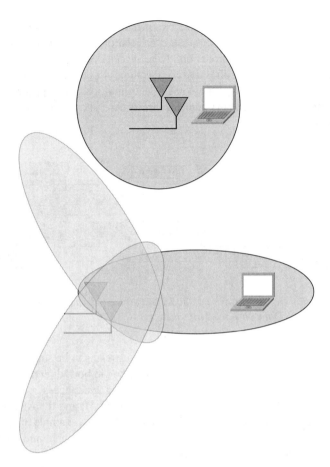

Figure 3-5 *Coverage Area Comparison Between Non-Beam Forming (Top) and Beam Forming (Bottom). Notice That Beam Forming Improves the Coverage Area for the Client with Additional Lobes Formed in Directions Away from the Client.*

Spatial Multiplexing

Spatial multiplexing sends a unique data stream on each transmitter and antenna in the antenna array, as shown in Figure 3-6. This technique relies on low correlation between the elements in the antenna array. Low antenna correlation means that the receiver can see the difference between the transmitters sending different data streams. The receiver antenna has a low degree of correlation if the characteristics of the transmission from two different transmitters are uniquely different. For example, if the delay and degree angle of arrival of the transmission from two different transmit antennas are very different, there would be a low degree of antenna correlation. If the antenna, and thus wireless channel, has a low degree of correlation, the receiver's DSP will be able to demodulate multiple data streams. The result is that large volumes of data can be sent in the wireless channel. The environment must have some level of multipath to support spatial multiplexing. The better the multipath environment, the greater the capability to support multiple spatial streams.

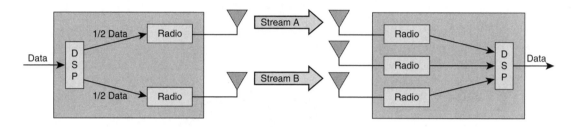

Figure 3-6 *Functional Representation of 802.11n Devices Using Spatial Multiplexing Sending a Different Data Stream of Data on Each Transmitter*

The 802.11n specification allows up to four spatial streams to be supported. The number of spatial streams used does not have to be symmetric in both directions of the conversation. For example, a 1x1:1 client communication with a 2x3:2 access point (AP) can communicate using one spatial stream from the client to the AP, and the AP can communicate to the client using a utilizing two spatial streams. 1x1:1 is an example of MIMO nomenclature that expresses the number of transmit and receive antennas and the number of spatial streams that are deciphered in the MIMO nomenclature section. One of the side effects of transmitting multiple spatial streams is unintentional beam forming, resulting in a degraded signal arriving at the receiver. To prevent unintentional beam forming with multiple spatial streams, cyclic shift techniques are similar to beam forming, with phase modification being performed to prevent beam-forming effects.

The number of spatial streams supported will be equal to or less than the number of the transmitter's transmit RF chains. Supporting four spatial streams requires four TX radio chains at the sender and four receive RF chains at the receiver. Supporting three spatial streams requires three TX radio chains at the transmitter end and three RX radio chains at the receiver end.

The number of spatial streams used will vary based on channel conditions and power. A transmitter and receiver might be capable of supporting more spatial streams; however, because of power consumption considerations, the transmitter might choose to use fewer transmitters to conserve power and thus battery life. The performance when using less than the number of maximum spatial streams will obviously be reduced. When checking performance for 802.11n clients using spatial multiplexing, the power profile of the mobile device needs to be understood and optimized to achieve the desired performance.

The number of spatial streams used can be less than the maximum number supported if the channel conditions indicate that spatial multiplexing will not provide the best performance. The transmitter and receiver autonegotiate the Modulation Coding Scheme (MCS) rate that will produce the best data throughput. MCS is a table of variables for HT data rates. For example, in an open outdoor environment, the correlation between the transmitter and receiver might be so high that it is not possible for the receiver to distinguish between the multiple spatial streams being transmitted. In this case, the communication link cannot use spatial multiplexing to improve the data-link performance, which would result in an MCS rate with a single spatial stream in the MCS rate table.

Transmit Diversity

Transmit diversity sends the same data out of multiple transmitters. By sending multiple copies of the data, the strongest representation of the original signal can be re-created at the receiver. While a number of different transmit diversity techniques are possible, the one specifically supported as an optional feature with 802.11n devices that use different algorithms is space-time block coding (STBC).

STBC is an optional technique in the 802.11n protocol to improve the signal strength at the receiver. STBC encodes redundant information across multiple transmitters, as shown in Figure 3-7. The result is a stronger signal at the receiver. STBC basically uses the power of multiple transmitters. Using STBC requires both the transmitter and receiver to support STBC. STBC was created to provide a means to increase signal strength for receivers that cannot utilize MIMO receiver techniques because of either the physical space constraints to support multiple antennas for an antenna array or the additional power requirements needed to support the multiple radio chains required for MIMO. Figure 3-8 shows the HT capabilities field, indicating device support for sending or receiving STBC transmissions.

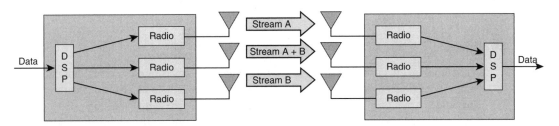

Figure 3-7 *Block Diagram Showing STBC Sending Redundant Information to the Receiver to Create a Stronger Signal at the Receiver*

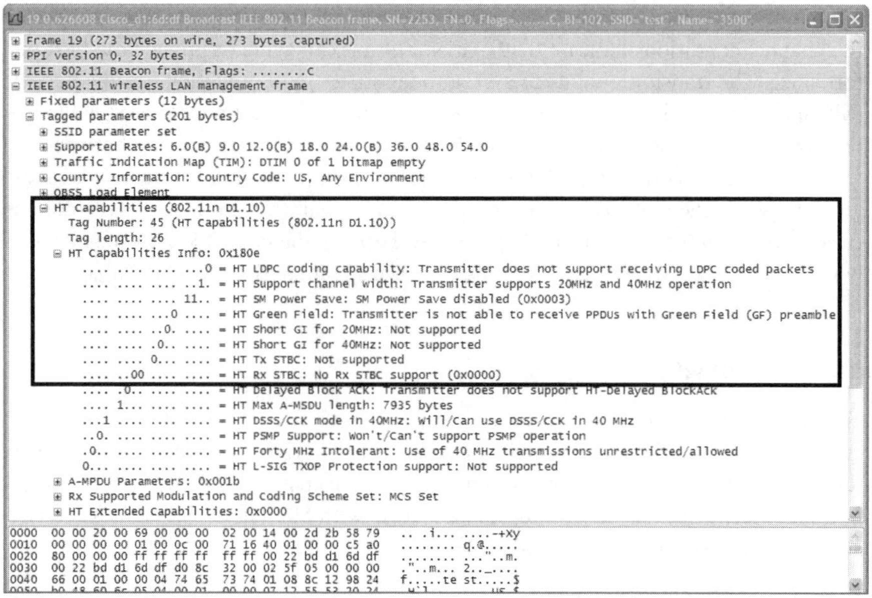

```
19 0.676608 Cisco_d1:6d:df Broadcast IEEE 802.11 Beacon frame, SN=2253, FN=0, Flags=........C, BI=102, SSID="test", Name="3500"   _ □ X
⊞ Frame 19 (273 bytes on wire, 273 bytes captured)
⊞ PPI version 0, 32 bytes
⊞ IEEE 802.11 Beacon frame, Flags: ........C
⊟ IEEE 802.11 wireless LAN management frame
  ⊞ Fixed parameters (12 bytes)
  ⊟ Tagged parameters (201 bytes)
    ⊞ SSID parameter set
    ⊞ Supported Rates: 6.0(B) 9.0 12.0(B) 18.0 24.0(B) 36.0 48.0 54.0
    ⊞ Traffic Indication Map (TIM): DTIM 0 of 1 bitmap empty
    ⊞ Country Information: Country Code: US, Any Environment
    ⊞ OBSS Load Element
    ⊟ HT Capabilities (802.11n D1.10)
       Tag Number: 45 (HT Capabilities (802.11n D1.10))
       Tag length: 26
    ⊟ HT Capabilities Info: 0x180e
       .... .... .... ...0 = HT LDPC coding capability: Transmitter does not support receiving LDPC coded packets
       .... .... .... ..1. = HT Support channel width: Transmitter supports 20MHz and 40MHz operation
       .... .... .... 11.. = HT SM Power Save: SM Power Save disabled (0x0003)
       .... .... ...0 .... = HT Green Field: Transmitter is not able to receive PPDUs with Green Field (GF) preamble
       .... .... ..0. .... = HT Short GI for 20MHz: Not supported
       .... .... .0.. .... = HT Short GI for 40MHz: Not supported
       .... .... 0... .... = HT Tx STBC: Not supported
       .... ..00 .... .... = HT RX STBC: No Rx STBC support (0x0000)
       .... .0.. .... .... = HT Delayed Block ACK: Transmitter does not support HT-Delayed BlockAck
       .... 1... .... .... = HT Max A-MSDU length: 7935 bytes
       ...1 .... .... .... = HT DSSS/CCK mode in 40MHz: Will/can use DSSS/CCK in 40 MHz
       ..0. .... .... .... = HT PSMP Support: Won't/Can't support PSMP operation
       .0.. .... .... .... = HT Forty MHz Intolerant: Use of 40 MHz transmissions unrestricted/allowed
       0... .... .... .... = L-SIG TXOP Protection support: Not supported
    ⊞ A-MPDU Parameters: 0x001b
    ⊞ Rx Supported Modulation and Coding Scheme Set: MCS Set
    ⊞ HT Extended Capabilities: 0x0000

0000  00 00 20 00 69 00 00 00  02 00 14 00 2d 2b 58 79   .. .i.. ....-+Xy
0010  00 00 00 00 01 00 0c 00  71 16 40 01 00 00 c5 a0   ........ q.@.....
0020  80 00 00 00 ff ff ff ff  ff ff 00 22 bd d1 6d df   ........ ...".m.
0030  00 22 bd d1 6d df d0 8c  32 00 02 5f 05 00 00 00   .".m... 2.._....
0040  66 00 01 00 00 04 74 65  73 74 01 08 8c 12 98 24   f.....te st.....$
0050  b0 48 60 6c 05 04 00 01  00 00 07 12 55 53 20 24   .H`l.... ....US $
```

Figure 3-8 *802.11n Capabilities Field Showing Whether Transmit or Receive STBC Is Supported*

Multiple Input, Multiple Output (MIMO)

MIMO support is a key addition that 802.11n uses to increase performance. A MIMO radio attaches to an antenna array, and the antenna is attached to a dedicated radio, which is referred to as an *RF chain*. Multiple RF chains work with advanced signal processing techniques to increase performance for both 802.11n devices and legacy a/b/g devices.

Multipath

Multipath is an effect produced when wireless signals reflect, scatter, or delay. Multipath results in creating multiple copies of the same wireless transmission arriving at the receiver at different points in time with different signal strengths. These multiple copies of the same signal will often result in destructive interference. Before the use of MIMO, multipath would degrade the signal seen by the receiver and the overall performance of the wireless communication link. Prior to the use of MIMO, wireless communication systems were designed to avoid multipath effects.

Each environment has different multipath characteristics. An 802.11n receiver must estimate the channel's multipath characteristics to utilize multipath to improve SNR and data transmission capacity. The 802.11n standard defines six channel models, as shown in Table 3-2. These are used by the receiver to classify the channel's multipath characteristics and by radio developers to predict performance. An 802.11n receiver uses the HT Long Training Fields (HT LTF) to estimate the channel characteristics.

Table 3-2 *802.11n Channel Models*

Model	Environment	Delay Spread in Nanoseconds
A	Theoretical ideal representation with no signal reflection	0
B	Residential	15
C	Small office	30
D	Typical office	50
E	Large office or indoor space	100
F	Large indoor or outdoor space	150

The characteristics used to distinguish between channel models is the amount of *multipath*. Multipath will vary based on the number of reflective surfaces in the environment. Those reflective surfaces will cause the RF to create multiple copies of the same RF signal to arrive at different times. The time difference between the first copy of the RF signal and reflected copies of the RF signal is referred to as *delay spread*. A subset of the IEEE channel models is commonly used for modeling performance, consisting of channel model B for residential environments, channel model D for average-size office environments, and channel model E for large indoor or outdoor spaces.

Some of the 802.11n performance improvements can be utilized in an environment with sufficient multipath. For example, spatial multiplexing requires sufficient multipath to operate. Most indoor environments will have sufficient multipath to operate, whereas most outdoor environments will have minimal multipath. Measuring and quantifying multipath is extremely complex, but there are tools that you can use to detect and measure multipath delay spreads to provide an indication of the amount of multipath in an environment. Figure 3-9 shows an example of an analyzer being used to measure multipath delay spread. 802.11n radios automatically adjust for different multipath delay spread, but a delay spread analyzer can be used to verify that the environment has sufficient multipath.

MIMO Nomenclature

The convention used to describe the MIMO characteristics varies depending on whether the MIMO device is being described from the perspective of the device or the channel. The MIMO nomenclature used by Cisco and used in this chapter is described in the text that follows.

MIMO devices use a convention N_{TX} (number of transmit radio chains) * N_{RX} (number of receive radio chains) : N_{STS} (number of spatial division multiplexing streams):

$$N_{TX} * N_{RX} : N_{STS}$$

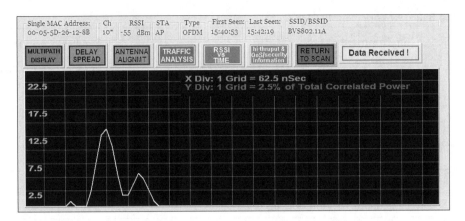

Figure 3-9   *Berkeley Varionic's Analyzer Measurement of the Multipath Delay Spread*

Figure 3-10 illustrates an example of a MIMO 2x3:2 802.11n AP. The nomenclature specifies the number of radio chains, where a radio chain is an antenna and radio. There are two types of radio chains:

■ **A receive-only radio chain:** The antennas will typically be marked with the Rx designation.

■ **A transmit-and-receive radio chain:** The radio will constantly change mode from receiver to transmitter as required. This type of radio chain is typically marked with a Tx/Rx designation.

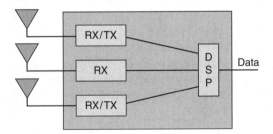

Figure 3-10   *Functional Representation of an 802.11n AP Providing MIMO 2x3:2 Support, Which Consists of Three RF Radio Chains with One Receive-Only and Two Receive Transmits*

For example, the AP in Figure 3-10 is a MIMO 2x3:2 that contains three radio chains for each band. On each band, it has two radio chains that support transmit and receive and one radio chain that is receive-only, which supports receiving and transmitting two spatial streams. This is discussed in more detail in the section, "Spatial Multiplexing," earlier in this chapter. The 802.11n standard mandates that APs support a minimum of MIMO 2x2:2 with optional support up to MIMO 4x4:4.

The 802.11n standard does not require 802.11n clients to support MIMO and multiple spatial streams. There can be many instances where the 802.11n clients support fewer MIMO capabilities than the 802.11n AP because of the potential device size not allowing enough room for multiple antennas or the battery life constraints not affording the power budget to support multiple radio chains. The lowest-capability 802.11n client adapter at press time is a MIMO 1x2:2, but some vendors are developing MIMO 1x1:1 802.11n client adapters for devices without enough space to support two antennas. Consider the case of a client device supporting MIMO. The number of spatial streams support is only two downlink spatial streams and one uplink spatial stream. A client device with 1x2:2 has one receive radio chain and one receive-transmit radio chain, allowing up to 300-Mbps downlink and 150-Mbps uplink speeds. Uplink is defined as transmission from the client to the AP, and downlink is defined as transmission from the AP to the client. A client device might be implemented with 1x2:2 support to reduce the number of trans-mitters, reducing power draw on the device battery. By not requiring multiple transmit-ters for the 802.11n client device, the battery life can be increased for the device. Some client devices will support more than one MIMO transmitter and use the embedded device management to disable one transmitter to conserve battery life. However, the 802.11n standard provides support for devices up to MIMO 4x4:4 if the devices can sup-port it.

Receiver Diversity

Diversity is a receiver technique used to provide a more robust signal at the receiver. Diversity uses multiple antennas to receive multiple copies of the signal in a different point in space. The fundamental concept with diversity is that each antenna provides a different copy of the transmitted signal such that the best signal can be used or created from the combination of the multiples received. The effect is a more consistent signal, with a greater SNR that will support greater data rates. Diversity provides legacy 802.11 wireless stations with a means to work around or avoid some of the negative effects of multipath.

The 802.11n standard, as well as the 802.11, does not specify any requirement to support receiver diversity or the diversity techniques to be implemented. The details for imple-menting receiver diversity are left to each vendor as there are no interoperability require-ments. 802.11n devices will have some form of an antenna array and MIMO support, which inherently provides support for receiver diversity. The level of performance improvements from receiver diversity will be vendor and device dependent.

802.11n devices provide diversity improvements to increase performance. The diversity improvements provided in an 802.11n device increase the number of receive antennas to produce additional copies of the signal and additional diversity signal-processing algo-rithms, which can produce a stronger signal. The type of diversity techniques used as well as antenna orientation with the diversity effect can produce different levels of SNR improvements. To better understand diversity and the importance of antenna orientation, the following sections present several receiver diversity methods.

Branch Selection Diversity

Many legacy 802.11 wireless devices use a branch selection diversity technique. This consists of a single receiver RF radio chain connected to two antennas through a combiner. This diversity method assumes that with sufficient spacing between the two antennas, the signal received at each antenna will fade independently. The combiner simply selects the antenna signal with the best average SNR for any point in time, as illustrated in Figure 3-11. The branch selection algorithm can also be implemented to use other triggers besides average SNR for branch selection.

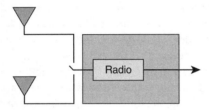

Figure 3-11 *Branch Diversity Selects the Antenna with the Strongest Signal*

An issue with branch selection is that that signal fade is often not equal across all frequencies with the 802.11 signals. For orthogonal frequency-division multiplexing (OFDM) modulated signals, this means that some sub-bands will have a lower SNR than other sub-bands. Some OFDM sub-bands might have a stronger signal on one branch, and others might have a stronger signal on the other branch. Branch selection provides improvements that select the better of the average signals seen on the two signal branches; however, branch selection does not have the capability to combine the best signal for each frequency or OFDM subcarrier.

Antenna selection (ASEL) is an optional feature added in the 802.11n protocol to provide a method to select the best antenna to use in each device when more antennas exist than radios. This could be considered another form of diversity, providing additional intelligence for selecting the best antenna to use over traditional diversity techniques. Figure 3-12 shows two 11n wireless devices (A and B), where each device has more antennas than radios. The selection of antennas is made based upon sounding packets sent between the devices to optimize the antenna selection for the channel state. Figure 3-13 shows the HT Capabilities field that identifies whether ASEL is supported.

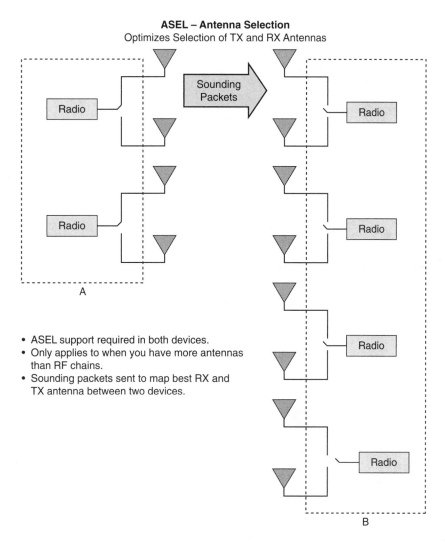

ASEL – Antenna Selection
Optimizes Selection of TX and RX Antennas

- ASEL support required in both devices.
- Only applies to when you have more antennas than RF chains.
- Sounding packets sent to map best RX and TX antenna between two devices.

Figure 3-12 *ASEL Sounding Packets Are Used to Select the Best Antenna Because of the 802.11n Device Having More Antennas than Radios*

Branch-Combining Diversity

Branch diversity combines the receive signal of all the receive antennas. In Figure 3-14, the DSP combines the received signal from each antenna and radio. Different techniques can be used for diversity combining to create a stronger signal across all frequencies or OFDM subcarriers. Some combining methods require more signal-processing capabilities in the device; however, the benefit is the capability to produce a stronger signal in environments with significant fade and multipath conditions. *Fade* is the characteristic of how the transmitted signal diminishes as it propagates through an area. The 802.11n device will automatically select the best diversity-combining algorithm for the environmental conditions. In Figure 3-14, the device receives a different signal on each antenna and uses the DSP to combine the multiple received signals.

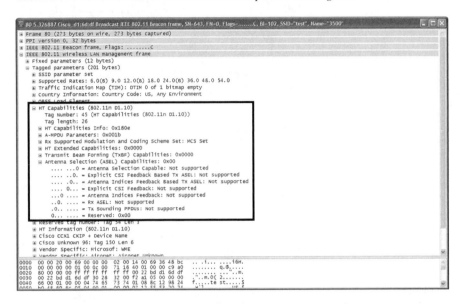

Figure 3-13 *HT Capability Field Indicating Whether ASEL Is Supported*

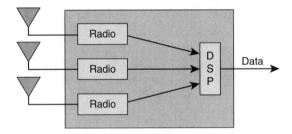

Figure 3-14 *MIMO Radio's DSP Using Branch-Combining Diversity to Create a Stronger Signal by Combining the Information from Three RF Chains*

The greater number of receive antennas, the greater the performance improvements will be from diversity combining. Each additional signal combination will increase both robustness and performance. The 802.11n standard specifies device support for up to four MIMO receive RF chains. This means that up to four signals can be combined through diversity combining if you have four receive RF chains.

Diversity branch combining can also be combined with diversity branch selection. This would consist of two antennas connected to one receive RF chain through a combiner. The combiner selects the signal with the best average SNR to supply to the RF chain. The

RF chain provides the selected signal to the signal processor to combine with the signal from the other RF chains. Many types of branch-combining diversity exist, with each type using a different approach or algorithm for producing the combined signal. The sections that follow describe three of the most-used diversity-combining techniques.

Equal Gain–Combining Diversity

With equal gain combining, the signal processor aligns the phase of the signal for each RF chain and adds the signals together. This method requires the receiver to have sufficient channel information to be able to cophase the signals and combine. This technique gives equal weight to all the signals being combined and results in a linear increase in the signal gain by up to the number of receive RF chains.

Maximum-Ratio-Combining (MRC) Diversity

Maximum ratio combing (MRC) is a common diversity-combining technique used in 802.11n devices. MRC is performed by the signal processor aligning the phase of the signal for each RF chain and adding the signals together as with equal combing. The difference is that the receiver's signal processor uses channel information to weight the values of the different frequency components in each branch. This method maximizes the SNR of the signal by emphasizing the signal components among the RF chains that have the best SNR. This method will produce a better SNR over equal-gain combining, which will produce a linear increase in the signal gain by up to the number of receive RF chains. The weighting process that MRC uses is analogous to how an audio equalizer can make the vocals or bass tracks in music more predominant.

Minimum-Mean-Square-Error (MMSE)-Combining Diversity

With minimum mean square error (MMSE) combining, the signal processor aligns the phase of the signal for each RF chain and adds the signals together, as with MRC combining. The difference is that the receiver uses channel information and error information to weight the signal components to minimize intersymbol errors. MMSE will outperform MRC when significant levels of noise are present in the channel.

Diversity Antenna Array, Type, Orientation, and Spacing

With just two antennas, the antennas are referred to as *diversity antennas*. With MIMO, there will often be more than two antennas, referred to as an *antenna array*. The antenna array influences the performance of the MIMO system. Regardless of which type of diversity is being used, the antennas in the antenna array should be the same type, gain, and orientation for diversity to be effective. The diversity antennas should be receiving the signal from the same coverage area, with the only difference being that they are approximately half a wavelength apart. Spacing the diversity antennas approximately half a wavelength apart provides a high probability that the fade between the antennas will be independent.

In a situation where the diversity antennas are covering different areas that have a different orientation, problems can occur. If the diversity antennas are hearing different areas, the multipath and signal improvements from diversity will be ineffective. Figure 3-15 shows a coverage example for a case where the antennas are not in the proper position, resulting in poor operation of the wireless devices. Figure 3-16 shows the coverage example with the antennas in the proper position to provide the best wireless performance.

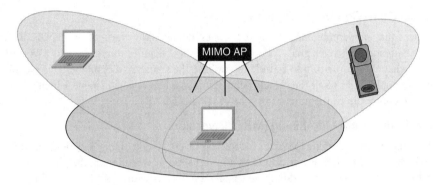

Figure 3-15   *Diversity Antenna Improperly Positioned to Cover Different Areas*

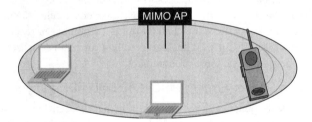

Figure 3-16   *Diversity Antennas Properly Positioned to Cover the Same Areas*

Transmit Beam-Forming Types

Beam forming is an optional feature that can be implemented with 802.11n devices. Cisco 802.11n APs provide beam forming to improve with legacy wireless client devices. This is different from the beam forming specified in the 802.11n device for 802.11n clients. 802.11n TxBF requires that both clients and APs support the specific type of beam forming being used. The three types of beam forming are as follows:

■   Legacy beam forming

■   Implicit beam forming

■   Explicit beam forming

The sections that follow cover these types of beam forming in greater detail.

Legacy Beam Forming

Legacy beam forming is where the 802.11n device provides beam forming to legacy clients. Legacy device beam forming is not specified in the 802.11n standard. For example, Cisco provides a form of legacy beam forming for OFDM legacy clients with the Client link feature. Legacy beam forming adjusts the transmit signal such that multiple copies of the same signal arrive at the receiver in phase to create constructive inference and produce a combined signal at the receiver that is several times stronger than any one signal. For an OFDM signal, an adjustment is made for each OFDM subcarrier. The 802.11n standard does not provide any protocol support for legacy beam forming. This means that the protocol has no fields to indicate that legacy beam forming is supported or in use. The feedback method to use this type of beam forming assumes reciprocity of the channel state information at the transmitter and receiver. The Cisco AP uses the channel state information from client device data and 802.11 ACK transmissions for optimizing the signal transmission for beam forming.

Implicit Beam Forming

Implicit beam forming is an 802.11n form of beam forming that will function only between 802.11n devices that support implicit beam forming. Implicit beam forming relies on reciprocity of the channel characteristics between the transmitter and receiver. It gathers the channel state information from sounding packets sent from the receiver. Implicit beam forming has no capability to provide feedback about the channel state information at which the receiver hears the transmitter. While in theory the channel state information should be the same at the client and receiver side of a RF link, this might not be true if there is interference in the environment or if one side of the link has more receive antennas or RF chains than the other. The type of beam forming that is supported is advertised in the transmit beam forming (TxBF) Capabilities field.

Explicit Beam Forming

Explicit beam forming is another optional 802.11n beam-forming method. With explicit beam forming, the 802.11n protocol provides a means for the client to communicate to the transmitter the channel state information (CSI), allowing the transmitter to optimize the beam-formed signal performance to the receiver's channel conditions. This allows the best performance and fast beam-forming adjustments as the client moves. Two types of explicit beam-forming CSI feedback are supported with 802.11n—explicit compressed or explicit uncompressed. The amount of data required to communicate the CSI information can easily be several kilobits of data because the CSI channel information is reported for every transmitter and every OFDM subcarrier. To improve protocol efficiency, utilization of channel capacity for reporting CSI information 802.11n defines a method to compress CSI data. Figure 3-17 shows an example of the fields in 802.11n provided for explicit beam-forming support. For explicit beam-forming support to be utilized, both the transmitter and the clients must support this optional 802.11n beam-forming feature set, with support for the exact type of beam forming used by the transmitter. For example, if the AP supports explicit uncompressed beam forming, the client must also support explicit uncompressed for beam forming to be utilized. Figure 3-17 shows the TxBF Capabilities field used to signal support for explicit beam forming.

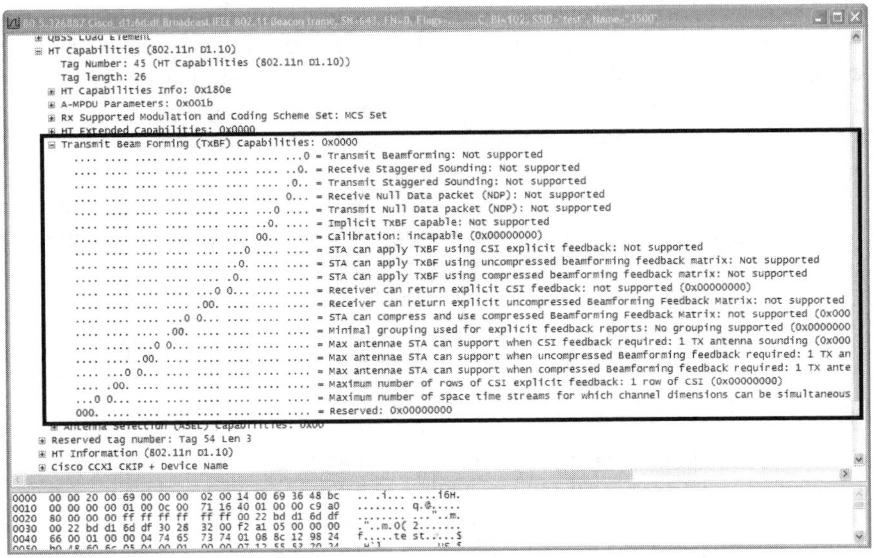

Figure 3-17   *802.11n Transmit Beam Forming Capabilities Field*

MIMO Antenna Array Coverage and Placement

To determine the placement and coverage for an antenna, an azimuth and elevation chart is typically used. The data for the azimuth charts is gathered in an anabolic chamber. This provides an ideal measurement of the antenna propagation, showing where the power has attenuated by 3 dB (that is, 50 percent less power). *Azimuth* is a top-down view of the antenna's propagation, and *elevation* is a side view of the antenna's propagation. Figures 3-18 and 3-19 provide an example of an antenna's azimuth and elevation chart. For a MIMO antenna array, there will be an azimuth and elevation chart for each antenna element in the array. What has to be considered when using these for a MIMO AP is that the anabolic chamber is a multipath-free environment. With an 11n MIMO AP, in a multipath-rich environment, the antenna array's propagation pattern might be very different than the propagation pattern shown for any signal element. A site survey might need to be performed with both sides of the RF (the AP and the client) using MIMO.

Coding

To ensure reliable data transmissions, coding is used to introduce redundancy in the data stream being transmitted. The additional information added to the data stream is used by the receiver to overcome noise, interference, and fading effects to the signal as it travels from the transmitter to the receiver. The common convention for coding rate is noted as the number of data input bits divided by the number of output bits. For example a coding rate of 1/2 means that for every 1 bit of data, 2 bits are transmitted. The better the SNR is for the signal, the lower the coding rate is needed.

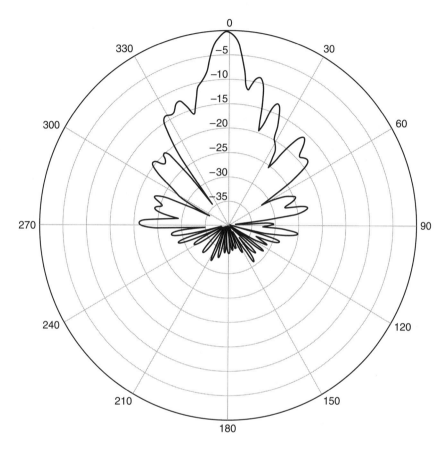

Figure 3-18   *Antenna Elevation*

Binary Convolutional Coding (BCC)

Binary Convolutional Coding (BCC) is the mandatory coding method with 802.11n. This is the same coding method used with 802.11a and 802.11g. The data rates shown in the 802.11n MCS rate charts are with BCC.

Low-Density Parity Checking (LDPC)

Low-density parity checking (LDPC) is optional encoding used with 802.11n MCS rates. LDPC is an alternative to BCC, which is used to improve the SNR up to 6 dB. Both the transmitter and receiver must support LDPC; otherwise, BCC will be used. For noisy channel conditions, LDPC will improve the performance and reliability of communications. Figure 3-20 shows the fields that indicate support for LDPC. Because of the data rate in the MCS charts for BCC, the data rates produced using LDPC should be higher than the rates listed in the MCS charts because of the coding gain.

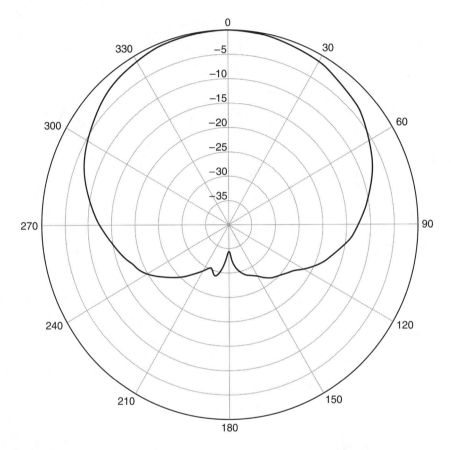

Figure 3-19   *Antenna Azimuth*

HT PHY and Operation

802.11n adds support for the HT PHY to the Physical Layer Convergence Protocol (PLCP) protocol data unit (PPDU) to support higher data rate communications. Besides supporting higher data rates, the PHY specifies modes of coexistence with 802.11a/b/g. Three possible modes of operation are possible with 802.11n:

- Legacy (non-HT)

- HT mixed (legacy and HT)

- Greenfield (HT only)

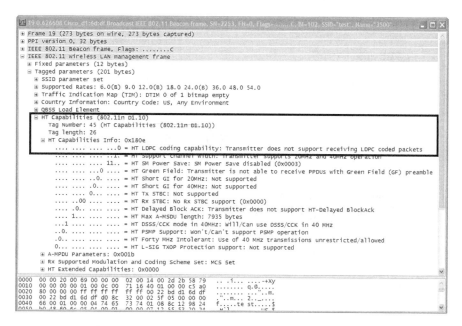

Figure 3-20 *Verifying LDPC Encoding*

The sections that follow cover the latter two modes of operation.

HT Mixed

The 802.11n standard requires 802.11n devices to support a mixed format of 802.11n HT devices and legacy devices. To meet this requirement, the HT packets must be enabled in the legacy packet to allow legacy 802.11 devices to detect HT transmissions for coexistence. Figure 3-21 shows the HT mixed PPDU. HT mixed mode support is a mandatory requirement with 802.11n because it is expected that an 802.11n device will interoperate with legacy devices. To indicate whether stations should be operating in HT mixed mode, the HT Capabilities field indicates the operating mode of the basic service set (BSS) and whether devices that support greenfield mode are present, as shown in Figure 3-22.

HT-Greenfield Format

Greenfield is an optional 802.11n feature where HT transmissions cannot be interpreted by legacy devices. However, legacy devices will detect the presence of HT transmission through their clear-channel assignment based on the RF energy present in the channel but will not understand the HT greenfield management and control transmission. This means the legacy device will not know how to show the differing transmissions and might interrupt HT-greenfield transmissions. This is why many 802.11n implementations have excluded HT-greenfield if any legacy devices are in the area. Figure 3-23 shows the HT fields indicating whether the 802.11n device supports receiving greenfield-mode transmissions.

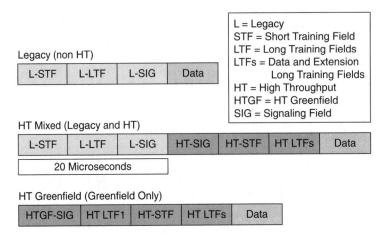

Figure 3-21 *Three Modes of Physical Layer Operation*

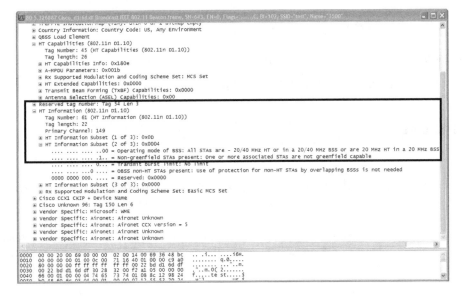

Figure 3-22 *HT Operating Mode Showing Whether Nongreenfield Stations Are Present*

```
19 0.626608 Cisco_d1:6d:df Broadcast IEEE 802.11 Beacon frame, SN=2253, FN=0, Flags=........C, BI=102, SSID="test", Name="3500"    [_][□][X]
⊞ Frame 19 (273 bytes on wire, 273 bytes captured)
⊞ PPI version 0, 32 bytes
⊞ IEEE 802.11 Beacon frame, Flags: ........C
⊟ IEEE 802.11 wireless LAN management frame
  ⊞ Fixed parameters (12 bytes)
  ⊟ Tagged parameters (201 bytes)
    ⊞ SSID parameter set
    ⊞ Supported Rates: 6.0(B) 9.0 12.0(B) 18.0 24.0(B) 36.0 48.0 54.0
    ⊞ Traffic Indication Map (TIM): DTIM 0 of 1 bitmap empty
    ⊞ Country Information: Country Code: US, Any Environment
    ⊞ QBSS Load Element
    ⊟ HT Capabilities (802.11n D1.10)
       Tag Number: 45 (HT Capabilities (802.11n D1.10))
       Tag length: 26
     ⊟ HT Capabilities Info: 0x180e
        .... .... .... ...0 = HT LDPC coding capability: Transmitter does not support receiving LDPC coded packets
        .... .... .... ..1. = HT Support channel width: Transmitter supports 20MHz and 40MHz operation
        .... .... .... 11.. = HT SM Power Save: SM Power Save disabled (0x0003)
        .... .... ...0 .... = HT Green Field: Transmitter is not able to receive PPDUs with Green Field (GF) preamble
        .... .... ..0. .... = HT Short GI for 20MHz: Not supported
        .... .... .0.. .... = HT Short GI for 40MHz: Not supported
        .... .... 0... .... = HT Tx STBC: Not supported
        .... ..00 .... .... = HT Rx STBC: No Rx STBC support (0x0000)
        .... .0.. .... .... = HT Delayed Block ACK: Transmitter does not support HT-Delayed BlockAck
        .... 1... .... .... = HT Max A-MSDU length: 7935 bytes
        ...1 .... .... .... = HT DSSS/CCK mode in 40MHz: Will/Can use DSSS/CCK in 40 MHz
        ..0. .... .... .... = HT PSMP Support: Won't/Can't support PSMP operation
        .0.. .... .... .... = HT Forty MHz Intolerant: Use of 40 MHz transmissions unrestricted/allowed
        0... .... .... .... = HT L-SIG TXOP Protection support: Not supported
     ⊞ A-MPDU Parameters: 0x001b
     ⊞ Rx Supported Modulation and Coding Scheme Set: MCS Set
     ⊞ HT Extended Capabilities: 0x0000
0000  00 00 20 00 69 00 00 00  02 00 14 00 2d 2b 58 79   .. .i....  ....+Xy
0010  00 00 00 00 01 00 0c 00  71 16 40 01 00 00 c5 a0   ........  q.@.....
0020  80 00 00 00 ff ff ff ff  ff ff 00 22 bd d1 6d df   ........  ..."..m.
0030  00 22 bd d1 6d df d0 8c  32 00 02 5f 05 00 00 00   ."..m...  2.._....
0040  66 00 01 00 00 04 74 65  73 74 01 08 8c 12 98 24   f.....te  st.....$
0050  b0 48 60 6c 05 04 00 01  00 00 07 12 55 53 20 24   .H`l....  ....US $
```

Figure 3-23 *HT-Greenfield Capabilities Fields*

Channel Bonding/40-MHz-Wide Channels

802.11n provides support for channel bonding, which is combining two 20-MHz-wide channels into a single 40-MHz-wide channel, as illustrated in Figure 3-24. Support for 40-MHz-wide channels is optional for both the 2.4-GHz and 5-GHz bands. 40-MHz operation will typically be enabled in the 5-GHz band and disabled in the 2.4-GHz band because 2.4 GHz has only three nonoverlapping 20-MHz-wide channels.

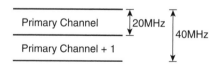

Figure 3-24 *Support for 40-MHz-Wide Channels*

The two 20-MHz-wide channels must be adjacent to be used for 40-MHz operations, with the secondary channel immediately above or below the primary channel. Figure 3-25 shows the HT information field indicating the primary channel number, the offset of the secondary channel operating above or below the primary channel, and the supported channel width, where the channel above or below is the next nonoverlapping adjacent channel. For example, for channel 36, the adjacent channel above would be channel 40. The primary channel is the common operating channel for all devices (stations, or STAs)

that are members of the BSS. Depending on the protection mode, management and signaling functions will occur on the primary channel.

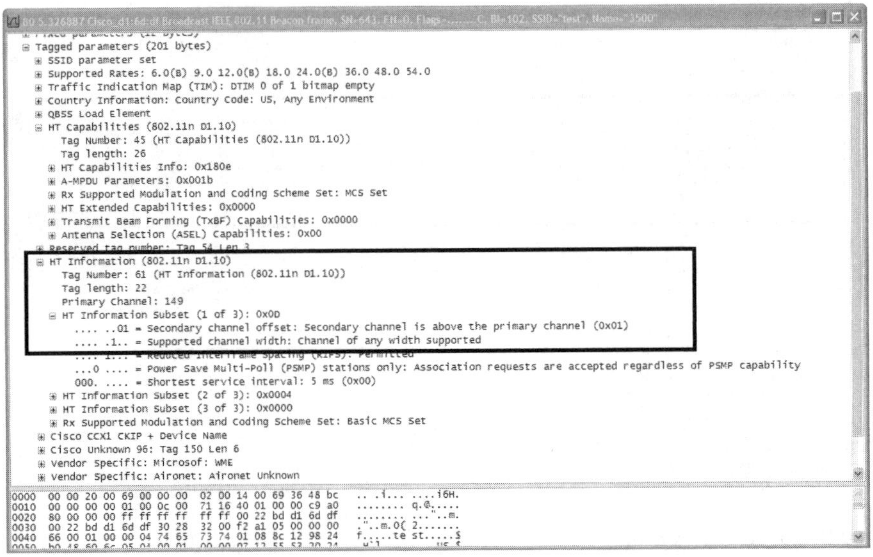

Figure 3-25 *40-MHz Support Channel Information*

If device in the BSS cannot tolerate 40-MHz-wide operation, it can set the 40-MHz intolerant bit for the BSS, as shown in Figure 3-26. This will prevent any 40-MHz-wide channel operations being performed in this BSS. It is common to see an 802.11n device set the
40-MHz intolerant bit in the 2.4-GHz band.

To support both 20 and 40 MHz in the BSS requires additional signal and protection
mechanisms to be implemented. Support of mixed 20-MHz and 40-MHz operation is
referred as *phased coexistence* (PCO), as shown in Figure 3-27. Notice that there is a gap
in time needed when shifting between 20-MHz and 40-MHz operations to prevent 20-
MHz or 40-MHz operations from colliding with each other. Figure 3-28 shows the HT
Capabilities field indicating support for PCO and the current PCO operation. In normal
40-MHz-wide operation, the AP beacons just on the primary 20-MHz channel. If 20-
MHz clients are present, they might need to beacon for both 20-MHz channels to provide protection, as shown in Figure 3-28.

Protection

Protection is needed to prevent HT-greenfield and legacy devices from disrupting each
other's communications. Protection is also needed to prevent transmissions using 40-
MHz-wide communication from disrupting communications when devices that only
understand 20-MHz-wide communications are present. One of four modes of protection
can be in use for a BSS with HT stations, depending on the device associated with and
heard by the BSS. Table 3-3 summarizes the four modes of protection specified with

802.11n. The protection mode used will be automatic but is dependent on the device's capabilities and how it is configured. If the device supports HT-greenfield, some 802.11n devices can be configured to operate only in HT-greenfield mode. If the 802.11n device supports 40-MHz-wide channels, the device might need to be configured to allow the use of 40-MHz-wide channels.

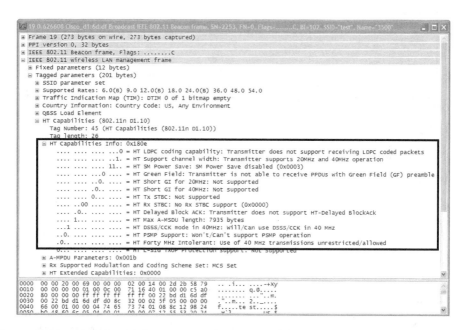

Figure 3-26 *40-MHz Intolerant Bit in the HT Capabilities Field Support Channel*

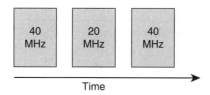

Figure 3-27 *PCO Operation with Changing Intervals Between 20-MHz- and 40-MHz-Wide Channel Operations*

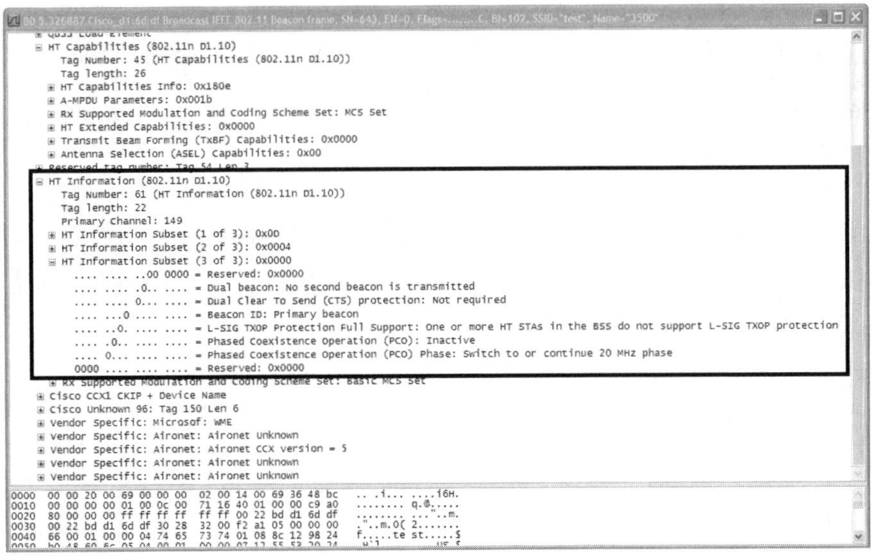

Figure 3-28 *HT Capabilities Fields Support PCO and Protection in 40-MHz-Wide Channel*

Table 3-3 *HT Operation Protection Modes*

Mode	Type of Protection	Description
Mode 0	None	Only HT devices associated to BSS, all supporting the same channel width
Mode 1	HT nonmember protection	Non-HT device heard by AP but not associated to AP
Mode 2	20-MHz protection	40-MHz BSS with 20-MHz devices associated
Mode 3	HT mixed protection	Non-HT devices associated to BSS

Power Management

802.11n adds support for spatial multiplexing power save (SMPS) and power save multiple poll (PSMP). SMPS provides the capability for a device that supports multiple transmitters to temporarily power down all but one transmitter to save power. Supporting this capability requires the protocol to signal the modes of SMPS supported and the current mode of operation. PSMP provides the capability for the uplink and downlink transmission schedule to be established, allowing the client to go into power save mode outside the SMPS schedule. Figure 3-29 shows the HT information field supporting SMPS and HT PSMP.

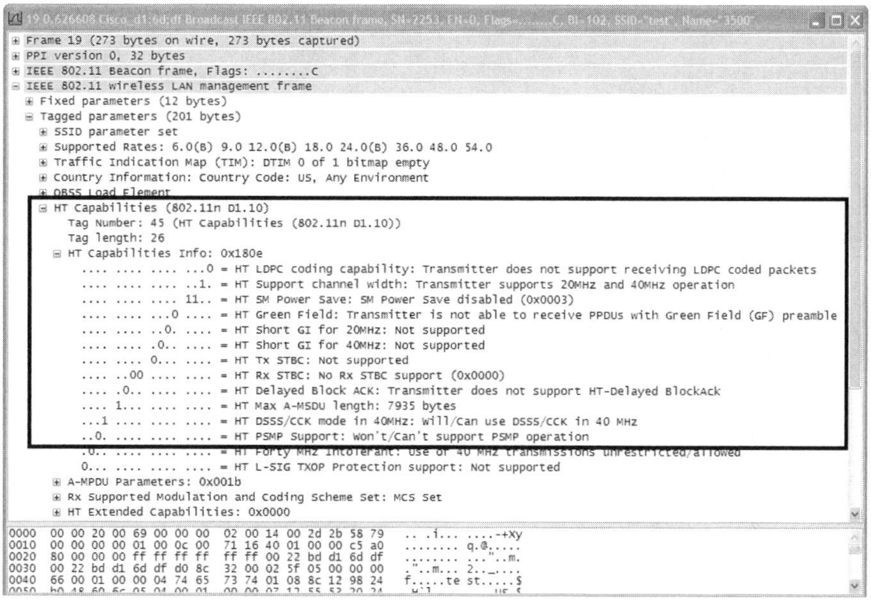

Figure 3-29 *Spatial Multiplexing Power Save HT fields*

Packet Aggregation

Packet aggregation is a key method for increasing performance with 802.11n. One of the key issues with 802.11a/g is that performance was limited because of the overhead of the protocol, especially with the transmission of small packets. With 802.11a and 802.11g, when transmitting a small payload, the throughput would drop to a few percent of the channel capacity; for example, a client with a 54-Mbps link might achieve only a throughput of 4 Mbps because of the 802.11 protocol overhead. The 802.11n protocol provides a means to reduce the protocol overhead by aggregating more data into each 802.11 transmission, thus increasing the effective throughput. 802.11n specifies two methods of packet aggregation—aggregate MAC protocol data unit (A-MPDU) and aggregate MAC service data unit (A-MSDU). All 802.11n devices are required to support the reception of either A-MSDU or A-MPDU. The device can optionally transmit either type of packet aggregation. The difference between A-MSDU and A-MPDU is that A-MSDU aggregates a maximum of 8 kb of MSDUs whereas A-MPDU aggregates a maximum of 64 kb of MPDUs. Figure 3-30 shows the HT Capabilities field indicating the maximum size of A-MPDU that can be received. Figure 3-31 shows the HT Capabilities field indicating the maximum size of aggregated A-MSDUs supported.

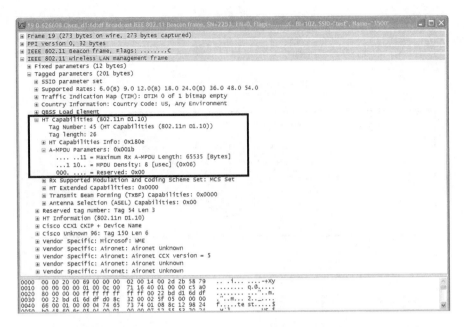

Figure 3-30 *A-MPDU Field*

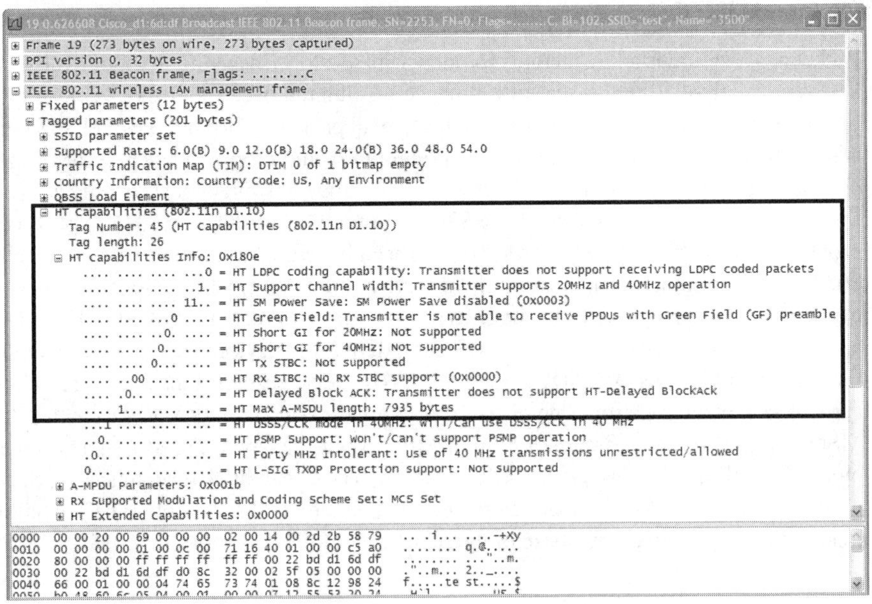

Figure 3-31 *A-MSDU Field*

Bursting/Block ACK (BACK)

Multiple packets can be sent using a bursting mode with 802.11n where the overhead of sending an 802.11 acknowledge (ACK) after each data packet can be reduced by using block acknowledge to acknowledge multiple data packet transmissions and signal whether any packets were not received. This provides additional efficiency improvements for 802.11, especially when used with packet aggregation. BACK support is mandatory with 802.11. The 802.11n stations must negotiate some parameters to signal the use of capabilities for using BACK. The capabilities exchanged are the number of blocks the receiver can accommodate. If the receiver can accommodate multiple blocks, it indicates support for delayed BACK with the add BACK frame. Some clients might not be able to support multiple blocks because of the buffering needed to reorder retransmitted blocks and will signal the need for immediate BACK support. For a client to initiate the use of block acknowledge, it must negotiate its BACK capabilities with an add block to the transmitter.

Short Guard Interval (GI)

The interval between symbol transmissions is the guard interval (GI). Radios require an interval between symbol transmission to distinguish where one symbol ends and the next symbol begins. The default guard interval is the long guard interval (L-GI), which is 800 nanoseconds (ns). A short guard interval (S-GI) can be used to increase performance by reducing the guard interval from the default of 800 ns to 400 ns. This allows more information to be sent in the channel. Reducing the GI is an optional 802.11n feature, and some 802.11n devices might not support an S-GI. Use of an S-GI has a downside in that it increases the odds for intersymbol interference. Using an S-GI will not usually be an issue for indoor environments, but is more likely to be an issue in outdoor environments. In an outdoor environment, the distance and packet flight could be long enough that use of an S-GI would cause intersymbol interference, resulting in an increased error rate. The radios must support the use of S-GI; otherwise, L-GI will be used by default. Figure 3-32 show the HT S-GI fields that indicate S-GI is supported for both 20-MHz-wide channel operations and 40-MHz-wide operations.

Reduced Inter-Frame Spacing (RIFS)

Reduced inter-frame spacing (RIFS) is used when sending a burst of multiple packets from one transmitter. This can reduce the spacing between packet transmissions from 16 microseconds to 2 microseconds. RIFS increases the efficiency of the consecutive transmissions of one transmitter. The time it takes to transfer a large amount of data is reduced when RIFS is utilized. Figure 3-33 shows the HT fields that signal whether RIFS is allowed in the BSS.

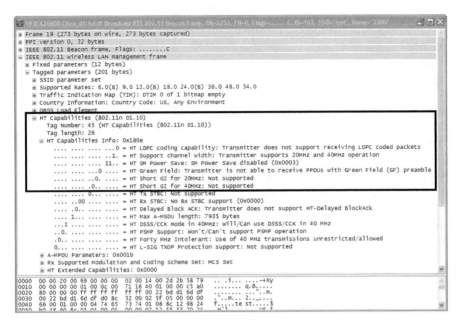

Figure 3-32   *HT Fields Indicating Use of S-GI*

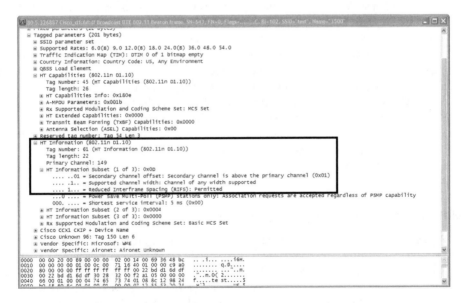

Figure 3-33   *HT Field Indicating Whether RIFS Is Supported*

Reverse Direction Protocol (RDP)

Reverse Direction Protocol (RDP) is an optional feature used to reduce the time and increase the efficiency for network traffic patterns that always have a transmission from one source followed by a return transmission; for example, a TCP SEND followed by a TCP ACK. RDP allows the media to be reserved for both the original transmission and the accompanying response. This saves the responding device from having to arbitrate for the media to transmit a response by using the current allocation created by the original transmitter.

Modulation and Coding Schemes (MCS)

The 802.11n standard defines a range of radio operation modes to define HT data rates. A number of variables need to be agreed upon between the HT transmitter and HT receiver. These variables include coding method, modulation type, number of spatial streams, and other physical attributes. Physical attributes include variables such as timing values, for example, guard interval—the time the radio must wait between transmissions to ensure that the receiver can determine the beginning and end of the transmissions. Modulation and coding schemes (MCS) are used describe these variables. The MCS value or index is used to establish the communication variables an HT transmitter and HT receiver will use. The MCS index can be used to determine the corresponding physical data rate. Table 3-4 illustrates MCS rates 0–31.

Table 3-4   *MCS Rates 0–31*

MCS Index	Modulation	Coding Rate	Spatial Streams	802.11n Data Rate			
				20-MHz		40-MHz	
				L-GI	S-GI	L-GI	S-GI
0	BPSK	1/2	1	6.5	7.2	13.5	15
1	QPSK	1/2	1	13	14.4	27	30
2	QPSK	3/4	1	19.5	21.7	40.5	45
3	16-QAM	1/2	1	26	28.9	54	60
4	16-QAM	3/4	1	39	43.3	81	90
5	64-QAM	2/3	1	52	57.8	108	120
6	64-QAM	3/4	1	58.5	65	122	135
7	64-QAM	5/6	1	65	72.2	135	150
8	BPSK	1/2	2	13	14.4	27	30
9	QPSK	1/2	2	26	28.9	54	60
10	QPSK	3/4	2	39	43.3	81	90

continues

Table 3-4   *MCS Rates 0–31   (continued)*

MCS Index	Modulation	Coding Rate	Spatial Streams	802.11n Data Rate			
				20-MHz		40-MHz	
				L-GI	S-GI	L-GI	S-GI
11	16-QAM	1/2	2	52	57.8	108	120
12	16-QAM	3/4	2	78	86.7	162	180
13	64-QAM	2/3	2	104	116	216	240
14	64-QAM	3/4	2	117	130	243	270
15	64-QAM	5/6	2	130	144	270	300
16	BPSK	1/2	3	19.5	21.7	40.5	45
17	QPSK	1/2	3	39	43.3	81	90
18	QPSK	3/4	3	58.5	65	121.5	135
19	16-QAM	1/2	3	78	86.7	162	180
20	16-QAM	3/4	3	117	130	243	270
21	64-QAM	2/3	3	156	173.3	324	360
22	64-QAM	3/4	3	175.5	195	364.5	405
23	64-QAM	5/6	3	195	216.7	405	450
24	BPSK	1/2	4	26	28.9	54	60
25	QPSK	1/2	4	52	57.8	108	120
26	QPSK	3/4	4	78	86.7	162	180
27	16-QAM	1/2	4	104	115.6	216	240
28	16-QAM	3/4	4	156	173.3	324	360
29	64-QAM	2/3	4	208	231.1	432	480
30	64-QAM	3/4	4	234	260	486	540
31	64-QAM	5/6	4	260	288.9	540	600

Seventy-eight MCS index values are defined by the 802.11n standard, MCS 0–77. The standard specifies the minimum set MCS index that must be supported by every 802.11n client and 802.11n access point. 802.11n APs must support MCS rates 0–15 for a 20- or 40-MHz-wide channel. 802.11 client stations must support MCS rates 0–7 for a 20-MHz channel.

An 802.11n device might use different transmit and receive MCS values because of differences in capability between the two devices. For example, an 802.11n MIMO 1x2:1 client device might be communicating with an 802.11n MIMO 2x3:2 AP. In this example, communication in each direction would use a different MCS rate because of different capabilities in the uplink and downlink direction, where downlink is the transmission from the AP to the client and uplink is the transmission from the client to the AP. In this case, the downlink will support the use of two spatial streams such as MCS 15. The uplink will support only one spatial stream because the client adapter only has one transmitter, such as MCS 7. Table 3-4 shows the data rates for MCS 0–31. Figure 3-34 shows the HT Capabilities field identifying the MCS sets supported.

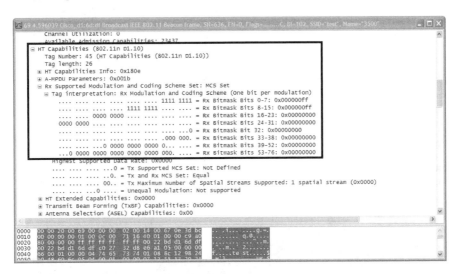

Figure 3-34   *MCS Sets Supported*

Configuration Requirements to Obtain HT Rates

For devices to communicate using the 802.11n HT data rates (MCS rates), specific configuration tasks are required for the WLAN and the global wireless network parameters. For the WLAN, QoS must be allowed for that service set identifier (SSID) and the encryption for the SSID must not allow Temporal Key Integrity Protocol (TKIP). This means either Advanced Encryption Standard (AES) encryption or no encryption for the WLAN. Figure 3-35 shows the Wireless LAN Controller (WLC) configuration to allow Wi-Fi Multimedia (WMM) QoS. Figure 3-36 shows the WLC configuration for allowing AES encryption for the SSID. With both of these items configured, the clients will be allowed to use HT rates. If QoS is not allowed or a non-TKIP encryption method is allowed on the WLAN, 802.11n devices will fall back to 802.11a or g data rates. The language in the 802.11n specification makes it mandatory that clients using HT rates do not use TKIP. This does not mean the WLAN cannot be configured to allow both TKIP and AES; only the device communicating HT rates cannot utilize TKIP encryption.

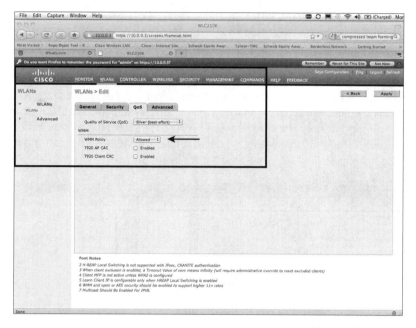

Figure 3-35 *WLAN Configuration to Allow Use of WMM QoS to Allow Clients to Use HT Data Rates*

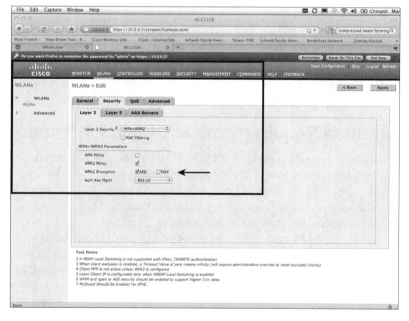

Figure 3-36 *WLAN Configuration to Allow AES Encryption, Which Allows Clients to Use HT Data Rates*

The global wireless parameters for the networks must be enabled to allow the use of HT rates. Figure 3-37 shows the configuration for enabling 802.11n mode and the various MCS rates. For the majority of situations, there is no downside to enabling 11n mode for 2.4 and 5 GHz (802.11g/h and 802.11a/n). The key difference for configuring 802.11n mode between 2.4 and 5 GHz is that 40-MHz-wide channels should be configured for 802.11n in the 5-GHz band, which is shown in Figure 3-38.

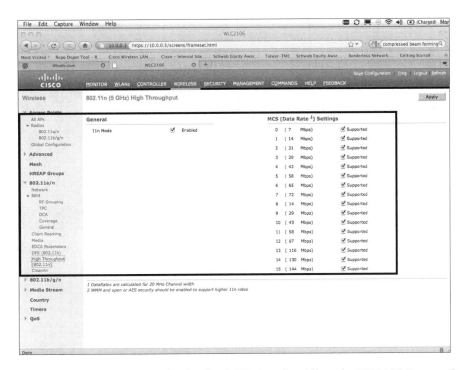

Figure 3-37   *Enabling HT Modes for the 5-GHz Band to Allow the HT MCS Rates to Be Allowed*

To ensure that downlink transmissions utilize packet aggregation, the WLC might require additional configuration. The WLC determines what packets to aggregate, with A-MPDU, based on the QoS priority marking on the packet. Priority level 0 will automatically be aggregated. Higher-priority packets might require configuring the WLC to use packet aggregation. This is because packet aggregation can add latency to the packet while the WLC delays transmission to accumulate several packets for aggregations. The WLC command-line configuration command **ampdu tx priority** {0-7} is used to specify which priority of packet will be aggregated.

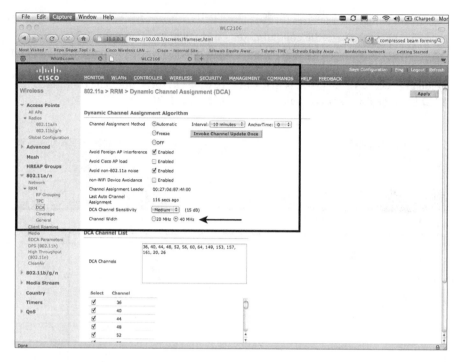

Figure 3-38   *Dynamic Channel Assignment (DCA) Configurations for 802.11n in the 5-GHz Band to Allow Use of 40-MHz-Wide Channels*

Predicting 802.11 Link Performance

With so many options, the task of predicting 802.11n performance is complex. Some 802.11n options might double performance, while others might only provide a few percentage points in improvement. Besides the 802.11n options affecting performance, other factors will also contribute to the potential performance gain, such as protocol, packet size, and number and type of wireless clients associated with and communicating within the wireless basic service set area. The first approach to help predict performance is to determine the data rate that clients will use to communicate with the AP based on 802.11 feature support and anticipated data rate. You can use the MCS charts to determine the possible physical data rates because of feature support. You can use the access point data sheet to predict the data rates based on client distance and SNR. Ideally, a site survey will be performed to predict performance or use of other performance-prediction tools that consider the 802.11n options utilized and application factors such as data packet size. Figure 3-39 shows an example of an application used to predict 802.11n performance.

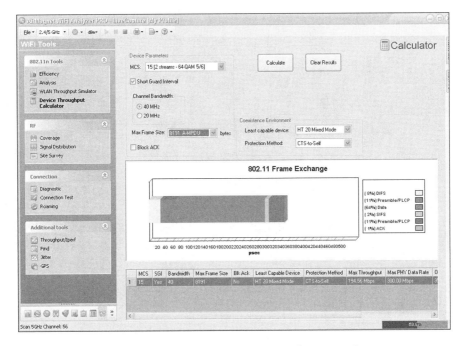

Figure 3-39 *AirMagnet Planner 802.11n Capacity Prediction Tool*

Summary

The various 802.11n features allow greater performance, capacity, and robustness to be achieved. Many of the 802.11n features are optional. Some of the optional 802.11n features might not be significant while others might be, depending on the environment and application. Many of the optional 802.11n features will improve performance only if both the transmitter and receiver support the feature. 802.11n performance will be the greatest in multipath-rich environments. The net effect of each feature has to be evaluated based on the traffic type and environment to determine which 802.11n features will have the greatest effect on performance, with some 802.11n features providing no or marginal performance improvement. 802.11n devices should provide improved performance and robustness over all legacy device deployments; however, the level of improvements can vary greatly depending on 802.11n device capabilities and environmental factors.

Chapter 4

Cisco Unified Wireless LAN Security Fundamentals

"New Vulnerability Allows Hackers to Penetrate Wireless Networks!" screams the headline in the newspaper or periodical. Perhaps the accompanying article describes some new theoretical vulnerability announced by a security research group that (surprise!) offers wireless LAN (WLAN) security consulting services. Or maybe it's a WLAN vendor that, quite naturally, not only "discovered" the new vulnerability but also offers the industry's "only" or "best" solution. Or maybe the accompanying article contains a sensationalistic description of how some "white hat" hacker demonstrated a new tool to exploit a WLAN or network attack vector at a security conference. Quite often, what's "new" is just a variant of what's old—a new exploit tool for a well-known vulnerability, for example. But then, every once in a while, articles of this ilk describe a significant new development that gravely impacts the industry.

Unfortunately, many journalists—even those writing for industry and technical publications—struggle to grasp even the fundamentals of WLAN technology, let alone the intricacies and complexities of WLAN security threats and their full ramifications on network design and implementation. It's shocking how often vulnerabilities common only in consumer WLAN implementations are applied in hysterical, sweeping generalizations to all wireless networks.

This is not to say that there aren't real security threats with WLAN networks; there definitely are some significant security challenges for WLAN network designers and operators. But the challenges are, for the most part, manageable when reality is filtered out of all the hype and the problem domain is well understood. Indeed, we often observe that the WLANs our customers deploy are more secure than their companion wired networks!

This chapter discusses the fundamentals of wireless LAN security in the context of the Cisco Unified Wireless Network (CUWN). An in-depth discussion and analysis of WLAN security can be its own book. In fact, there are already a number of excellent books available on the topic of WLAN security. Some favorites are listed in the references at the end of this chapter.

This chapter begins with an introduction of the security risks with WLAN technologies and continues with an explanation of technology building blocks that address and mitigate the risks.

When you are done reading this chapter, you should have sufficient background information on WLAN security. The security concepts discussed in this chapter are woven throughout the fabric of the CUWN. Indeed, one of the real benefits of the CUWN architecture is that it simplifies the design, deployment, and operations of security for your WLAN.

Understanding WLAN Security Challenges

You should know the vulnerability points of any network you are trying to secure and understand how the bad guys try to exploit them. How else do you separate the real from the hype and design sensible security policies and select the right WLAN security technologies?

This would be a good place for one of those hackneyed quotes about the importance of knowing your enemy from the likes of Sun Tzu's *The Art of War*. But all the good quotes we know of have already been used *ad nauseum* by other authors. So we'll spare you (and ourselves).

Instead, let's move right into discussing the security risks. The discussion that follows centers on the places where WLANs have security exposures as opposed to specific attacks and flaws. Basically this is because books have a long life, and by the time you read this, today's latest, greatest WLAN exploits might be old news. But the risk points remain the same. The risks discussed are as follows:

- Vulnerabilities inherent to the radio transmission medium

- Vulnerabilities inherent to the standards definitions

- Vulnerabilities inherent to mobility

- Readily available profiling and attack tools

- Misconfigured wireless devices and clients

- Rogue access points and devices

After concluding the following sections, you should have a good overview of the real risks associated with WLANs and be ready to take a closer look at the building blocks that address these vulnerabilities.

Vulnerabilities Inherent to the Radio Transmission Medium

WLANs have inherent vulnerabilities arising from the use of the airwaves and radio waves as the transmission medium. The two significant problem areas are

- Physical containment of transmissions

- Use of the unlicensed radio spectrum

The sections that follow look at these problem areas in greater detail.

Physical Containment Problem

With an Ethernet LAN, eavesdropping or attacking the network from the inside requires physical access to the network. Typically, an attacker must be able to connect a machine to a switchport in the network somewhere. Violating the network's security requires violating physical security.

This is not the case with WLANs. The basic physics of the transmission medium creates a physical containment problem. WLANs use radio signals over the air as the physical transmission medium. After a radio signal leaves its source, whether it is an access point or a wireless client, the signal travels through the air in many directions, and you have little or no control over the signal propagation.

Any listener with an antenna tuned to the right frequency and within range of the WLAN can "hear" the transmissions of both clients and access points. Skilled attackers know how to use high-gain directional antennas to profile and eavesdrop on WLAN networks from far away. But even relatively unskilled attackers can hear your WLAN pretty easily with simple tools.

If an attacker can hear transmissions in the unlicensed spectrum using readily available equipment from the WLAN coverage area, it's only logical that the attacker can also transmit into the WLAN coverage area relatively easily to cause big problems. Attackers might do this for one or more reasons. For example, the attacker might simply be trying to create a denial of service by using up available radio channel time. The attacker could also be trying to spoof a legitimate wireless device. It's not uncommon for an attacker to spoof a legitimate access point to try to trick wireless clients into connecting to the attacker.

Unlicensed Radio Spectrum Problem

The physical containment problem is exacerbated by the use of the unlicensed radio spectrum in both the 2.4-GHz and 5-GHz bands. Other types of wireless networks—for example, the cellular phone carrier networks—enjoy a certain amount of "security by obscurity" because they have a dedicated radio spectrum allotted to them by a regulatory agency. While that doesn't solve the physical containment problem, it makes it much harder for an eavesdropper or attacker because he has to obtain or build special equipment and tools to attack the network. This typically requires sophisticated knowledge and technical skills. It is also illegal.

On the other hand, with WLANs, attackers can use off-the-shelf equipment and open-source software attack tools. The skills and knowledge level required are moderate. Also, because the spectrum is unlicensed, the legal questions are much more abstruse.

WLANs can be susceptible to competition with non-802.11 devices that use the same radio channels in the unlicensed spectrum. From the 802.11 WLAN's perspective, this competition is considered noise, and if strong enough, can significantly degrade the network's performance. Common products that use some of the same spectrum as the WLAN are Bluetooth wireless devices, 2.4-GHz cordless phones, and microwave ovens. Legitimate devices don't represent a security problem per se, but they can affect WLAN availability, creating a de facto denial of service. Malicious attackers can use jammers to the same effect.

One of our favorite stories from Cisco sales lore comes from a customer bake-off between Cisco and a competitor for a large WLAN deal. The Cisco pilot was going very poorly and Cisco engineers were completely baffled because every failed test case in the pilot environment worked perfectly in Cisco labs. After many sleepless nights and much consternation, the mystery was solved. The competitor was camping out in a van outside the test environment with a doorless microwave oven jamming the airwaves during the pilot!

While this story is almost certainly apocryphal, it does illustrate how a legitimate product can be used nefariously and how the unlicensed spectrum makes the WLAN susceptible to RF jamming attacks.

Vulnerabilities Inherent to the Standards Definitions

The underlying IEEE 802.11 standards definitions have some inherent vulnerabilities, which fall into two categories:

■   Authentication and encryption weaknesses

■   Unauthenticated management and control frames

The sections that follow look at some of the details.

Authentication and Encryption Weaknesses

Put simply, authentication controls access to the network and networked resources by using techniques that identify who and which devices are allowed onto the network and those that are not. Encryption protects data frames in transit on the network, using cryptographic algorithms to obfuscate the frame content. When you consider the vulnerabilities inherent to the transmission medium, it's pretty obvious why both authentication and encryption are really important security concepts with WLANs.

The original IEEE 802.11 specification was released in 1997 and called out a mechanism for authentication and data privacy called Wired Equivalent Privacy, or WEP for short. This name is telling because it reflects the original goals of the standards designers—to provide a wireless data privacy mechanism roughly equivalent to what you get with a wired Ethernet network. In other words, it was supposed to be as hard to break WEP encryption as it is to violate an enterprise's physical security to gain access to the wired network. The WEP standard was designed to be a trade-off between "reasonably strong" security and implementation simplicity and exportability.

WEP is based on the shared-secret concept. Both end devices of a WLAN connection share a secret WEP key. The WEP key can be used to authenticate wireless devices; if a device has the secret WEP key, it must be authorized!

The WEP key is also used to encrypt data transmissions between each end of the WLAN connection. The original 1997 version of the 802.11 specification called out 40-bit WEP keys. In 1999, the specification allowed expanding the key length to 104 bits. These keys are statically configured on the devices that will use the WLAN.

As 802.11 WLAN technology started to take off, a lot of smart people in the cryptographic community started to take a good look at WEP as a security mechanism. In 2000 and 2001, several landmark papers were published detailing critical problems with WEP. If you're really interested, these papers are listed in the references at the end of this chapter, and they make for excellent reading to combat insomnia.

Not long after these papers were published, exploit tools appeared on the scene. These tools are now readily available on the Internet and are pretty easy to use, even for novices. So the most important thing to know about WEP is that it is irreversibly cracked and should never be used. It bears repeating: WEP is totally ineffective for data privacy because of cryptographic flaws; don't use it.

Recognizing that WEP was not the answer to WLAN security, the IEEE formed the 802.11i task group to come up with a robust security scheme for the future. The 802.11i task group's work was ratified in 2004.

While the 802.11i standard was in draft form, the Wi-Fi Alliance released its own requirements based on a subset of the 802.11i standard. The first iteration of these requirements was called Wi-Fi Protected Access (WPA). An update to these requirements is based on the complete, ratified 802.11i standard and is called Wi-Fi Protected Access Version 2 (WPAv2). The industry as a whole has moved toward 802.11i/WPAv2-based security, and that's where you should be too. Later in the chapter, you will learn more about WPAv2.

Unauthenticated Management Frames

Recall from the basics of 802.11 WLANs that there are three kinds of frames: control, management, and data frames. Discussions of WLAN security weaknesses are incomplete without noting that the 802.11 specification lacks an authentication mechanism for management frames.

The lack of authentication for management frames opens the door to a variety of denial of service (DoS) attacks. For example, an attacker runs a tool that spoofs disassociation and/or deauthentication management frames from the access point.

These DoS attacks can be run in conjunction with other attacks. For example, if you have a WLAN using Lightweight Extensible Authentication Protocol (LEAP) for authentication, an assailant could spoof deauthentication messages to all the users connected to an access point in the hopes of capturing username and password hash combinations when the client devices reauthenticate. If some username and password hash combinations get retrieved, an offline dictionary attack is used to crack as many passwords as possible.

LEAP is covered later in the chapter, but the attack just described is why LEAP should not be used anymore. Coverage of LEAP has been included solely for historical and educational reasons.

Vulnerabilities Inherent to Mobility

The freedom offered by mobility is why we love wireless technologies; however, when it comes to WLANs, the same mobility that is the primary driver for adopting the technology also creates some security challenges.

One of the big challenges in an enterprise is figuring out how to handle roaming end users securely. Wireless clients regularly leave their association with one access point to reassociate with another access point. These wireless clients cannot just reassociate; they must be reauthenticated and generate new encryption keys. This means that the wireless client devices must carry some kind of security context with them so that the system can support fast reauthentication and rekeying if you want to avoid adversely affecting latency-sensitive applications like voice.

There are other problems inherent to mobility that are less related to technology and more related to end-user behavior. Suppose that you've deployed a secure WLAN in your enterprise, using the strongest authentication and encryption technologies available. You are confident in the strength of your WLAN security in your enterprise. But then, how do you secure the laptops of your road warriors when they connect to public hotspot WLAN networks in airports and coffee shops?

Consider what could happen when a senior executive in your enterprise uses her laptop to connect to an open network in an airport. There is probably some of your enterprise's important intellectual property and strategic information stored on that laptop in the form of documents, spreadsheets, PowerPoint presentations, and emails. You don't want an attacker compromising that valuable data. You also don't want that laptop catching a virus from another computer connected to the same wireless network. That laptop needs to be protected!

A similar problem arises with home WLAN networks. Home WLAN devices are very common these days. Usually, these are commodity devices from the local electronics megastore that don't always support the strongest security. Most end users aren't all that technical and don't pay much attention to security. These users get easily confused configuring security settings. Walk around any neighborhood with a WLAN sniffer and you will see that most home users don't give much attention to the physical containment problem either. Now when your enterprise users take their laptops home and connect to their home WLANs, how do you trust that the device is not vulnerable?

It can get worse too. A former neighbor of ours is a telecommuter, working as a marketing consultant for a large Fortune 500 company. His employer supplied him with a hardware Virtual Private Network (VPN) solution. Quite innocently, he decided it was a great idea to add a wireless access point so that he could enjoy working outside on nice days. And as you'd expect from a marketing consultant, his access point was configured with weak security. It never occurred to the neighbor that computers connected behind the hardware VPN client have a free ride onto his employer's corporate network through the VPN tunnel.

Misconfigured Wireless Devices and Clients

The previous section reviewed some of the security challenges inherent to mobility. Another issue that is often related is misconfigured wireless client devices. Client devices usually get misconfigured when users tinker with the client supplicant settings on their own, usually when they are trying to set up their home WLAN or connect to a public WLAN hotspot.

Wireless network devices, like access points, can get misconfigured too. We've been on a customer site where we (temporarily) crippled WLAN security during troubleshooting. This isn't necessarily a dumb thing to do; in this customer's case, we were troubleshooting issues with wireless client associations and were eliminating authentication and encryption as variables while working on RF issues. But it's pretty easy to forget to turn the security back on, especially after an all-night troubleshooting session!

Enterprise-class WLAN implementers can be presented with a dizzying array of configuration options, especially when it comes to some of the authentication and encryption settings. Even the most experienced network manager can make mistakes and inadvertently leave the network exposed in some way.

Rogue Access Points and Devices

Consider an enterprise with a wireless network deployment utilizing Extensible Authentication Protocol–Transport Layer Security (EAP-TLS) authentication and Counter Mode with Cipher Block Chaining Message Authentication Code Protocol (CCMP) for privacy. Don't worry if these concepts are foreign to you because they'll be explained shortly. Suffice it to say, for now, that this is a very strong authentication and encryption approach.

Now suppose though, that in some of the buildings, the access points are placed improperly so that some labs and conference rooms along the building periphery get poor radio coverage and users have difficulty connecting to the wireless network, and when they do connect, they experience very bad performance. Take it as axiomatic that people love the freedom of wireless mobility, so the poor end-user experience in the conference rooms and labs creates an unintended incentive for employees to deploy "rogue" access points.

Some employee, almost inevitably and quite innocently, will bring a cheap, commodity access point from the local electronics superstore into one of the conference rooms or labs with poor coverage, find a free Ethernet jack, and deploy an unauthorized, rogue access point, probably with weak security at best.

Clearly, this represents a catastrophic network security hole. The conference room or lab locations along the periphery of the building almost guarantee that the access point radio signals will be accessible from outside the building. Attackers frequently look for poorly secured WLANs to exploit, and it doesn't take much in the way of technical skill to find them. If and when an unauthorized user associates to the rogue, the user has free access to the enterprise network and can do all sorts of nefarious things.

In this example, the authorized wireless network is securely implemented with strong authentication and encryption. But while there is no glaring weakness with the official wireless network, there is a serious wireless security problem!

This example illustrates what Cisco has often called the "frustrated insider" rogue access point. These are rogue access points deployed by insiders out of frustration because of no wireless access or rotten WLAN performance.

There's an entire different class though of "malicious attacker" rogue access points and devices. These are rogue wireless devices implemented by the bad guys for the singular purpose of compromising your network. It's not hard to imagine a parasitic attacker tail-gating an employee in your enterprise to bypass building security, then finding an available Ethernet jack and deploying a rogue access point that he can later exploit from outside the building.

There is also software readily available that can turn any computer with a wireless network interface card into a software-based access point. Attackers use these software-based access points to entice wireless clients to connect to them. After a wireless client connects, the attacker attempts to trick the wireless client into giving up valuable information, or else the attacker compromises the client device in some way. This attack vector is especially effective in public hotspot environments.

Readily Available Profiling and Attack Tools

So far, you've learned about the vulnerability characteristics of the radio transmission medium, vulnerabilities in the standards definitions, vulnerabilities introduced by mobility, and the challenge of rogue access points.

All the problems are exacerbated by the proliferation of profiling and attack tools on the Internet that exploit the basic vulnerabilities in WLANs. Many of these tools are very easy to get started and not hard to use. There are bootable Linux CDs that include all the latest tools and client card drivers that make running these attacks "chimp simple."

Addressing the WLAN Security Challenges

The security challenges presented by 802.11 WLANs can seem daunting; however, do not despair, because there are solutions! Based on experience, WLAN deployments are usually more secure than their parallel, wired networks. Now that you've been introduced to the major vulnerabilities in 802.11 WLANs, this section takes a look at the solutions.

Table 4-1 documents a mapping between the major WLAN security challenges and the solutions.

Table 4-1   *WLAN Security Challenges and Solutions*

WLAN Security Challenge	WLAN Security Solution(s)
Vulnerabilities inherent to the radio transmission medium	Strong authentication and privacy
Vulnerabilities inherent to the standards definitions	Strong authentication and privacy, Management Frame Protection
Vulnerabilities inherent to mobility	Fast, secure roaming; secure management and policies
Misconfigured wireless devices and clients	Secure management and policies
Rogue access points and devices	Rogue AP management and wireless intrusion prevention systems, secure management and policies
Readily available profiling and attack tools	Secure management and policies

The sections that follow take a more in-depth look at the solutions.

Background on Strong Authentication and Privacy

If you think about the challenges presented by the radio transmission medium and the standards definition, the most logical and only practical mitigation strategies introduce strong authentication and data privacy through encryption. The need for strong authentication and data privacy extends to roaming clients, which must be reassociated and reauthenticated quickly while securely preserving data privacy. But what are the specific requirements for strong authentication and privacy? To answer that question, you need to consider how the 802.11 WEP-based security model is flawed.

How WEP Encryption Works

Previously, this chapter established that WEP is broken on the cryptographic front and shouldn't be used; however, it's useful to look briefly at how WEP works to establish some baseline knowledge for later in the chapter.

The WEP encryption is based on the symmetric RC4 cipher algorithm developed by Ron Rivest at RSA Security Inc. A symmetric cipher algorithm uses the same encryption key for encryption and decryption. Figure 4-1 illustrates the entire WEP processing model for a packet.

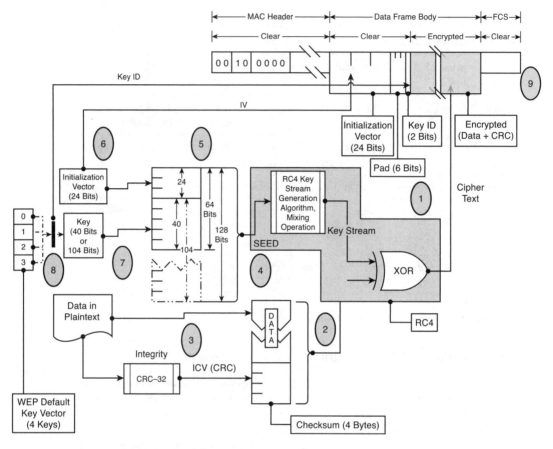

Figure 4-1   *WEP Processing Model*

There are a couple of things to note about RC4 first. RC4 encrypts data one byte at a time. This is because RC4 is a stream cipher, as opposed to a block cipher, which operates on chunks of data. For each byte of data input into the encryption algorithm, an encrypted byte of data is output. Note also that the RC4 algorithm is reversible. Inputting plain text and the encryption key into the RC4 algorithm yields cipher text. Inputting the cipher text and the same encryption key into the RC4 algorithm yields the plain text.

Notice how the WEP key is prepended with an IV, or initialization vector, prior to being fed into the RC4 algorithm. The IV is a 24-bit value that is different per packet, ensuring a different encryption key per packet. Note that we said *different* instead of *unique*. You can never truly have a unique encryption key per packet in the WEP processing model because the WEP key portion is static and there are only 2^{24} IVs available. Eventually, the IV space will be exhausted and the WEP processing model needs to start reusing IVs. Also, the encryption key per packet cannot be unique because there will be multiple client devices using the same connection. Each client has its own IV sequence, meaning that multiple clients could use the same IV.

The IV is not kept secret because the receiver needs to know which IV has been used to encrypt the packet in order to decrypt the packet. In fact, as Figure 4-1 shows, the IV is transmitted in the clear.

The combined IV and WEP key are fed into the RC4 algorithm. Specifically, the combined value is used to seed the RC4 *key stream generator*. The purpose of the key stream generator is to output a pseudorandom sequence of bytes, called the *key stream*, that are used to scramble the plain text. Remember though, that every time an identical IV and WEP key pair are input into the RC4 algorithm, the same key stream will be generated.

The plain text is a combination of the data in the MAC protocol data unit (MPDU), which is a chunk of data from a higher-layer application and a 4-byte Integrity Check Value (ICV). The ICV is a value computed over the MPDU data using the CRC-32 algorithm. The ICV is intended to provide protection against message tampering in transit. That's why the CRC-32 value is computed before encryption.

The combined data and ICV are then encrypted by the RC4 algorithm using the key stream. The encryption mechanism used by the RC4 algorithm is simply the bitwise exclusive OR (XOR) operation. The plain text is XORed with the key stream, and the result is considered the cipher text.

The cipher text is inserted into the data frame body along with the clear text IV and the key ID of the WEP key used for this particular packet. Remember that the 802.11 specification calls for up to four WEP keys, so the receiver needs to know which key to use for decryption. The MAC header is prepended to the data frame body, and the frame check sequence (FCS) is computed. Next, the entire frame is handed down the protocol stack to be transmitted by the radio.

When the frame is received on the receiving end, the process is essentially reversed. The IV is stripped out of the frame's data body, the key ID is used to select the correct WEP key, and the IV and WEP key are combined and fed into the key stream generator. The encrypted cipher text is extracted from the frame body and XORed with the key stream, yielding the plain text. The ICV is computed over the data portion and compared to the ICV computed by the sender. If it matches, the data in the frame has not been tampered with and it is accepted. If the ICV does not match, the frame is rejected because the system assumes that the data has been modified in transit.

So now that you understand the WEP processing model, the section that follows examines how the 802.11 specification uses WEP and why it's broken!

How WEP Is Broken

To determine why WEP isn't a good security solution, you need to look at some practical problems and then look at the cryptographic problems with WEP.

For now, ignore the cryptography and consider just the practical aspects of using static WEP for data privacy. Remember that WEP keys have the following properties:

- **They are static:** They can't be changed except by reconfiguring all access points and stations.

- **They are shared:** All access points and stations share the same WEP keys.

The static property of WEP keys creates a management headache when it comes to key distribution. It isn't much of a challenge to configure WEP keys in a small office or home network when there are only one or a few access points and a few end stations. If there are many access points and end stations, however, this is a major problem. Configuring WEP keys isn't just a problem when devices are initially provisioned; as you are about to learn, WEP keys should be frequently rotated to mitigate some cryptographic weaknesses.

Now, think about the shared key property. Basically, this means that every WLAN device on the network has the capability to decrypt any other device's encrypted frames. Maybe that doesn't matter in some deployments, but then again, it probably does in others. Do you want your colleagues decrypting and reading some of your email messages?

Those are just some of the practical problems intrinsic to the specification. There are some major cryptographic problems with WEP, too. As previously noted, as 802.11 WLAN technology started to take off, a lot of smart people in the cryptographic community took a good long look at WEP as a security mechanism and identified catastrophic flaws.

We'll keep it simple here and not go into all the details of birthday paradoxes, bit-flipping, and weak IVs. The reference material at the end of the chapter provides that information. In a nutshell, the big cryptographic problems center around several areas: IV choice, reuse, transparency, flaws in the integrity-checking mechanisms, and weak RC4 keys.

802.11 Authentication

In the base 802.11 specification, there are basically two kinds of authentication: open authentication and shared-key authentication. Figure 4-2 illustrates open authentication.

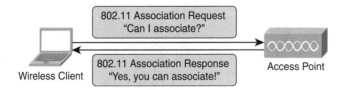

Figure 4-2   *802.11 Open Authentication*

As you can see, open authentication is exactly that—completely open. It isn't designed to authenticate the end-user device in any way. As long as the association request includes a valid service set identifier (SSID) on the access point, the device is allowed access to the network. When open authentication is used with static WEP encryption, there is some access control because each end-user device needs to know the WEP key to transmit any data after associating with an access point.

You might ask, why would a standards body allow free and open access to the WLAN? Well, there are many applications where open access to the network satisfies business objectives. Many universities view the WLAN as an open resource and thus provide no authentication or access control. Open authentication is sometimes used for guest access solutions in enterprises and supplemented with some kind of portal-based access control. It's also used in most public hotspots, typically supplemented with the service providers' access and authentication framework layered on top of the 802.11 open authentication.

Now what about shared-key authentication? Figure 4-3 illustrates shared-key authentication.

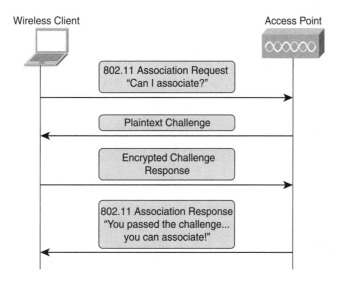

Figure 4-3 *802.11 Shared-Key Authentication*

As you can see from Figure 4-3, the authentication is provided by a challenge, challenge-response mechanism. The access point sends an arbitrary 128-bit value as challenge text to the station requesting access. The station encrypts the challenge text using the WEP key and sends this as the challenge response. If the WEP key is shared correctly between the AP and the end-user device, the AP should be able to decrypt the challenge response and compare it to the challenge text. If it matches, the station is allowed access. Simple enough.

If you take a closer look, however, there's a mutual authentication deficiency. The AP is authenticating the station, but what allows the station to trust that the challenge response is from the correct AP? The answer is...nothing! The station has no way of knowing whether the challenge text comes from a legitimate AP or an AP impersonator.

But it gets worse. An eavesdropper watching this transaction just saw a plain-text message (the challenge) and its corresponding cipher text (the challenge response). Now, if the eavesdropper takes the plain text and XORs it with the cipher text, she gets the key stream corresponding to that IV!

Unfortunately, the 802.11 specification allows for IV reuse, so if the vendor implementation is sloppy, the eavesdropper might be able to use the recovered material to authenticate herself and start sending packets into the network. Worse, the next time the eavesdropper sees a frame with that IV, she can use the recovered key stream to decrypt the cipher text by simply XORing the cipher text with the key stream. If she's patient, she can build enough of a key stream database to decrypt a lot of cipher text.

As you can see, shared-key authentication is worse than no authentication because it provides a false sense of security.

Oh, and maybe you noticed something else about both open and shared-key authentication. Curious? There is no user-based authentication. Device-based authentication, like 802.11 open and shared-key authentication, does not prevent unauthorized users from accessing networked resources from authorized machines. Think of the problem presented by lost or stolen assets!

Addressing the Strong Authentication and Privacy Challenges

After having reviewed the issues with the base 802.11 specification and WEP for authentication and privacy, a set of basic requirements for real authentication and privacy emerges:

■   User-based authentication

■   Mutual authentication

■   Dynamic, per-session, and per-user cryptographic keys

■   Larger IV space than 2^{24}

■   Stronger cryptographic algorithms than RC4

■   Backward compatibility with RC4-only-capable client devices

■   Strong message integrity checks

■   Scalability and manageability

These are the basic requirements for strong authentication and privacy addressed by the IEEE 802.11i task group charter. The work of the 802.11i task group resulted in a new 802.11 amendment that defines the following:

■   **Two types of networks:** The Transition Security Network (TSN) and the Robust Security Network (RSN)

- **New data privacy and integrity models:** Temporal Key Integrity Protocol (TKIP) and CCMP

- An authentication framework based on IEEE 802.1X and EAP

- Dynamic cryptographic key management

TKIP includes techniques to protect cryptographic keys through key mixing and packet counters and a Message Integrity Check (MIC) algorithm. TKIP is designed to be backward compatible with legacy WEP equipment.

CCMP is an algorithm for data privacy and integrity based on the Advanced Encryption Standard (AES). CCMP is stronger than TKIP but is not backward compatible with legacy equipment that cannot support AES.

The IEEE 802.1X standard defines an algorithm for port-access control that requires client devices to authenticate before being given network access. The authentication is accomplished through the EAP and RADIUS protocols. The key management algorithm is designed to generate dynamic cryptographic keys to address the weaknesses in WEP.

An RSN is a network that allows only TKIP and/or CCMP. A TSN allows both RSN and WEP machines.

While the IEEE 802.11i task group was working on completing the 802.11i standard, the Wi-Fi Alliance adopted Wi-Fi Protected Access (WPA) as an industry standard. WPA was based on the parts of the 802.11i standard that were available and uncontroversial at the time. After 802.11i was ratified, though, the Wi-Fi Alliance adopted the full document as its WPA Version 2 standard.

In a nutshell, WPA includes TKIP, 802.1X authentication, and dynamic key management. WPAv2 adds CCMP. Both WPA and WPAv2 have the following modes:

- **Personal mode:** Allows pre-shared keys for authentication

- **Enterprise mode:** Requires 802.1X authentication

We will look at the enterprise mode here.

Cisco literature often uses a four-ingredient model, as illustrated by Figure 4-4, to abstract basic wireless security requirements:

- **The authentication framework:** The scaffolding necessary for the authentication and encryption algorithms

- **The authentication algorithm:** Provides a secure way of validating user credentials

- **The data privacy algorithm:** The cryptographic mechanism for obfuscating data in transmission

- **The data integrity algorithm:** Protects messages in transit from tampering

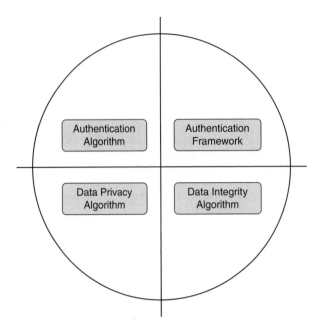

Figure 4-4   *WLAN Authentication and Data Privacy*

Authentication Framework

The authentication framework provides the scaffolding for the authentication and encryption algorithms and mechanisms by specifying the protocols and processes. In the raw 802.11 specification, the authentication framework is provided by the authentication management frame. This management frame facilitates the open and shared-key authentication algorithms, without doing the actual authentication.

802.11i specifies the use of the IEEE's 802.1X port-based access control specification for access control and the IETF's EAP authentication framework with RADIUS as the protocol for enterprise-grade wireless authentication.

EAP is an authentication framework defined in IETF RFC 3748 and RFC 3579 that is used to authenticate supplicants. After the supplicant is authenticated, the authenticator removes the port access restrictions and the authenticated device can begin transmitting and receiving data frames.

EAP, as defined in RFCs 2284 and 3579, is an authentication framework only. There are many different authentication algorithms based on the EAP framework, defined either in other RFCs or as proprietary protocols. The following section covers EAP types in more detail.

RADIUS is the protocol used to authenticate the supplicant. EAP over RADIUS messages, as defined in RFC 2869, transport the authentication messages between the authenticator and authorization server. In RADIUS terminology, the authenticator is the Network Access Server (NAS) or RADIUS client.

Figure 4-5 illustrates the 802.11i authentication framework.

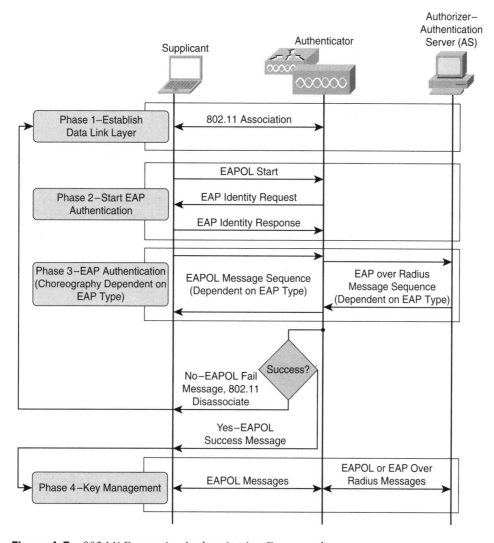

Figure 4-5 *802.11i Enterprise Authentication Framework*

Note that 802.1X authentication has three parties:

- **Supplicant:** The client device requesting access to network resources.

- **Authenticator:** The network unit that controls access to the network. It acts as an intermediary between the supplicant and the authentication server. In the CUWN, the WLAN controller is the authenticator.

■   **Authentication server:** Grants or denies permission to the supplicant based on the authentication algorithm and user-based access credentials. The authentication server is the RADIUS server.

Initially, the wireless station (the supplicant) establishes data link layer connectivity through the standard 802.11 open authentication. Immediately then, the authenticator blocks further wireless station access to the network.

Next, the client typically issues an Extensible Authentication Protocol over LAN (EAPoL) start message to begin the authentication process. The authenticator, the WLC, responds with an EAPoL Identity request.

In the next phase, the device identity is authenticated through an exchange of EAP and RADIUS messages. We've deliberately abstracted this phase at this point because the mechanics vary by EAP algorithm. Suffice it to say, though, that in this phase, some type of mutual authentication is necessary to establish two-way trust. The network trusts the supplicant only after it is authenticated, and the supplicant can only trust the network after it authenticates the network in some way. The supplicant cannot implicitly trust the network because some attacker could be spoofing the network elements.

Assuming success in authentication, the key management phase follows. We'll look at key management in more detail in the context of data privacy. During key management, a dynamic encryption key is negotiated for the particular session.

Now finally, after full authentication and session key derivation, the authenticator lifts the 802.1X port restrictions and the supplicant is allowed access to the network.

Authentication Algorithm

Recall in the previous sections that the authentication framework includes the use of the EAP, but the authentication algorithm performs the actual authentication of devices based on some type of credentials. The authentication algorithm is defined by an EAP type, of which there are many. Neither 802.11i nor the Wi-Fi Alliance specifies an EAP type, but the Wi-Fi Alliance currently certifies interoperability with several EAP types as part of the WPA certification tests: EAP-TLS, EAP Tunneled Transport Layer Security (EAP-TTLS), Protected EAP (PEAP), and EAP Subscriber Identity Module (EAP-SIM). Additionally, there are Cisco-developed EAP types—Lightweight EAP (LEAP) and EAP with Flexible Authentication through Secure Tunneling (EAP-FAST)—that are widely adopted.

The sections that follow cover all of these EAP types, though some in greater detail than others, starting with the Cisco-developed EAP types.

LEAP

Prior to the ratification of 802.11i and the WPA certifications, Cisco introduced a proprietary EAP type called Lightweight Extensible Authentication Protocol (LEAP). Some literature refers to LEAP as Cisco-EAP.

Initially, LEAP support was limited to Cisco Aironet–branded client cards and supplicant software. Cisco drove wide adoption of LEAP into the market through the Cisco

Compatible Extensions (CCX) program by making LEAP a mandatory part of the CCX version 2 specification.

Let's look at the choreography of LEAP in Figure 4-6 because it illustrates some important things.

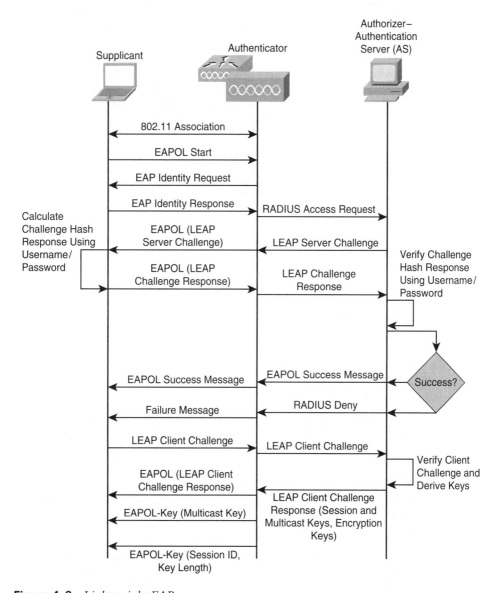

Figure 4-6   *Lightweight EAP*

As shown in Figure 4-6, LEAP has several important characteristics. It includes mutual authentication and is password based. It is also *lightweight* in the sense that all that is really needed to deploy LEAP is support for it on the three parties of the 802.1X authentication model.

But notice also in Figure 4-6 how there is nothing in LEAP's choreography to obfuscate the mutual challenge/challenge-response messages. In 2004, a tool called ASLEAP was released that exploited weaknesses in the hashing mechanisms in those challenge/challenge-response messages to recover user credentials. ASLEAP attacks can be mitigated with strong passwords, but that adds more management overhead and isn't totally effective.

So LEAP is now deprecated and should not be used. But the wide adoption of LEAP was a watershed industry development. LEAP was the first EAP type defined specifically for WLANs. It also provided a viable alternative to WEP at a time when this alternative was desperately needed and there was not a standards-based alternative. Most importantly, it proved the viability of 802.1X with EAP as an authentication framework for WLANs before standards ratification.

EAP-FAST

EAP-FAST is an acronym for EAP with Flexible Authentication through Secure Tunneling. Cisco has published the EAP-FAST specification as IETF RFC 4851.

EAP-FAST preserves the lightweight characteristic of LEAP but provides a mechanism to protect the exchange of credentials during authentication. EAP-FAST uses something called a *Protected Access Credential (PAC)* as a unique shared-secret between the supplicant and server. The PAC is used during the EAP-FAST algorithm to establish a TLS tunnel that protects the exchange of user authentication messages. The tunnel establishment is called the *outer authentication*; the user authentication inside the tunnel is called in the *inner authentication*.

Figure 4-7 illustrates the EAP-FAST choreography.

During EAP-FAST Phase 0, the PAC is provisioned on the supplicant using the Authenticated Diffie-Hellman Protocol. The supplicant can subsequently securely store the PAC, obviating Phase 0 for future authentications.

During Phase 1, the PAC is used for mutual device authentication that results in a session tunnel key. This session key is used to secure the authentication exchanges in Phase 2.

Finally, in Phase 2, the user authentication is performed in the TLS tunnel established during Phase 1.

Now, it's important to note that the devil is in the details of EAP-FAST implementation. When automatic PAC provisioning is enabled, an attacker can intercept the PAC and subsequently use that to compromise user credentials.

There is also a potential attack vector, where an attacker deploys a rogue AP offering service to clients. During Phase 1, the attacker rejects the PAC during Phase 1, triggering a return to the PAC-provisioning phase. Many supplicants are configured to prompt the user to accept a new PAC. If the target in this attack accepts the new PAC, the attacker can compromise user credentials when EAP-FAST moves to Phase 2 on the rogue network. Strong rogue AP management and proper supplicant configuration mitigate this attack.

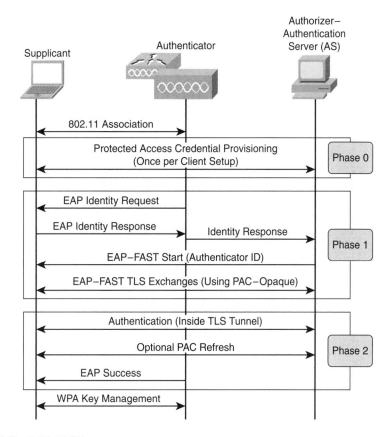

Figure 4-7 *EAP-FAST*

The PAC is issued on a per-user and per-authentication server basis, so if a new user logs in to the network from a device, or if a device is logging in to a part of the network serviced by a different RADIUS server, a new PAC file must be provisioned. This does present some obvious challenges from a management perspective in light of the potential attack vectors just discussed.

EAP-FAST allows manual PAC provisioning and server certificate use during the PAC provisioning phase to mitigate the threats and management challenges.

PEAP

Protected EAP (PEAP) is similar to EAP-FAST in that it establishes a TLS tunnel to protect authentication messages; however, PEAP uses a server certificate for outer authentication and to negotiate the cryptographic keys necessary for the TLS tunnel. Figure 4-8 illustrates the choreography of PEAP.

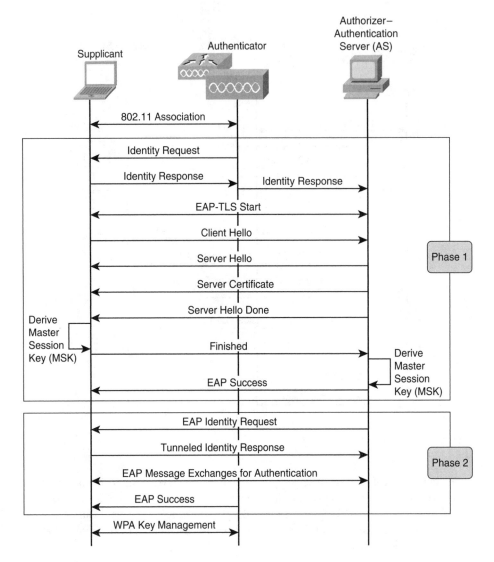

Figure 4-8 *PEAP*

PEAP inner authentication in the TLS tunnel comes in two flavors:

- **PEAP-MSCHAPv2:** PEAP-MSCHAPv2 is the most common version of PEAP, so common in fact that usually when people use the term *PEAP*, they are referring to this version of PEAP. PEAP-MSCHAPv2 uses the Microsoft Challenge Handshake Authentication Protocol version 2 (MSCHAPv2) for the inner authentication method.

- **PEAP-GTC:** GTC is an acronym for Generic Token Card, which represents the inner authentication method, which uses hardware token cards to generate one-time passwords for users.

EAP-TLS

RFC 5216 defines EAP-TLS. Like PEAP, EAP-TLS uses certificate exchanges for outer authentication in establishing a TLS tunnel. But, as shown in Figure 4-9, EAP-TLS adds client-side authentication: The client device must present a certificate that is authenticated by the server.

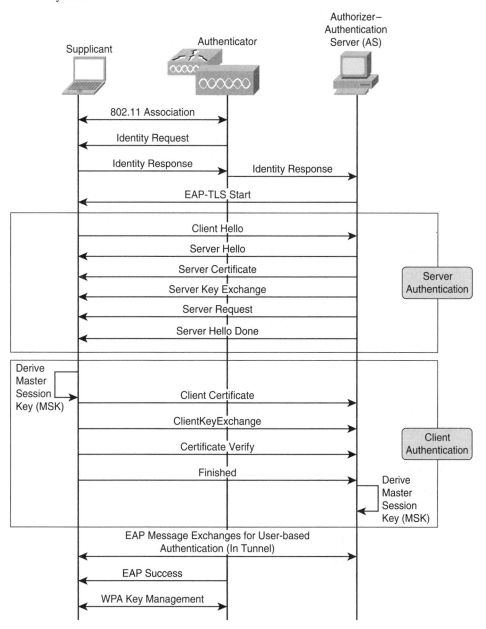

Figure 4-9 *EAP-TLS*

The power of this mutual certificate exchange is that it mitigates theoretical man-in-the-middle attacks to which other authentication types might be vulnerable.

After the mutual exchange is completed, the inner authentication takes place, leading up to the keying phase.

EAP-TTLS

RFC 5281 defines EAP-TTLS as an authentication algorithm extending the functionality of EAP-TLS to a number of legacy inner authentication methods. It is listed here for completeness because the Wi-Fi Alliance includes EAP-TTLS in its WPA interoperability certifications.

EAP-SIM

RFC 4186 defines a protocol for authentication and session key derivation through Global System for Mobile Communications (GSM) Subscriber Identity Modules (SIM) infrastructure. The choreography of EAP-SIM is out of the scope of this book but is listed because it is included in the Wi-Fi Alliance WPA test suite.

Selecting an EAP Type

After all this discussion of EAP choreography, which EAP type should you use? The answer is, it depends.

One of the decision criteria is what EAP types are supported on your client devices. At the time of this writing, the latest versions of Microsoft Windows have native support for PEAP, EAP-TLS, LEAP, and EAP-FAST (with the appropriate patches). The latest versions of Mac OS have support for LEAP, PEAP, EAP-FAST, EAP-TLS, and EAP-TTLS.

If your device's OS does not support the EAP type you select, you'll have to install additional supplicant software. You might decide to do this anyway because add-on supplicants often have additional features you want. Sometimes add-on supplicants just work better than native OS supplicants.

The other major decision factor customers wrestle with is how much management overhead to incur. Each EAP type requires some setup and maintenance, and there are usually trade-offs between manageability and security.

For example, EAP-TLS is probably the most secure of the EAP types covered; however, it's also the most difficult to manage because it requires a PKI infrastructure and certificates on every client device. You might decide that a lighter-weight authentication algorithm such as PEAP or EAP-FAST is good enough.

Data Privacy and Integrity

The previous section looked at how the 802.11i and WPA standards address the problem of missing access control and authentication in WEP. This section looks at how the standard addresses encryption key management.

Remember that with WEP, there were two big problems with key management:

■ A big management challenge distributing WEP keys.

■ The keys are shared between all devices in the WLAN.

The 802.11i standard addresses these problems by calling out a mechanism for dynamic encryption key generation.

Before going into detail, consider the two kinds of keys:

■ **Master keys:** Used to generate transient keys. The master key exists as long as a supplicant's authentication is valid, so it can exist across multiple 802.11 associations.

■ **Transient keys:** Change with each session.

The two phases of the key management process are

■ Master key establishment

■ Key exchange

With master key establishment, the master key is shared between station and authenticator and is subsequently used to negotiate keys that are used to encrypt data. There are two types of master keys:

■ **Pairwise master key (PMK):** Used for unicast traffic; there is a PMK instance for each supplicant.

■ **Group master key (GMK):** Used for multicast and broadcast traffic; group keys are shared among all stations and the AP.

When using 802.1X/EAP authentications, the PMK is established following mutual authentication between the supplicant and authentication server. Figure 4-10 illustrates the key management phase.

In Figure 4-10, you can see that following mutual authentication, the PMK is established between the supplicant and the authentication server. The supplicant and the authentication server derive the PMK separately. The authentication server then hands the PMK to the authenticator. The 802.11i specification does not dictate how the PMK is passed to the authenticator, although it does recommend EAPoL; WPA on the other hand, specifies that this must be done through RADIUS.

After the PMK is handed off to the authenticator, the supplicant and authenticator negotiate a pairwise transient key (PTK) through a cryptographic four-way handshake. As you can see in Figure 4-10, the four-way handshake begins with the authenticator and supplicant each generating a cryptographic nonce value. In the first message then, the authenticator sends its nonce to the supplicant. As shown in Figure 4-11, the supplicant uses the two nonces and the PMK to generate the PTK.

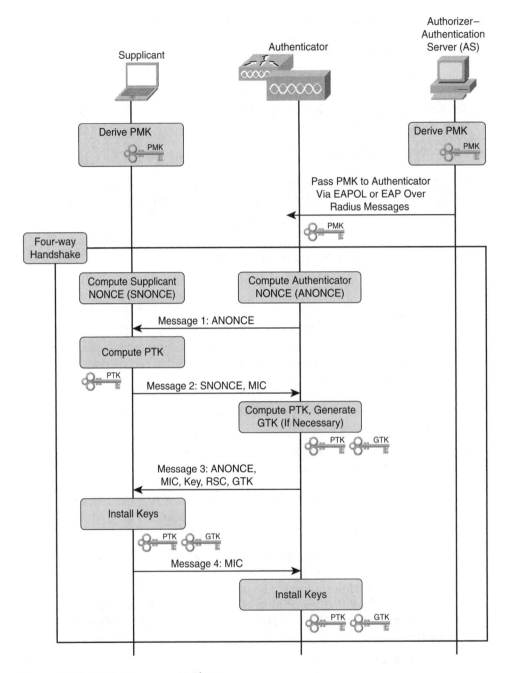

Figure 4-10   *Key Management Phase*

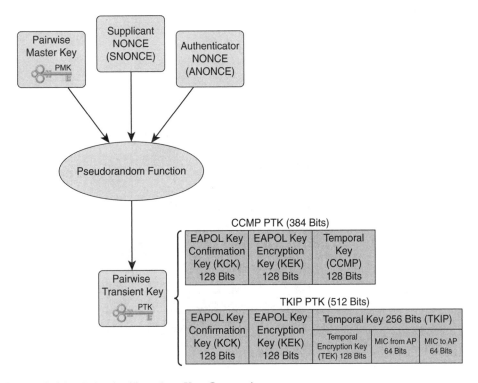

Figure 4-11 *Pairwise Transient Key Generation*

In Figure 4-10, you can see that after generating the PTK, the supplicant sends a message back to the authenticator with its own nonce and a message integrity check (MIC) that proves the supplicant knows the PMK. After verifying the MIC, the authenticator generates the PTK using the methodology shown in Figure 4-11.

The authenticator will generate a group transient key (GTK) from the GMK if necessary. The GTK is used for encrypting multicast and broadcast traffic. Figure 4-12 illustrates the process for generating the GTK.

In the third message of the four-way handshake illustrated in Figure 4-11, the authenticator sends its nonce, a MIC based on the PMK, the receive sequence counter (RSC), and the GTK. The RSC is the current sequence counter for the GTK. The GTK requires a sequence counter to prevent an attacker from replaying a broadcast message. After the supplicant verifies the MIC, it installs the PTK and GTK. It then sends the confirmation message to the authenticator that includes a MIC. After the authenticator confirms the MIC, it installs the PTK and GTK. At this point, the wireless station can begin sending and receiving data. The data is encrypted with part of the PTK.

Take a moment to revisit the generation of the GTK. Figure 4-12 illustrates the process for generating the GTK from the GMK.

An obvious question is, where does the GMK come from? The answer is that the authenticator generates the GMK. The authenticator then uses the GMK to generate the GTK.

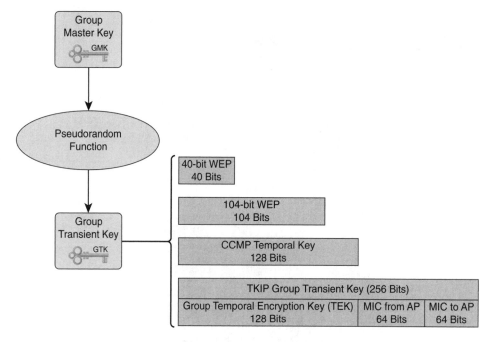

Figure 4-12   *Group Transient Key Generation*

As you probably have deduced, all devices associated to an AP share the GTK. The GTK will be regenerated in the following situations:

■   When a MIC failure occurs (more on that in the next section)

■   When a client disassociates or is deauthenticated

■   After a specified interval

When a new GTK is generated, it is sent in an encrypted message to each associated wireless station. This is a two-way handshake process, as illustrated in Figure 4-13.

You should have noticed in Figures 4-11 and 4-12 that there is both a pairwise and group key hierarchy and that this hierarchy is different for CCMP and TKIP. The sections that follow examine CCMP and TKIP in greater detail. For now, note that the PTK is made up of several keys:

■   EAPoL Confirmation Key

■   EAPoL Encryption Key

■   Temporal Key

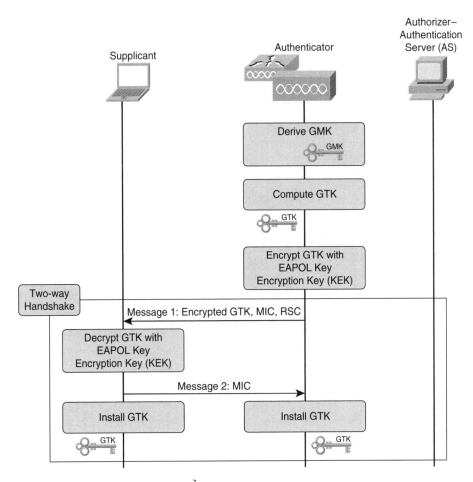

Figure 4-13 *Group Transient Key Two-Way Handshake*

In the case of TKIP, the Temporal Key is actually a Temporal Encryption Key and the MICs from the four-way handshake. The Temporal Encryption Key is used in the data encryption and decryption. The EAPoL keys are used to secure transactions across the air whenever encryption keys need to be sent from the authenticator to the supplicant.

Temporal Key Integrity Protocol (TKIP)

At this point, you should understand how the standards bodies have addressed WEP deficiencies when it comes to authentication and key management. Now it's time to look at how the cryptographic flaws have been addressed. This section looks at TKIP in detail, while the next section examines CCMP.

Recall that the basic cryptographic problems with WEP centered on the following items:

■ IV choice and reuse

■ ICV flaws

■ "Weak" RC4 keys

The design challenges before the standards bodies for TKIP were that TKIP had to "fix" the WEP cryptographic deficiencies and at the same time had to work with legacy 802.11 equipment. Basically, this meant that TKIP had to work within the mechanical framework of WEP using RC4.

The TKIP designers settled on a solution that involves three protocols to supplement WEP:

- Michael MIC

- TKIP Sequence Counter (TSC)

- Key-mixing algorithm

Michael MIC is a message integrity check mechanism to augment the WEP ICV. Remember that the WEP ICV failed to protect against bit-flipping. TKIP uses the Michael hashing algorithm instead that is not vulnerable to bit-flipping. Essentially, the Michael MIC is a hash value calculated from a 64-bit key derived from one-half of the lower-order 128 bits of the PTK (see Figures 4-11 and 4-12) and a padded MAC service data unit (MSDU) from the network layer. The padded MSDU is the MSDU with some additional fields, including the source and destination MAC addresses and some additional special octet values. This padded MSDU is used only for the Michael MIC calculation.

The Michael MIC was selected because it is computationally inexpensive. The 802.11i task group felt that this was important because the algorithm needed to run on legacy hardware with limited CPU horsepower. As such, Michael MIC is a trade-off between cryptographic strength and computational complexity. The 802.11i amendment itself calls Michael MIC "weak protection against active attacks."

So the 802.11i amendment calls out some countermeasures. Specifically, 802.11i requires that all Michael MIC failures be logged and that, in the event that two Michael MIC failures (on either the AP or the client) occur within one minute, both the station and AP are to disable all packet reception and transmission and the AP is to deauthenticate and disassociate all wireless clients. The ICV is always checked before the MIC to make it harder for an attacker to create deliberate MIC failures, which in itself could be a DoS attack.

The TKIP Sequence Counter (TSC) is used to strengthen the IV and prevent replay attacks on the system. The TSC is a 48-bit counter that starts at 0 and is incremented with each packet.

The TSC protects against replay attacks in two ways:

- Each device records the highest TSC value it has seen for a MAC address. If a packet arrives with a TSC value less than or equal to the current highest TSC value, the packet is discarded because the receiver assumes that the packet has been replayed.

- The TSC is used in the key-mixing algorithm for both encryption and decryption algorithms, so if the TSC is tampered with in transit, the ICV and MIC will fail and the packet will be discarded.

Figure 4-14 illustrates the TKIP packet format.

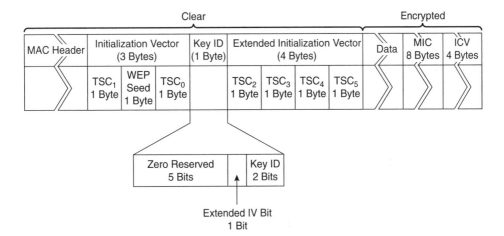

Figure 4-14 *TKIP Packet Format*

In Figure 4-14, you can see that the 48 bits of the TSC are split up into 6 bytes, TSC_0 through TSC_5. The low-order bytes, TSC_0 and TSC_1, are joined with a specially crafted byte to create a standard 24-bit IV that is designed to avoid FMS weak keys. Bytes TSC_2 through TSC_5 are placed in a new field called the Extended IV field. A bit is set in the Key ID byte to indicate that the Extended IV is in use. We will see shortly how all 6 bytes of the TSC are used in the key-mixing algorithm.

The TSC protects against IV reuse because a TSC is never repeated for a given key; when a new key is generated, the TSC is reset to 0. So even if an attacker were to retrieve a key stream for a packet, the key stream would be worthless.

The third protocol that TKIP introduces is a key-mixing algorithm that ensures a unique per-packet 128-bit WEP key generated from the Temporal Encryption Key (TEK). As shown in Figures 4-11 and 4-12, the TEK is the high-order 128-bits of the PTK.

Figure 4-15 illustrates the TKIP key-mixing algorithm.

In Phase 1, the most significant 32 bits of the TSC are "mixed" with the transmitter's 48-bit MAC address and the high-order 80 bits of the TEK. The output is an 80-bit TKIP Transmit Address and Key (TTAK).

The TTAK is "mixed" with the entire TEK and TSC in Phase 2. The output is a 128-bit WEP key that is used to seed the RC4 keystream generator. The first 24 bits of the 128-bit key are the IV constructed from the least significant TSC bytes and the specially crafted byte, as shown previously in Figure 4-14.

TKIP provides strong protection, but the 802.11i task group wanted to do better. Particularly important was to have a solution that satisfies the U.S. government FIPS-140-2 certification requirements and that calls for AES encryption. That solution is CCMP.

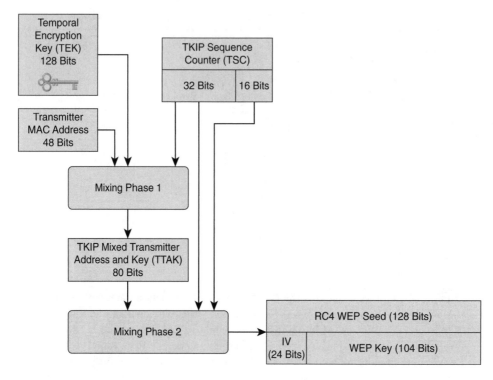

Figure 4-15   *TKIP Key-Mixing Algorithm*

Counter/CBC-MAC Protocol (CCMP)

CCMP is the strongest confidentiality, integrity, and replay protection protocol suite available for WLAN security. It is based on AES and is the core of the 802.11i RSN and the WPAv2 specification. CCMP is thus the preferred solution if all the WLAN devices in the system can support it.

An in-depth discussion of AES is beyond the scope of this chapter. We will just look at it in the abstract as it is applied to CCMP. The *Counter* part of the CCMP name is from an AES *counter mode* that provides the data privacy. The *CBC-MAC* part of the name comes from the *Cipher Block Chaining Message Authentication Code* that is used as a message integrity check.

WEP and TKIP rely on the RC4 stream cipher for encryption. In contrast, AES is a block cipher. A block cipher operates on chunks of data as opposed to a stream of bytes.

Figure 4-16 illustrates how AES counter mode works to encrypt plain text.

The plain text is chopped into 128-bit chunks. A 128-bit counter is AES encrypted and then XORed with the first 128-bit chunk of plain text. The counter is then incremented and the process repeated on the next 128-bit chunk. The process is repeated until the entire plain text is exhausted. Then the 128-bit chunks of cipher text are concatenated to produce the full encrypted text.

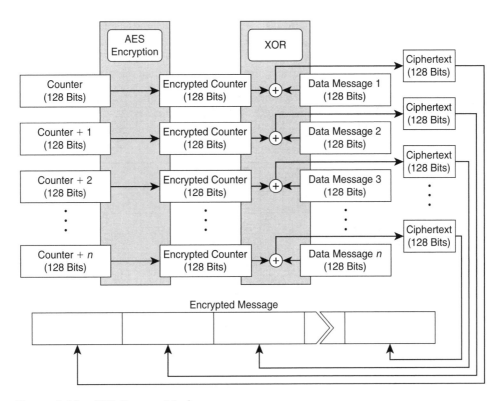

Figure 4-16   *AES Counter Mode*

Now, the decryption of this encrypted text is really simple. The decrypting entity chops up the encrypted text into 128-bit chunks. It then uses the same algorithm shown in Figure 4-16, starting with the same counter value. But instead of XORing the encrypted counters with plain text, the encrypted counters are XORed with the 128-bit chunks of cipher text. The output is the decrypted chunks of plain text. These chunks are then reassembled as the full plain-text message.

Figure 4-17 illustrates the AES CBC-MAC mode.

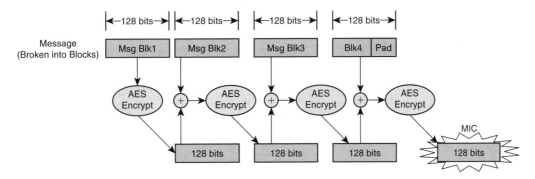

Figure 4-17   *AES CBC-MAC Mode*

As you can see from Figure 4-17, the plain text is again broken into chunks. The first chunk is AES encrypted to produce a chunk of cipher text. This chunk of cipher text is then XORed with the next block of plain text and then AES encrypted. The process is then repeated until the plain-text chunks are exhausted. The final value is the MIC.

So now that you understand the mechanics of the CCM algorithm, the next step is to see how it is applied. Figure 4-18 shows the CCMP packet format.

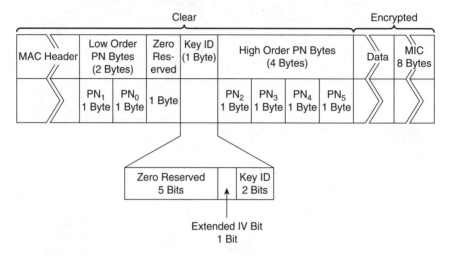

Figure 4-18 *CCMP Packet Format*

What you'll notice is that this looks a lot like the TKIP packet format. Instead of the TSC, though, CCMP uses a 48-bit packet number (PN) that is split into two parts. The Extended IV bit is also set in the KeyID field.

The MIC is a 64-bit value computed with CBC-MAC mode. The plain-text input into the CBC-MAC mode is the plain-text data plus the parts of the MAC header that cannot be changed in the event of a retransmission. The parts of the MAC header included in the MIC calculation are called the *Additional Authentication Data (AAD)*.

Figure 4-19 shows the CCMP encapsulation process.

You've already seen how the CCM algorithm encrypts the data using AES counter mode and computes the MIC through CBC-MAC. The encryption key input into the AES encryption algorithm is the CCMP Temporal Key derived from the PTK.

Remember that AES counter mode needs a counter value that is unique per packet. This counter value is the nonce shown in Figure 4-19. The nonce is assembled from the priority and source address fields from the MAC header and the packet number.

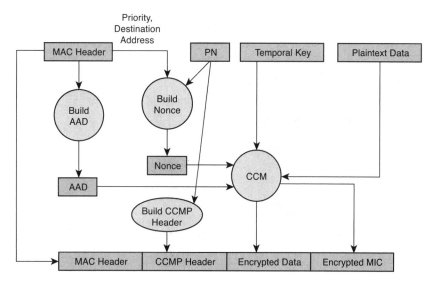

Figure 4-19   *CCMP Encapsulation Process*

Figure 4-20 shows the CCMP decapsulation process.

When a packet is received, the receiver extracts the PN and compares it against the value it has stored. If the PN has increased, the receiver knows that the packet has not been replayed.

The receiver knows the CCMP Temporal Key and can compute the nonce from the MAC and CCMP headers. It can then run the AES counter mode algorithm to decrypt the cipher text. As we've already seen, AES counter mode decryption is essentially the same as AES counter mode encryption, except that the operations are performed on the cipher text.

The MIC is then computed and compared to the decrypted MIC value to verify that the packet has not been tampered with.

Alternative Approaches to Authentication and Data Privacy

There are, of course, alternative approaches to WPA/WPAv2 Enterprise. A full 802.1X/EAP authentication solution is overkill for most home and many small-office WLAN implementations. The IEEE standards and WFA committees recognized this from the beginning and so allow an implementation using pre-shared keys (PSK). In a PSK implementation, there is a shared secret—the pre-shared key (PSK)—between the wireless station and authenticator. This shared secret is used as a passphrase to negotiate per-session encryption keys with the authenticator, as described in the key management sections.

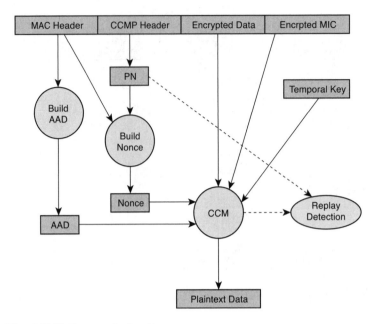

Figure 4-20   *CCMP Decapsulation Process*

We'd be remiss if we didn't at least mention overlay options as an approach to securing WLANs. Overlays typically allow 802.11 open authentications to the wireless network and leverage back-end mechanisms for user authentication and data privacy and to protect networked resources. Some customers, usually universities, don't bother with user authentication and data privacy, treating the WLAN as a public resource.

Some WLAN implementers simply don't trust anything other than VPNs, or for some reason cannot or won't implement 802.1X authentication. Typically, VPN solutions treat the 802.11 network as completely untrusted, treating the WLAN as a logically separate entity from the rest of the network. Usually, the WLC is firewalled off from the rest of the network and the APs reside on their own VLAN infrastructure. Traffic aggregated at the controller is directed to the VPN concentrator. You can see how this creates a lot of complexity in the wired network, which is why VPN overlay solutions have mostly been deprecated in favor of the wireless standards-based approaches.

Another overlay variant is to use browser redirects for web authentication, either through the native capabilities on the controller or through an external web-authentication box. These architectures were discussed in the context of guest access.

Rogue Access Point Detection and Wireless Intrusion Prevention

Remember the earlier discussion of rogue access points and devices and the other potential vulnerabilities presented by readily available profiling and attack tools? A comprehensive wireless security approach usually requires some type of rogue device detection and wireless intrusion prevention system (WIPS).

The most crude detection technique is "sneaker net." An IT staffer laces up his or her "sneakers" and walks the campus with a WLAN sniffer or other reconnaissance tools, looking for unauthorized wireless devices and potential attackers. This isn't a bad approach for small deployments, where it's usually pretty effective and good exercise too!

However, sneaker net just doesn't scale to a large or geographically dispersed deployment. Furthermore, it's pretty easy to defeat and pretty low yield for the amount of effort. One large enterprise we frequently work with used sneaker net to find rogues. At first, the IT staff found the sneaker net technique pretty effective. But after a few months, they began to find the technique was pretty much good only as physical exercise. It was a lot of effort for a pretty low yield; they rarely found rogues but still suspected there were many of them out there connected to their network.

After reevaluating their approach, they decided to take advantage of embedded rogue detection and location capabilities in their Cisco WLAN. Sure enough, as soon as they began using the embedded tools, many rogues were identified and located. One of the employees guilty of rogue deployments confessed that he had figured out the IT staff's rogue hunting schedule and simply removed the rogue until the IT staffer walked by!

All modern WLAN vendors including Cisco implement over-the-air rogue detection and WIPS using the entire WLAN system. Typically this involves sampling the RF environment at the AP radio interfaces and applying higher-level forensic analysis at the WLC or management software. For WIPS, this involves comparing traffic patterns against signatures that profile known attacks. For rogue AP detection, this involves collecting 802.11 beacons from the environment and culling out the beacons that are sourced from devices not belonging to the WLAN system. Can you see the problem with this approach, though?

We've run a WLAN sniffer in the Cisco office in midtown Manhattan and identified upwards of 350 different WLAN networks by simply capturing beacons. Each of these networks is probably a legitimate network belonging to someone. The beacons are just propagating out of their coverage area. You should be able to see that separating real rogues from other legitimate 802.11 networks is nontrivial, especially if you're trying to make the classification manually.

Cisco has tools that give you pretty granular location of rogue APs, and this is pretty helpful in classifying true rogues. Cisco has also implemented algorithms for identifying rogue devices as connected to the wired network and tracing the rogue to an actual switchport. When you can determine that a rogue AP is connected to your network, you can be pretty certain that it is in fact a rogue AP.

After you classify an AP as a rogue, Cisco gives you tools to suppress the rogue. The most effective of these techniques allows you to shut off the switchport the rogue is connected to. Essentially, this renders most rogues useless. Cisco also has the ability to do *over-the-air containment*. When the WLAN system sees legitimate wireless clients connecting to a rogue, 802.11 deauthentication frames with the rogue MAC source spoofed are sent to the client.

The CUWN has two tiers of offerings. Figure 4-21 shows the base-level rogue AP and WIPS solution.

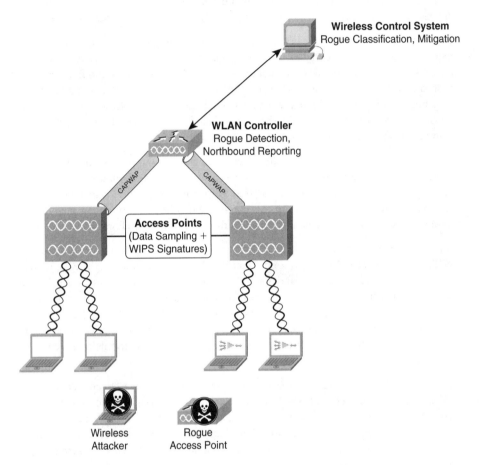

Figure 4-21   *Rogue AP and WIPS Base Solution*

In this base solution, the APs sample the environment during normal operation. APs have on-board WIPS signatures that, when triggered, create alerts that get forwarded through the WLC to WCS, where logic and rules are applied.

As far as rogue AP detection is concerned, the WLC collects sampled data from the APs and identifies potential rogue devices. The WCS takes this information and applies classification logic. After it is classified, the network administrator can initiate rogue AP containment strategies.

Figure 4-22 shows the more sophisticated solution with Cisco Adaptive WIPS running on the Mobility Service Engine (MSE) platform.

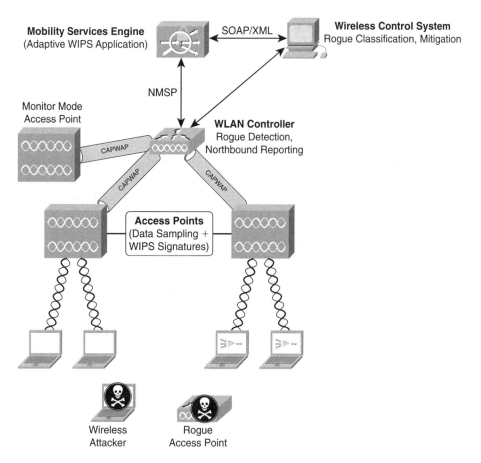

Figure 4-22   *Rogue AP and WIPS Base Solution*

This more advanced solution contains a superset of the base solution's functionality. There are more signatures and a more accurate and sophisticated classification engine running on the MSE. Also, this solution potentially uses dedicated *monitor mode* APs, dedicated to sampling the air, so there is significantly more data for the system to work with.

Further details on rogue AP management and WIPS are a chapter unto themselves. Furthermore, at the time of this writing, the details and nuances of both solutions were under analysis and discussion by the Cisco engineering teams, so any details we might include now might be obsolete when you read them. We suggest you work closely with your Cisco representatives for the details if you're interested in these topics.

Secure Management and Security Policies

It's always important to remember that any device in a network can be attacked. WLAN infrastructure devices are no different in this respect than routers and switches. It's always a good idea to follow sensible secure management practices.

A discussion on secure management practices is a chapter unto itself. We won't spend much time on it. Basically, you should try to follow these general security recommendations:

■ Use centralized authentication and authorization (TACACS+ for example) for administrative device access if possible.

■ Select secure management protocols such as SSH, HTTPS, and SNMPv3 over insecure protocols such as Telnet, HTTP, SNMPv1, and SNMPv2, if possible.

■ When you can't use centralized authentication and authorization and/or secure management protocols, try to find other ways of securing access. For example, use obscure and strong passwords and SNMP community strings. You can also use access control lists (ACL) to restrict management access to specific hosts.

■ Disable all unnecessary services on WLAN devices.

■ Limit management connectivity to specific platforms using ACLs or an equivalent mechanism.

This is obviously not a comprehensive list, but you get the idea. There are some good papers referenced at the end of the chapter that will help you with secure management practices.

Protecting WLAN client devices is fundamentally a desktop management problem. The best thing you can do is make sure that your mobile users are running host-based security solutions like personal firewalls and maintaining current antivirus software. Furthermore, you can eliminate many of the problems related to misconfigured wireless clients by preprovisioning supplicant profiles for your end users. There's a little bit more work up front, but it's definitely worth it.

It's always a good idea to periodically audit your WLAN configurations to be sure that there aren't any unintentional security holes. Cisco offers tools to periodically check AP configurations and provide alerts when security policies are violated. The CUWN enforces security policies at the controllers, so policy monitoring and enforcement are de facto parts of the architecture.

Summary

There is a lot of information in this chapter about WLAN security. We examined the potential vulnerabilities in an 802.11 WLAN. The risks discussed were as follows:

- Vulnerabilities inherent to the radio transmission medium

- Vulnerabilities inherent to the standards definitions

- Vulnerabilities inherent to mobility

- Readily available profiling and attack tools

- Misconfigured wireless devices and clients

- Rogue access points and devices

We then looked in detail at how the 802.11 WEP standard was broken and how the newer 802.11i, WPA, and WPAv2 standards solve the WEP problems and allow strong authentication and data privacy through 802.1X/EAP and TKIP and CCMP. We also looked at overlay options.

The chapter concluded with a look at other aspects of WLAN security, including rogue device detection and mitigation, wireless intrusion detection and protection, secure management practices, techniques for protecting WLAN client devices, and security configuration policy monitoring and enforcement, as well as how to deal with RF containment challenges.

This has been a lot of information for sure, but you should now know enough about WLAN security to understand what it takes to secure a WLAN deployment.

References

For additional insight on wireless LAN security fundamentals, consult the books, RFCs, standards, white papers, and technical documentation listed in the sections that follow.

Books on WLANs, WLAN Security, and General Network Security

1. Shankar, K., Sundaralingam, S., Balinsky, A., and Miller, D. *Cisco Wireless LAN Security*. Indianapolis, Indiana: Cisco Press; 2005.

2. Fleck, B. and Potter, B. *802.11 Security*. Cambridge, Massachusetts: O'Reilly; 2002.

3. Edney, J. and Arbaugh, W. *Real 802.11 Security: Wi-Fi Protected Access and 802.11i*. Reading, Massachusetts: Addison-Wesley; 2003.

4. Flickenger, R. *Wireless Hacks*. Cambridge, Massachusetts: O'Reilly; 2003.

5. Vladimirov, A.A., Gavrilenko, K.V., and Mikhailovsky, A.A. *Wi-Foo: The Secrets of Wireless Hacking*. Reading, Massachusetts: Addison-Wesley Professional; 2004.

6. Peikari, C. and Fogie, S. *Maximum Wireless Security*. Indianapolis, Indiana: Sams Publishing; 2002.

7. Swaminatha, T.M. and Elden, C.R. *Wireless Security and Privacy: Best Practices and Design Techniques*. Reading, Massachusetts: Addison-Wesley; 2002.

8. Roshan, P. and Leary, J. *802.11 Wireless LAN Fundamentals*, Indianapolis, Indiana: Cisco Press; 2003.

9. Convery, S. *Network Security Architectures*. Indianapolis, Indiana: Cisco Press; 2004.

10. Kaeo, M. *Designing Network Security*. Indianapolis, Indiana: Cisco Press; 1999.

11. O'Hara, B. and Petrick, A. *IEEE 802.11 Handbook*. Piscataway, New Jersey: IEEE Press; 2005.

Relevant RFCs and Standards Documentation

1. RFC 2196, "Site Security Handbook." Fraser, B. IETF. ftp://ftp.rfc-editor.org/in-notes/rfc2196.txt. September 1997.

2. RFC 3579, "RADIUS (Remote Authentication Dial In User Service) Support For Extensible Authentication Protocol (EAP)." Aboda, B. and Calhoun, P. IETF. ftp://ftp.rfc-editor.org/in-notes/rfc3579.txt. September 2003.

3. RFC 3748, "Extensible Authentication Protocol (EAP)." Aboda, B., Blunk, L., Vollbrecht, J., Carlson, J., and Levkowetz, H. IETF. ftp://ftp.rfc-editor.org/in-notes/rfc3748.txt. June 2004.

4. "Wi-Fi Protected Access: Strong, standards-based, interoperable security for today's Wi-Fi networks." www.wi-fi.org/membersonly/getfile.asp?f=Whitepaper_Wi-Fi_Security4-29-03.pdf. Wi-Fi Alliance. April 2003.

5. "Deploying Wi-Fi Protected Access (WPA™) and WPA2™ in the Enterprise." www.wi-fi.org/membersonly/getfile.asp?f=WFA_02_27_05_WPA_WPA2_White_Paper.pdf. Wi-Fi Alliance. March 2005.

White Papers on WLAN Security

1. "SAFE: Wireless LAN Security in Depth—version 2." Convery, S., Miller, D., Sundaralingam, S., et al. www.cisco.com/en/US/partner/netsol/ns340/ns394/ns171/ns128/networking_solutions_white_paper09186a008009c8b3.shtml.

2. "Wireless LAN Security White Paper." www.cisco.com/en/US/partner/products/hw/wireless/ps430/products_white_paper09186a00800b469f.shtml.

Technical Documents Describing WEP Flaws

1. "An Inductive Chosen Plaintext Attack Against WEP/WEP2." Arbaugh, W.A. Submission to the IEEE-802.11. doc# IEEE 802.11-01/230. www.cs.umd.edu/~waa/attack/v3dcmnt.htm. May 2001.

2. "802.11 Denial-of-Service Attacks: Real Vulnerabilities and Practical Solutions." Bellardo, J. and Savage, S. Proceedings of the USENIX Security Symposium, Washington, D.C. www.cs.ucsd.edu/users/savage/papers/UsenixSec03.pdf.

3. "Intercepting Mobile Communications: The Insecurity of 802.11." Borisov, N., Goldberg, I., and Wagner, D. 7th Annual Conference of Mobile Computing and Networking. July 2001.

4. "Weaknesses in the Key Scheduling Algorithm of RC4." Fluhrer, S., Mantin, I., and Shamir, A. In Proc. 8th Workshop on Selected Areas in Cryptography. LNCS 2259. www.crypto.com/papers/others/rc4_ksaproc.ps. Springer-Verlag. 2001.

5. "Using the Fluhrer, Mantin, and Shamir Attack to Break WEP, Revision 2." Stubblefield, A., Ioannidis, J., and Rubin, A.D. AT&T Labs. www.uninett.no/wlan/download/wep_attack.pdf. August 21, 2001.

6. "Unsafe at Any Key Size: An Analysis of the WEP Encapsulation." Walker, J. IEEE doc# 802.11-00/362. October 2000.

Chapter 5

Design Considerations

The increased demands for greater performance and availability on wireless LANs (WLAN) create new requirements for the next-generation design of WLANs. The additional requirements are driving additional design considerations beyond the earlier-generation WLAN designs. The next generation of wireless networks is no longer just a convenience or an extension to the existing wired network. The next generation of WLANs will be the primary access method for most clients. This will require careful consideration about the design requirements for the WLAN to ensure adequate coverage, capacity, and availability to meet the increased requirements of the WLAN being the primary or only access network. Next-generation WLANs might also need to support many advance mobility services, such as location, advanced security, voice, and roaming between wireless and cellular technologies. The WLAN will need to be designed to support advanced mobility service or need to be designed with the flexibility to evolve to support future mobility applications and increased usage scenarios, including a 100 percent wireless access layer.

100 Percent Wireless Access Layer

For the next-generation WLANs, many organizations might choose to migrate toward a 100 percent wireless access layer in the LAN. WLAN technology has evolved to the point that the capacity, reliability, and security capabilities of controller-based WLANs make it feasible to support a 100 percent wireless access layer. The number of devices exclusively using the WLAN as the preferred access method will continue to increase, while the number of wired Ethernet ports decreases with the migration to wireless networks as the primary access method. This does not mean all situations are appropriate for migrating to a 100 percent wireless access layer. Many situations or usage cases would not make use of wireless over wired as the primary access method feasible. The usage requirements for the access network need to be understood before making access layer deployment choices in your network. In most situations, the usage case will allow migration of a large percentage of the access layer to wireless. The percentage of the LAN access layer that becomes wireless will depend on a number of factors, including the client application's data communication requirements. The following factors should be considered when determining which clients can be moved to wireless access and what is needed for a wireless access layer to replace a wired access layer in the LAN:

- Client device power

- Radio frequency (RF) vulnerabilities

- Volume of network traffic

The sections that follow cover these considerations in greater detail.

The attributes of the data traffic for a wired access must be considered when moving to a primary wireless access layer. For example, a wired client, which is a high-data-rate IP multicast source, might not be desirable to run on the WLAN because 802.11 converts IP multicast to a broadcast, potentially having a high rate of data loss.

Client Device Power

One consideration when migrating from wired to wireless as the primary network is client power. Many client devices rely on Cat5 cabling to provide the Ethernet LAN connectivity as well as power for the client device using Power over Ethernet (PoE). In some situations, it might be less expensive to run Cat5 cabling to a device to provide PoE power over the costs to provide an AC power circuit. PoE provides an inexpensive means to power many clients. A wide variety of devices provide the capability to utilize POE power, including surveillance cameras, door access control systems, access card readers, clocks, radios, PA systems, telemetry, and sensors. The usage of PoE continues to increase. A more recent trend with PoE is to use the power it provides to recharge the batteries in a mobile device while connected to the Ethernet. The use of PoE also provides a means to centrally turn on or off the power supplied to a device remotely. An inventory on which devices use PoE and how they are used should be taken to determine whether or how many access layer ports must remain to support devices needing PoE power. Of course the access points (AP) themselves will need PoE ports for their power as well for the same reason that clients use PoE—because it is the most economical and flexible means to power many devices.

RF Vulnerability

The transition from a wired access to wireless access might expose the access layer to different attack vectors and corresponding vulnerabilities. It is fairly trivial, with some help from articles on the Internet, for people with malicious intent to launch an RF jamming attack on a WLAN. A jamming attack could cripple all wireless communications in an area. A jammer device is any transmitter that transmits at enough power on the same frequencies that the WLAN uses, to block all wireless communications in the area. A jamming attack will typically be across all the 802.11 channel frequencies. As a result of the jamming attack, legitimate wireless clients see the wireless channel as utilized, defer transmitting, and seek another channel to switch to.

One actual example of an 802.11 jamming attack occurred at a storage lot that used a WLAN to take feeds from wireless cameras for surveillance. An attacker launched a jamming attack to block the transmission of the cameras to avoid detection while stealing an expensive vehicle. While a jamming attack is a low probability, contingency planning or use of a wired Ethernet connection might be prudent depending on the nature of the WLAN use and the organization's activities. 802.11 wireless is not the only wireless technology vulnerable to jamming attacks. All current civilian wireless communication is susceptible to jamming attacks. While wireless is vulnerable to RF jamming attacks, wired networks do not have this vulnerability. The analogous attack on a wired network would consist of cutting the Cat5 cabling. The cutting of the cabling in most situations is much less likely than an RF jamming attack because cutting cable requires an attacker to be physically present on the premises. There have been situations where the move to wireless access was driven by the cabling to the client occasionally being cut or damaged. The solution for wireless jamming is to plan for the contingency of an RF-jamming situation and to use spectrum management tools to alert about and to mitigate such attacks.

Volume of Network Traffic

The volume of traffic to and from a device should be considered before deciding whether it should be using wireless links. WLANs are shared media networks, which can provide a few hundred megabits per second (Mbps) of data shared between the number of active concurrent users per AP or cell. If the wired device requires a Gigabit Ethernet connection or is exceeding tens of Mbps average data rate usage, it might be more practical to keep or move that client to a wired Ethernet connection.

Increased and Difficult WLAN Coverage Requirements

The increased usage of the WLANs might increase the WLAN coverage requirements, requiring ubiquitous access. Many newer applications used for the WLAN, such as voice, paging, and surveillance, will require WLAN coverage everywhere the user could wander. Users will expect to receive phone calls or pages everywhere from the elevators and restrooms to in their car in the parking lot or parking decks. Autonomous machines or robots that require a continuous connection to the WLAN might also be operating in your environment. For example, many hospitals use robots to deliver supplies and medications. If the robot loses its connection to the WLAN, it might become stranded or not receive updated orders. Supporting autonomous machines requires coverage anywhere the robot could potentially roam, including through tunnels and access doors that people do not normally enter.

Location services will require WLAN access everywhere the device being tracked can roam to. The number of specialized applications using the WLAN will increase the coverage requirements. Examples of specialized applications using the WLAN include digital signs, sensors, and building controls. Some of the specialized applications using the WLAN might require wireless coverage in nontraditional areas, including areas such as stairwells, restrooms, and elevators. Some usage scenarios might even require coverage in areas such as the inside of coolers, freezers, or storage areas. Applications exist where the WLAN is used to monitor the status of items in storage to ensure proper and safe storage conditions. Some items might use active RF ID tags that connect to the WLAN to track the item's location and condition. These types of WLAN uses require pervasive wireless coverage, potentially including coverage to be provided in outdoor areas, underground tunnels, and walkways between buildings and possibly inside the shipping containers or truck trailers. Many of these new areas of wireless coverage present unique challenges that should be identified as early as possible in the design requirements process.

Elevators

The requirement for pervasive wireless coverage is driving the need to support WLAN usage within elevators. Elevators are potentially the most challenging and costly areas in which to provide wireless coverage. The construction of some elevator shafts often consist of heavily reinforced concrete walls that attenuate wireless signals to unusable levels. Some elevator cars are steel boxes, blocking all wireless signals. The solution options allowed vary by each building's design and location. Building ordinances in each municipality restrict what is allowed or not allowed in the elevators and elevator shafts. The building ordinances might restrict the approaches that might be considered for each location and might dictate what solution can be used to provide WLAN coverage in the elevators. The most common methods to provide wireless coverage in elevator shafts are as follows:

- APs adjacent to the elevator shaft providing bleed-through

- APs radiating RF into the elevator shaft

- APs installed in the elevator car

The sections that follow cover these approaches in more detail.

External Bleed-Through

Using APs external or adjacent to the elevator shaft to radiate signals into the elevator shaft and car is the least costly approach. This method works only in some buildings. If the elevator car is not a solid metal box and the shaft walls do not attenuate all of the RF signal, it is possible to provide good wireless coverage with APs placed adjacent to the elevator shaft. To determine whether this method can be used often requires a site survey. The site survey will consist of establishing whether APs installed in the hallway adjacent to the elevator can provide sufficient coverage when the elevator doors are closed, with the elevator moving from floor to floor.

If this method provides sufficient coverage, additional steps are required to determine whether any roaming issues exist. Because the clients in the elevator shaft could potentially pass through coverage between a different AP on each floor, fast roaming and reauthentication techniques might be required to ensure continuous client connectivity.

Elevator Shaft Coverage

When WLAN coverage is not possible using RF bleed-through from external APs, radiating the RF signal into the elevator shaft is often the only alternate inexpensive method. This method will work if the elevator car is not a solid metal box. The elevator cars would need to be inspected to determine whether all sides of the elevator car are solid metal that might prevent a wireless signal from propagating into the car from the outside. This is usually accomplished using a wireless site survey, with an AP radiating into the elevator shaft and taking readings from inside the elevator car. Assuming that there is a means to propagate the wireless signal into the elevator car, the next hurdle is to determine whether the building ordinances allow APs or antennas to be installed in the elevator shaft. If allowed, the preferred approach would be to install only the antenna in the elevator shaft and cable it to the access point with low-loss RF cabling or with a distributed antenna system. Keeping the AP out of the antenna shaft will make servicing easier. The common approach is to install a patch antenna in the elevator shaft pointing toward the elevator car to provide coverage inside the elevator car.

The AP providing the coverage in the elevator shaft should be configured with Radio Resource Management (RRM) disabled. The channel and transmit power levels should be configured manually to provide sufficient power for when the car is the farthest distance from the AP's antenna. Depending on the client, the placement and power levels of the elevator APs might require additional adjustments to prevent undesired roaming when the elevator door opens, and the Receive Signal Strength Indicator (RSSI) levels for exterior APs could trigger roaming every time the car door opens. Each client device vendor's roaming algorithm makes roaming decisions based on RSSI level and error or retry rates. To prevent roaming, the client's RSSI from the AP should be stronger than -70 dBm. Besides tuning the AP transmit power, the client device's roaming aggressiveness might need to be reduced to prevent roaming whenever the elevator car door opens. To summarize, the best practice is to manually configure the AP's channel and transmit power to always provide a signal stronger than -70 dBm in the elevator and to test for roaming issues in the elevator car and when leaving the elevator car using the critical client devices.

Access Point Installed in Elevator Car

The surest method to provide WLAN coverage in the elevator is to install an AP in each elevator car. This method is often the only viable method because of building ordinance or elevator car construction. This method might also be the most expensive. To install the AP in the elevator car will require that Cat5 Ethernet cabling be installed in the traveler cable to the elevator car. The traveler cable is the cable bundle that supplies power and telephone communications to the elevator. By default, most elevator cable bundles do not include Cat cables in the traveler cable to support Ethernet. To have Cat5 Ethernet cabling added in the traveler cable bundle will require contracting with the elevator vendor to have a qualified elevator mechanic install the cabling needed to support the AP in the car.

The AP installed in the elevator should be configured with RRM disabled, with the channel and power configured manually. The goal is to operate the AP in the elevator in the car at the lowest power setting to reduce interference with the WLAN coverage outside the car when the car door is open. The lowest power level configured in such deployments should provide a strong enough RSSI in the elevator car such that the client does not roam every time the car door opens, minimizing cochannel interference when the door is open. Such deterministic fine-tuning often depends on the client device's roaming algorithm and your understanding of it. A good test to perform after deployment would be with a voice over wireless device or other device that panic roams.

Note   A *panic roam* occurs when the client device does not have a cache of a candidate AP to roam to and will be disconnected from the WLAN until a new AP can be found with which to associate.

The tests should determine the client's roaming behavior at various RSSI levels on the AP inside the elevator to find the value at which the client does not roam when the door opens on each floor.

Continuous Availability and Outage Planning

The increased usage of the WLAN requires the WLAN to provide increased uptime. The WLAN might be the primary or the only access network in some areas. For areas where the WLAN needs to be designed and implemented for high availability, the dependency of many clients on the wireless WLAN will require determining what the appropriate levels of resiliency should be for the WLAN infrastructure. WLAN uptime prediction is difficult to put in the same terms of the standard five nines of uptime because of the increased number of uncontrolled variables in the end-to-end system. While models to predict WLAN uptime do not exist because variables such as uncontrolled RF interference cannot be predicted, the designer can design for 99.999 percent uptime for each component layer in WLAN systems. To implement this level of uptime requires redundancy at each layer and configuration tuning to achieve 99.999 percent uptime.

The WLAN is becoming the primary network access technology or even the only network edge access technology in many organizations. This requires careful consideration of a number of factors in the design of the WLAN to prevent outages or minimize the downtime when failure occurs. This also requires contingency planning for essential applications if an extended WLAN outage occurs. The factors that affect availability and for which the design considerations should be made to make the wireless deployment resilient include the following:

- Power loss:
  - Equipment failures: APs, wireless LAN controllers (WLC), and backhaul network
  - Back office services: Authentication servers, mobility services servers
- RF interference:
  - Denial of service attacks
  - Business operations continuity in the WLAN era

The sections that follow describe these factors in greater detail.

Power Loss

WLAN equipment and support infrastructure is subject to the risk of a power outage disrupting communications. With voice or any essential service running on the WLAN, the appropriate level of planning must be taken to ensure uninterrupted operation during a power outage. The recommendations would be to use PoE for all APs and to provide backup power for the switches to which the APs are attached, as well as the distribution and core network components needed to support the WLAN's operation. This will include the wireless controllers and other network infrastructure components. Besides the network infrastructure, the authentication service used by the WLAN must also have backup power support to allow usage of the WLAN during a power outage.

Equipment Failures: APs, WLCs, and Backhaul Network

Planning must be done to ensure that equipment failures will not cause a WLAN service outage longer than a period acceptable for the usage of the WLAN. Various redundant equipment and device configuration options exist to provide high availability. The failover strategy for equipment should consider each element of the hardware chain to provide redundancy at each link. Part of redundancy planning might require specific configuration options for each device type, where priority to a failover resource might need to be configured for situations that could result in oversubscription of the failover resources.

AP Failover

To design for AP failover, the common approach is to design with APs providing overlapping coverage sufficient to support a single AP failure. The WLC will increase the power to provide coverage for a failed AP as a part of the RRM algorithms. To incorporate this in the AP RF design requires designing and performing site surveys with the AP operating at one-half or one-fourth of the maximum transmit power.

The potential outage time from a user perspective for an AP failure will be the time an unexpected or panic-roam event takes to occur. This is not usually very long, but the actual time a panic roam takes will be determined by the client vendor's roaming algorithms and should be tested for situations where this is critical with exact client devices expected to be used.

WLC Failover

To design for WLC failover requires allocating spare WLC resources to support a WLC failure event. The key consideration is where to place the failure WLC resources and determine what is an allowed or acceptable length of time for WLC failure (seconds, minutes, more?).

The WLC failover resource must be in a location that has a high probability of being available, with the sufficient bandwidth and network connectivity to other essential network-based services to support the WLAN during a primary controller's failure condition. The unified wireless network architecture supports placing the failover WLC almost anywhere, but higher levels of resiliency will dictate the best location. For example, having the backup controller at a central site across a WAN could increase the risk of outage because during a WLC failure, the resiliency and capacity of the WAN will determine the resiliency of the WLAN. Careful analysis must be performed to determine where the critical application services reside to determine the WLC resiliency strategy with the WAN and the application services resiliency plan.

As fairly evident and obvious, the failure of a WLC will cause an outage in the WLAN. The length of time of the WLAN outage is affected by the WLC failover strategy and the WLAN architecture and configuration of the WLC. Several methods exist to support different WLAN architectures, each influencing the outage time. The AP mode, explained in the text that follows, will determine outage behavior. A redundancy design option might consider using Control and Provisioning of Wireless Access Points (CAPWAP) local mode versus Hybrid Remote Edge Access Point (HREAP) mode. HREAP mode provides the ability to continue operation without a connection to the WLC at the cost of requiring traffic being locally switched and additional configuration tasks to push user accounts to the AP or site authentication server.

The most common approach for controller failure that uses the fewest number of controllers is a many WLCs plus one (N+1) WLC failover approach. When a WLC fails, the AP connection to the WLC will time out and the AP must discover, select, and join a different controller to establish the CAPWAP control and data channels. The timeout, discovery, selection, and join process all take time. The failover configuration and adjustment of CAPWAP timers can be used to reduce outage time.

For faster failover or higher levels of resiliency, a one-to-one (1:1) failover approach should be considered.

Back Office Services

Back office services can be an essential element to supporting WLAN high availability. Access to a back office server that can run the application the WLAN user accesses is an important part of the WLAN availability planning. What is sometimes overlooked are the authentication services needed by the WLAN infrastructures. The WLAN infrastructure must authenticate the clients against back-end authentication servers and databases. If their services are down or inaccessible through the network, effectively a WLAN outage could occur. Many times, a WLAN with redundant everything from the network side has had an outage because of a failed authentication server. Lack of a backup authentication server, or a backup WAN link to provide access to authentication services, will cause WLAN service disruption.

In addition to authentication services, other services might be critical to the usage for the WLAN. For example, location service might be a critical function in the WLAN for a business process or for safety services such as Enhanced 911 (E911). The mobility services servers might also need some level of resiliency to ensure availability of service. Many mobility applications are dependent on infrastructure and mobility application servers for continued operation and thus should be considered when doing a high-availability design.

RF Interference

The capacity and healthof the WLAN require managing the RF spectrum. Managing the effects of RF interference on the WLAN's operation is essential to continuous high-capacity WLAN operation. RF interference can originate from other devices transmitting on the same frequencies that the WLAN is using. Many sources of RF interference are unintentional because the device user is not conscious that his device uses the WLAN frequencies. Examples include Bluetooth headsets, wireless analog cameras, microwave ovens, and many other wireless consumer products. An outage can occur when devices cause interference on the same frequency the WLAN is using in a particular area. Spectrum management is an essential element to managing RF interference to prevent or mitigate outages because of interference issues.

The first element for spectrum management is allowing the unified wireless system to automatically adjust to the current spectrum conditions. The RRM features of the WLC should be used to allow APs to adjust usage to different channels to avoid outages from RF interference. The AP and WLC will report to the Wireless Control System (WCS) indications about air quality.

The second element to spectrum management is to use spectrum-monitoring and correlation services. Cisco spectrum intelligence services, referred to as CleanAir, provide various devices as part of the WLAN infrastructure to provide spectrum-monitoring, spectrum device recognition, and event correlation services to manage the RF spectrum. This service allows the source of interference to easily be identified down to the device type and to correlate client outages to the activity of devices creating wireless interference. The only way to ensure continuous WLAN operations is to monitor the RF spectrum for interference that causes outages.

Denial of Service Attacks

Any determined attacker could launch a successful denial of service attack very easily when it comes to wireless networks. The two most common means are RF jamming attacks and management frame attacks.

RF jamming attacks are attacks where the attacker creates RF noise or interference on the RF channels to disrupt all WLAN communications in an area. If the attacker is not attacking all WLAN channels, the WLAN might be able to move the AP to another channel. An intentional attack would typically jam all the channels. An example of where this has occurred is in situations where wireless security cameras were using the WLAN to monitor a storage area. The attacker jammed the RF channel to prevent the identification and immediate detection of theft of equipment.

Denial of WLAN service could be caused by any type of high-duty-cycle RF interference. RF interference is difficult to prevent but can be detected, and the location of the interference source can be determined. The use of CleanAir APs with WCS is the best way to characterize and report the impact of any type of RF interference in a centralized and scalable manner.

Management frame denial of service attacks are attacks on a weakness of 802.11 protocols and their lack of authenticating management frames. Management frames control the association, disassociation, and use allocation of the wireless medium. An example of a denial of service attack is a deauthentication flood to prevent wireless clients from using the wireless network. This type of attack can be mitigated by enabling Management Frame Protection (MFP), which is a Cisco WLAN notion and part of the IEEE 802.11w standard. Because not all clients support MFP, monitoring the spectrum for protocol denial of service attacks might be needed to detect and mitigate outages. Adaptive intrusion detection along with WCS is used to identify and alert to denial of service attacks.

Business Operation Continuity in the WLAN Era

Business continuity is the capability to continue operations in the event of a disaster. Leveraging wireless access technologies provides a number of options for rapidly establishing access to the LAN at a variety of locations. Next-generation wireless technologies allow increased agility for business continuity during a disaster situation. The nature of using wireless allows the end device to be mobile, with the organization systems being anywhere in an organization's services cloud. Disaster planning often implements dual data centers to continue operations if the primary data center fails. Often, disaster planning designates an off-site facility to move work to in the event of a disaster at a main facility. WLANs increase the agility of an organization in disaster situations by allowing clients and devices to easily move to a new facility because they are untethered. Wireless networks allow the wireless network to be extended to any location the user may be providing the same level of services and security. This could make the disaster recovery and plan potentially easier but might need to be considered when designing the WLAN.

One option for disaster planning is to use the Office Extend AP (OEAP) as a method to quickly turn up the WLAN in the event of a disaster. OEAP is a function in the next-generation wireless feature set that allows the wireless service cloud to extend to where the user is currently located. In a disaster situation, the workers in the organization might need to work from home, a hotel, or an ad hoc work site. Anyplace a broadband or Internet connection is available allows the user to attach an office-extended AP to the Internet and extend the organization WLAN to where the users need to carry out business.

The movement of more client devices toward a 100 percent wireless access layer also facilitates the options available for business contingency planning. With the majority of client devices being wireless, it is easier to move them to a new location, and the time it takes to place them back into service is decreased because of the untethered nature of wireless access.

Power Conservation

The controller-based wireless network provides the capability to reduce the power consumption of the WLAN by scheduling the WLAN radios to turn off after hours. This provides a means to reduce power consumption, which reduces greenhouse gas emissions produced by the power plants while reducing the WLAN's operating costs with a reduced power bill. Depending on when and how the WLAN is used will determine whether or how power reduction can be obtained with the WLAN.

There might be areas of the building that require the WLAN to be operational to support video surveillance, access control, or even Voice over Wi-Fi. Even though the people are not in the building, sensors or monitoring might require the WLAN to be active. Those areas must be identified to ensure that the WLAN is not configured to turn off the radios after normal hours of operation. The security and possibly emergency response personal might use the WLAN for voice or other uses during an emergency. Perhaps the security guard who walks the facilities uses a Voice over Wi-Fi phone or PDA to monitor the cameras. This might prevent turning down some or all of the WLAN to save power. Perhaps only a few devices need WLAN access, and the trade can be made to move a few devices to a wired Ethernet connection to allow the power saved by turning much of the WLAN down during off periods.

Flexibility

WLANs are very often designed and implemented with a very specific use case in mind; however, you will often encounter situations where the WLAN is being used for applications or in ways it was not designed or in ways it was not intended to be used. This results in a WLAN without enough capacity or coverage for data or voice applications. Many a WLAN engineer has completed a rollout of a WLAN for data applications when Voice over Wi-Fi or other unknown uses start appearing on the WLAN for which it was not designed to support. The more flexible WLAN designs will be those that consider the design for higher-capacity data usage and voice and location services. Even though certain services are not current requirements, by going through the exercise of looking at what would be required, flexibility can be built into the WLAN design to ease the transition.

Even simple things, such as installing service loops of an extra 20 feet of Cat5 cable to the APs, will create deployment flexibility by making it easier to later move APs to support additional services. For example, an AP that was installed at a particular location for data might need to be moved by only a few feet (either for density or because other APs are being added) in the future to support additional services such as voice or location. Very often, a little planning and consideration to potential WLAN usage scenarios can influence the WLAN design to better support future scenarios. The more up-front planning that is done for current and future application scenarios, the easier it will be to evolve the WLAN for future requirements. This will often mean that WLAN coverage design should be created for 5 GHz instead of 2.4 GHz to allow future capacity requirements.

WLAN Capacity

The increased usage of the WLAN as the primary network has placed additional capacity requirements on the WLAN. The number of users and the type of usage will continue to drive up the utilization of the WLAN. High-bandwidth applications such as system backup and video applications will be common in the next-generation WLANs. In the past, the WLAN engineers often focused on coverage. The next-generation WLAN engineer must focus on capacity modeling and planning. The fundamental principle for providing increased capacity in the WLAN revolves around increasing the number of cells and making the cell size smaller, which means fewer users per cell sharing the media, where the cell is the service area of the AP for a specific data rate and greater. Note that the AP's cell size is not just a factor of transmit power but also the data rates it is configured to support. Disabling the lower data rates on the AP will reduce the cell size.

Utilizing more channels also helps increase the WLAN capacity in area. This is typically done by using utilizing all the nonoverlapping 2.4-GHz and 5-GHz channels the client devices can support. Achieving maximum WLAN capacity also requires managing the RF spectrum for the intended usage; any interference and or unmanaged spectrum usage will reduce the capacity of the WLAN. To optimize spectrum management, all Wi-Fi devices in an area would be placed on the same WLAN versus operating multiple WLANs in the same area. Operating one WLAN allows controlling the priority that can be given to the devices that should have priority to use the spectrum (that is, QoS). The amount of time a client spends transmitting will impact the capacity of the WLAN. To minimize the amount of air time each client takes to send data, a measure should be taken to ensure that the clients are communicating at the highest data rates possible. This is accomplished by providing the greatest signal-to-noise ratio for the client so that it communicates at a greater data rate, thus spending less time transmitting and utilizing less spectrum.

Summary

Many factors need to be considered in the design and implementation of WLANs. This chapter presented some new areas that are becoming important considerations for WLAN deployments. It is impossible to predict future WLAN requirements with any precision. What is certain is that the demands on the WLAN will increase, with new mobility applications and devices continuing to drive new and increasing usage. More clients will use the WLAN as the primary network, making it critical for the WLAN being up 24/7 with little tolerance of outages. WLAN engineers need to plan for current and future WLAN growth by designing in support for as much capacity, resiliency, and flexibility as their budgets will allow.

Chapter 6

Cisco Unified Wireless LAN Architectures

Earlier chapters looked at the reasons for the controller-based wireless solution called the Cisco Unified Wireless Network (CUWN). You also looked in detail into the protocols that enable the CUWN, especially Control and Provisioning of Wireless Access Points (CAPWAP).

This chapter focuses on how the CUWN enables powerful systems-level features and flexible, scalable, resilient services-rich network architectures.

The chapter begins with a review of the basic CUWN architecture and then delves into how the architecture is flexible, scalable, and resilient and how it supports seamless and scalable mobility. Finally, the chapter concludes with an investigation of some examples of flexible, scalable, and resilient network architectures.

Cisco Unified Wireless LAN Architecture Review

Chapter 1, "The Need for Controller-Based Wireless Networks," and Chapter 2, "Wireless LAN Protocols," already covered the details of the CUWN architecture. As a brief review, consider the CUWN architecture (see Figure 6-1), which was first introduced in Chapter 2.

The CUWN architecture centralizes wireless local-area network (WLAN) configuration and control into a device called a wireless LAN controller (WLC). This allows the entire WLAN to operate as an intelligent information network that uses wireless as the access medium to support advanced services. The CUWN simplifies operational management by collapsing large numbers of managed endpoints (autonomous access points) into a single managed system comprised of the WLAN controller(s) and the corresponding, joined access points (AP).

In the CUWN architecture, APs are *lightweight*, meaning that they cannot act independently of a WLC. APs are typically *zero-touch* deployed, and no individual configuration of APs is required. The APs learn the IP addresses of one or more WLCs through a controller discovery algorithm and then establish a trust relationship with a controller through a *join* process. After the trust relationship is established, the WLC pushes firmware to the AP if necessary and a runtime configuration. APs do not store a configuration locally.

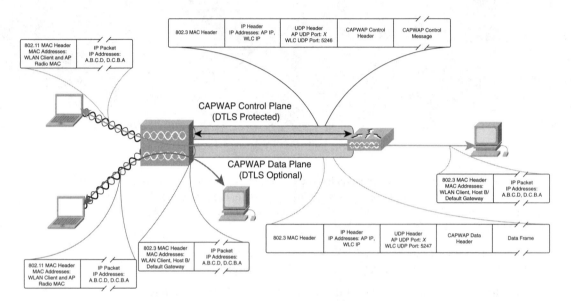

Figure 6-1   *Cisco Unified Wireless Network Architecture*

After they are joined to a controller, the APs are also lightweight in the sense that they handle only a subset of 802.11 MAC functionality. Typically, this subset includes only real-time 802.11 MAC functionality, with the controller handling all non-real-time 802.11 MAC processing. This division of 802.11 labor is called *split MAC* and enables the architecture to support seamless mobility and a number of advanced features in an elegant and scalable manner.

As can be seen from Figure 6-1, APs interact with the WLAN controller through the CAPWAP protocol. Chapter 2 covered CAPWAP in detail, so recall that CAPWAP defines both a control messaging protocol and format and a data path component. CAPWAP supports both a distributed and centralized data path.

CAPWAP control messages are exchanged between the WLC and AP for a variety of reasons, including the controller discovery and join process, AP configuration and firmware push from the controller, and statistics gathering and wireless security enforcement. WLC control messages are also used to support wireless station access, authentication, and mobility. CAPWAP control messages are secured in a Datagram Transport Layer Security (DTLS) tunnel.

In a centralized data path, the WLAN client data packets are encapsulated in CAPWAP between the AP and WLC. When a WLAN client sends a packet, it is received by the AP and encapsulated with a CAPWAP header and forwarded to the controller. At the controller, the CAPWAP header is stripped off and the frame is switched from the controller onto a VLAN in the switching infrastructure. When a client on the wired network sends a packet to a WLAN client, the packet first goes into the WLC, where it is encapsulated with a CAPWAP header and then forwarded to the appropriate AP. The AP strips off the CAPWAP header and then bridges the frame onto the RF medium. The CAPWAP data path between the controller and AP can be secured through DTLS.

Certain network architectures require some level of "hybrid" deployment, or distributed data plane. CAPWAP supports bridging data frames onto the wired network at the AP, too. The CUWN implementation of this distributed data path architecture is called Hybrid Remote Edge Access Point (HREAP). Recall from Chapter 2 how more of the 802.11 MAC processing is pushed to the network edge at the AP, and some data traffic might be bridged onto the Ethernet LAN at the AP instead of being encapsulated in CAPWAP and carried to the controller.

The sections that follow describe this basic architecture and consider how it helps you to build flexible, scalable, and resilient networks.

Architectural Flexibility, Scalability, and Resiliency

The CUWN is a flexible, resilient, and scalable transport architecture for mobility. The architecture is largely driven by the power and versatility of CAPWAP.

Architectural Flexibility

Figure 6-2 illustrates all the places in the network that a controller can be deployed and all the solutions that are enabled.

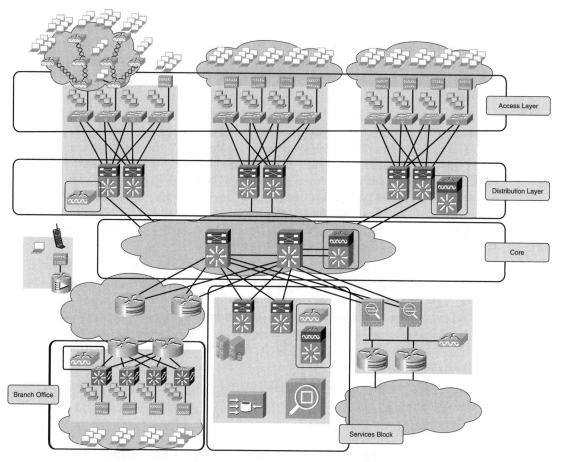

Figure 6-2 *Cisco Unified Wireless Network Architectural Flexibility*

Note that controllers can be placed at the campus access layer or distribution layer. Many CUWN customers place their WLAN controllers in services blocks in the campus network core or in their data center. For branch and satellite locations, controllers can be placed on-site or centralized. Access points can even be placed in teleworker and mobile user locations.

IT architects can select integrated or standalone controllers, depending on their needs, and can choose to centrally switch their data traffic at the controller or distribute the data switching to the network edge. Finally, access points can be deployed indoors or outdoors.

While this might appear to present the IT architect with dizzying complexity, what is truly unique and important is that regardless of the architectural design choices made—large or small, integrated or standalone controller, locally or centrally switched data traffic, coverage indoors or outdoors—the deployment and administrative experience is basically the same because of CAPWAP. IT architects have the flexibility to make architectural choices that best serve their business needs.

Architectural Resiliency

The CUWN leverages the flexibility of CAPWAP for system resiliency and redundancy. The CAPWAP protocol allows dynamic redundancy and load balancing of access points across controllers. Recall from Chapter 2 how APs use CAPWAP to discover and join controllers dynamically. CAPWAP specifies that the AP will attempt to join the least-loaded controller, defined as the controller with the greatest available AP capacity, by default. This dynamic load balancing is the basis for a dynamic controller redundancy scheme.

This dynamic load balancing can be a basis for a dynamic controller redundancy scheme. After an AP joins a WLC, it sends a CAPWAP heartbeat to its WLC at a predetermined heartbeat interval, which is every 30 seconds by default. The WLC responds to the CAPWAP heartbeats from the APs in the form of unicast heartbeat acknowledgments. When an AP misses a heartbeat acknowledgment, it resends up to five heartbeat messages at 1-second intervals. If no acknowledgment is received after the five resends, the AP resets and initiates a new WLC hunting and discovery process to find a new controller.

Remember that when an AP joins a controller, it learns the IP addresses of the other controllers in the mobility group from its joined WLC. Subsequently, the AP sends CAPWAP Primary Discovery Request messages to each of the WLCs in the mobility group. The WLCs respond with a Primary Discovery Response to the AP. The Primary Discovery Response includes information about the WLC type, total capacity, and current AP load. As long as the joined WLC has the "AP Fallback" parameter enabled, the AP might decide to change over to a less-loaded WLC. This is how the system supports dynamic WLC redundancy.

This algorithm helps dynamically balance the AP load across the mobility group. However, it is important to consider how it could also have some unintended consequences. For example, suppose that you have configured two controllers' management interfaces in Option 43 in the DHCP scope. When you deploy the first AP, it might join one controller. Now when you deploy the second AP, it might join the second controller. The next AP will join one of the two controllers, the fourth AP might join the other controller, and so on. By the time you've completed the AP deployment for the area, some of the APs will have joined one controller and the other APs will have joined the other controller. The APs will likely be joined to controllers in a random "salt-and-pepper" fashion, where APs are joined to the controllers in no particular order or sequence.

This random joining has several potential challenges. First, more client roaming across controller boundaries is inevitable. While client roaming across controllers is highly optimized, intracontroller roaming is still more efficient than intercontroller roaming. The random, salt-and-pepper layout makes operational tasks like troubleshooting and code upgrading more challenging. The client load-balancing feature also works on a per-controller basis, so this feature is not useful when the AP RF coverage layout assumes the salt-and-pepper configuration.

CUWN customers have the option to override the dynamic behavior of CAPWAP by assigning APs to specific controllers to balance the load and engineer AP layout by assigning APs a primary, secondary, and/or tertiary controller to each AP. By doing this, WLC redundancy behavior is deterministic. Figure 6-3 illustrates deterministic WLC redundancy.

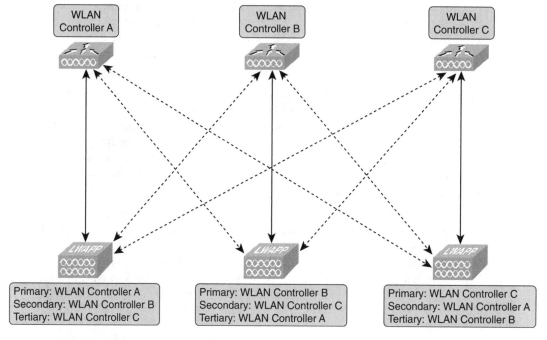

Figure 6-3   *Deterministic WLC Redundancy*

When an AP declares its primary controller unreachable because of missed heartbeat acknowledgments, it will attempt to join the secondary controller. If it fails to join the secondary controller, it attempts to join the tertiary controller. If the primary, secondary, or tertiary controller is not available, APs will resort to the dynamic Lightweight Access Point Protocol (LWAPP) algorithms to connect to the least-loaded available controller.

The WLC has a configurable parameter for *AP Fallback*. When the WLC AP Fallback option is enabled, APs will return to their primary controllers after a failover event when the primary controller comes back online.

The flexibility and resiliency of the CUWN CAPWAP architecture provide three primary options for controller redundancy:

■ N:1 redundant configuration

■ N:N redundant configuration

■ N:N:1 redundant configuration

Each of these redundancy architectures is easy to deploy and is highly manageable.

N:1 WLC Redundancy

A popular WLC redundancy option is an N:1 redundant configuration. This is a good option when there are many WLC controller devices and capital expenditure costs are a big consideration. Figure 6-4 illustrates N:1 redundancy with deterministic redundancy.

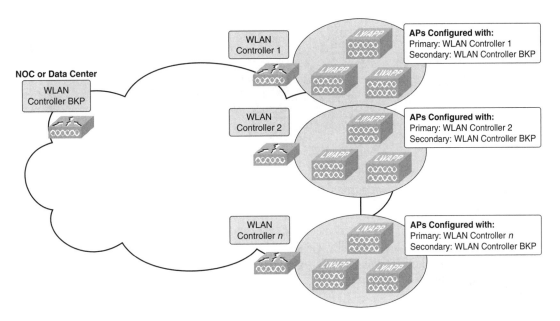

Figure 6-4 *N:1 Redundancy Architecture*

In this configuration, the redundant controller is placed in a network operations center (NOC) or data center and acts a backup for multiple WLCs. Each AP is configured with a WLC as primary, and all APs point to the "1" redundant controller as secondary.

In this architecture, the redundant controller could become oversubscribed with APs if there are multiple primary WLC failures, which is usually unlikely.

N:N WLC Redundancy

Many IT architects choose not to take the risk that the redundant controller could become oversubscribed with APs and so select an N:N redundancy architecture, as illustrated in Figure 6-5.

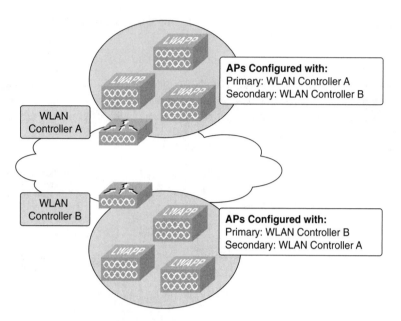

Figure 6-5   *N:N Redundancy Architecture*

In this configuration, there are two controllers. Some of the APs are configured with controller A as primary and controller B as secondary. The other APs are configured to use controller B as primary and controller A as secondary. In this design, AP capacity is load balanced across both controllers.

N:N:1 WLC Redundancy

A third redundancy option is an N:N:1 configuration, as illustrated in Figure 6-6.

In this configuration, some of the APs are configured with controller A as primary and controller B as secondary, and all APs are configured to use the same backup controller as tertiary. Typically, the primary and secondary controllers are placed at the network distribution level, and the "1" tertiary controller is placed in an NOC or data center. Multiple distribution blocks can be configured with the same tertiary controller.

The critical point is that IT architects have the flexibility to design and deploy a redundant wireless network that meets their business needs.

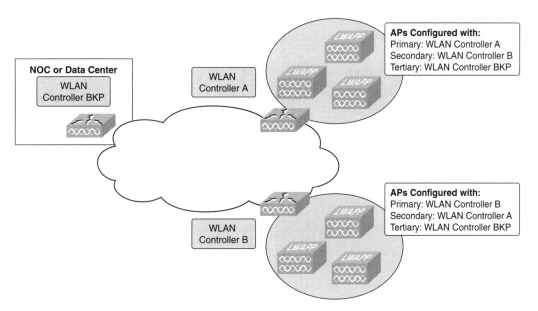

Figure 6-6   *N:N:1 Redundancy Architecture*

Architectural Scalability

One can argue that the real killer benefit derived from wireless networks is mobility; however, mobility introduces challenges in a network implementation. A WLAN client must be able to maintain its association seamlessly from one AP to another, securely, and with as little latency as possible, and the architecture needs to be able to scale the roaming domain as needed. These mobility requirements are completely supported by the Cisco Unified Wireless Network architecture.

Mobility

A wireless client roams when it moves its 802.11 association from one AP to another AP. Wireless client devices initiate roaming based on the internal roaming algorithms programmed into the client radio firmware. Typically, a client's roaming logic is triggered by crossing a Received Signal Strength Indication (RSSI) or signal-to-noise ratio (SNR) threshold that causes the client to look for a better signal from a new AP. Device roaming behavior and performance differ by vendor, so it is wise to characterize device roaming and look to device configuration best practices from the client vendor.

WLAN clients are always reauthenticated by the system in some way on a roam; this is always necessary to protect against session spoofing and replay attacks. Normally, the reauthentication requires a full authentication transaction. In the case of 802.1X authentication, a full Extensible Authentication Protocol (EAP) reauthentication and rekeying will be required. However, the CUWN supports two methods of fast secure roaming that shortcut the reauthentication process while maintaining security:

- Cisco Centralized Key Management (CCKM)

- Proactive Key Caching (PKC)

While no special client software is required for basic device roaming, Cisco CKM and PKC do require supplicant support. Additionally, Cisco supports the emerging 802.11R fast roaming standard, although at press time, no client devices yet support this standard. CCKM, PKC, and 802.11R each define mechanisms for inserting unique cryptographic identifiers in a roaming client's reassociation request to a new AP. These unique cryptographic identifiers allow the infrastructure, specifically the WLC, to reauthenticate roaming clients without a full authentication exchange with the RADIUS server.

From a roaming client's perspective, it is only roaming between APs; however, there is a considerable amount of choreography going on in the infrastructure that is opaque to the client. When a wireless client associates and authenticates to an AP, the AP's joined WLC places an entry for that client in its client database. This entry includes the client's MAC and IP addresses, security context and associations, and quality of service (QoS) context, WLAN, and associated AP. The WLC uses this information to forward frames and manage traffic to and from the wireless client. When a client roams, this client database information must be updated and possibly copied or moved to another controller.

CUWN client roaming comes in three "flavors":

- Intracontroller roaming

- Intercontroller Layer 2 roaming

- Intercontroller Layer 3 roaming

Figure 6-7 illustrates the first case, intracontroller roaming.

When the wireless client moves its association from one AP to another, the WLC simply updates the client database with the new associated AP context. The client is reauthenticated to establish a new security context.

Consider what happens when a client roams from an AP joined to one WLC and an AP joined to a different WLC. Figure 6-8 illustrates an intercontroller roam in the event of a Layer 2 roam.

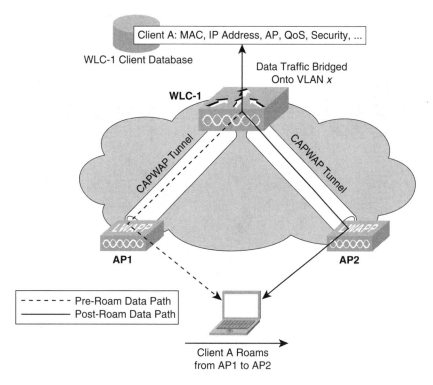

Figure 6-7   *Intracontroller Roaming*

A Layer 2 roam occurs when the controllers bridge the WLAN traffic on and off the same VLAN and the same IP subnet. When the client reassociates to an AP connected to a new WLC, the new WLC exchanges mobility messages with the original WLC and the client database entry is moved to the new WLC. The client is reauthenticated to establish a new security context, and the client database entry is updated for the new AP with which the client is associated.

Figure 6-9 illustrates an intercontroller roam in the event of a Layer 3 roam.

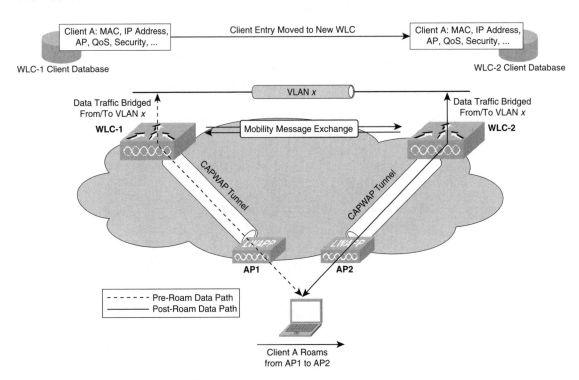

Figure 6-8 *Layer 2 Intercontroller Roaming*

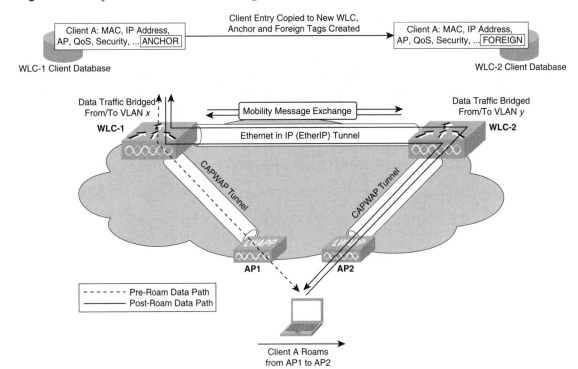

Figure 6-9 *Layer 3 Intercontroller Roaming*

A Layer 3 roam occurs when the controllers bridge the WLAN on and off different VLANs and IP subnets. The intercontroller roaming is similar to Layer 2 roaming in that the WLCs exchange mobility messages on the client roam. However, instead of moving the client's entry to the new controller's client database, the original WLAN controller marks the client with an *Anchor* entry in its own client database. The database entry is copied to the new controller client database and marked with a *Foreign* entry in the new WLC. The client is reauthenticated to establish a new security context, and the client database entry is updated for the new AP with which the client is associated. The choreography on the back end is totally opaque to the wireless client, and the wireless client maintains its original IP address.

If a wireless client subsequently roams to a new AP joined to a different WLC, the Foreign client database entry is moved from the original Foreign WLC to the new Foreign WLC, but the original Anchor WLC is always maintained.

Note that the client's data traffic is tunneled symmetrically to and from the anchor controller. This means that roamed clients reside logically in their anchor controller, and traffic patterns between the anchor and foreign controllers operate fully as a point-to-point symmetric tunnel. This feature allows the underlying wired network architecture to fully support features such as reverse path forwarding/filtering (RPF) on intermediary Layer 3 interfaces or stateful security.

Mobility Domains

The flexibility, resiliency of, and support for mobility in the CUWN are the ingredients for true architectural, systems scalability. A real, scalable architecture is an architecture that is right-sized to current business needs with the capability to scale easily as these business needs grow.

Cisco clusters a group of up to 24 controllers of any model in something called a mobility group. As will be shown shortly, the mobility group is really a mobility subdomain. Figure 6-10 illustrates the mobility subdomain concept.

Mobility groups, or subdomains, can be linked into a larger mobility domain of up to three mobility groups, or 72 controllers total. Wireless clients roam seamlessly across a subdomain. Fast roaming with CCKM, PKC, and 802.11R are supported in a mobility subdomain. Wireless clients can roam seamlessly across a full mobility domain in the sense that they maintain a single IP address as they roam, but fast roaming is only supported within a single mobility subdomain. Figure 6-11 illustrates the full mobility domain.

These concepts are very powerful; an IT architect can design to exactly the controller capacity required by the business needs with the assurance that as business needs grow, controllers can be added very easily to meet the growing capacity needs. But, IT architects do not have to deploy a lot of excess capacity in the network just for future proofing.

Configuring mobility groups and domains is trivial. Consult the WCS and WLC User Guides for detailed instructions.

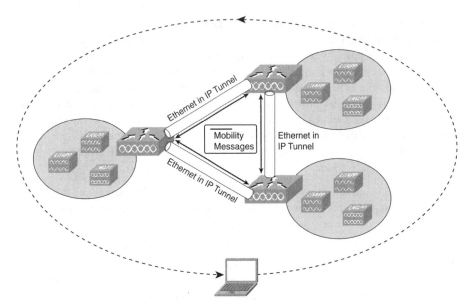

Figure 6-10   *Mobility Subdomain*

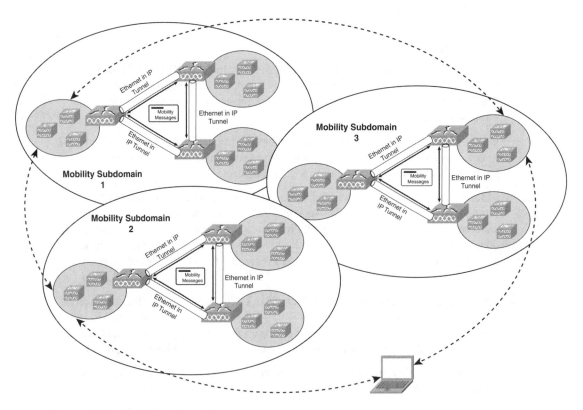

Figure 6-11   *Mobility Domain*

Campus Architectures

The following sections present conceptual design ideas for "places in the network" for controllers in enterprise campuses. The sections present ideas for the following:

■ Enterprise wiring closets

■ Distribution layer deployments

■ Services block deployments

■ Campus HREAP

Enterprise architects should select the design that best fits their needs.

Enterprise Wiring Closet Deployment

One option for controller placement is in the enterprise wiring closet, as shown in Figure 6-12.

Typically, these deployments use the 3750G Integrated WLAN controller as a "top-of-stack" solution but can also be implemented with the 440x series controller. Controller redundancy can be achieved in an N:N fashion within the switch stack.

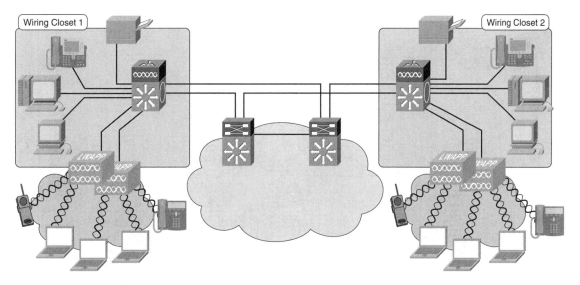

Figure 6-12   *Enterprise Wiring Closet Controller Placement*

Some advantages of these deployments are that access layer traffic is kept at the access layer, taking advantage of the integrated 3750G switch access layer features. There is also the advantage of having cost-effective, Layer 3 uplink redundancy from the edge of the network. Also, the 3750G has 802.3af-capable Power over Ethernet (PoE) ports that can power APs.

However, this architecture might present challenges in supporting intercontroller roaming across wiring closets. This can be quite common in a typical enterprise campus.

Enterprise Distribution Layer Deployment

Another option is to deploy controllers at the distribution layer, as shown in Figure 6-13. Because the distribution layer is where traffic is aggregated and policies enforced in campus LAN design, the distribution layer is a natural place to deploy controllers.

Typically, these deployments are done with WiSM blades in distribution layer Catalyst 6500 switches, or with 440x series standalone controllers. The 3750G Integrated WLC can also fit into distribution block deployments easily.

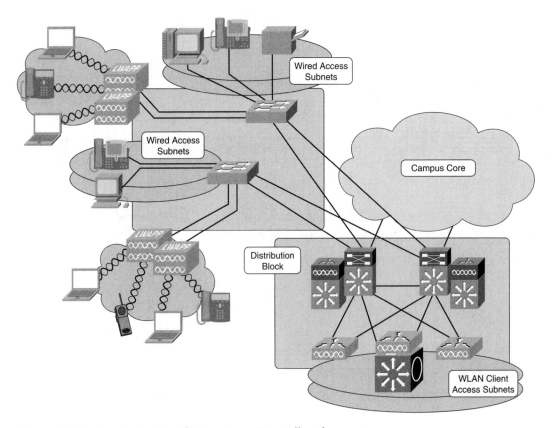

Figure 6-13 *Enterprise Distribution Layer Controller Placement*

Redundancy and AP load balancing are easy to implement when the controllers are deployed at the distribution layer, as shown previously in Figure 6-11. Distribution layer deployments naturally fit into an N:N and N:N:1 redundancy architecture.

From the campus LAN design perspective, these deployments in effect collapse the access layer (WLAN) into the distribution layer. So, consideration should be given to what access layer switching features need to be implemented in the distribution layer switches and applied to the WLAN traffic ingressing and egressing the controller.

Data Center or Services Block Deployments

The most common campus controller deployments for large campuses are in centralized services blocks. A *services block* is a central point of aggregation for control and data, where various network services can be easily applied. Figure 6-14 shows several services block options.

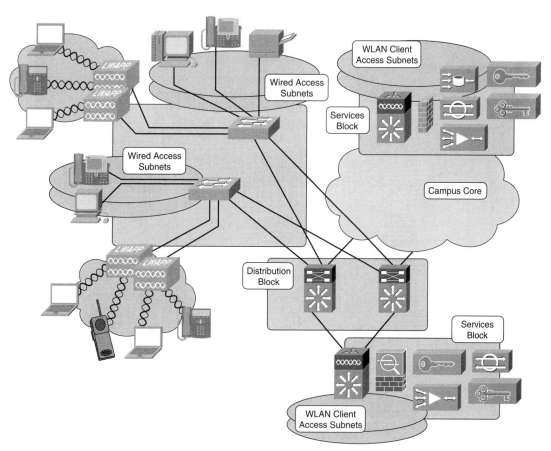

Figure 6-14 *Enterprise Services Block Deployment*

Typically, services block deployments use one or more WiSM blades deployed in Catalyst 6500 switches deployed as "appliances" but can also be deployed with 440x controllers.

Services block deployments are especially good for integration with other Catalyst 6500 services modules. These deployments usually lead to highly efficient intercontroller mobility and simplified network management. For large campuses, there is also an incremental economy of scale as the network grows larger.

Where to place a services block is another design challenge. Often, services blocks are deployed in data centers where there is high-availability routing and switching and power. Also, data centers tend to be managed and operated by the most skilled network staff. On the other hand, when deploying a services block in a data center, all WLAN data traffic must traverse the network core, so core bandwidth and latency are important considerations.

In many large campuses, services blocks can be deployed in a redundant arm off of distribution switches. These are particularly valuable when core bandwidth is at a premium, such as when there are several large distributed campuses connected through a metropolitan-area network (MAN).

Campus HREAP

Another option is to deploy APs in HREAP mode with local switching of some or all data traffic. These deployments typically locally switch authenticated data traffic while centrally switching guest WLAN traffic. This type of deployment, with locally switched, authenticated traffic, and centrally switched guest access, is shown in Figure 6-15.

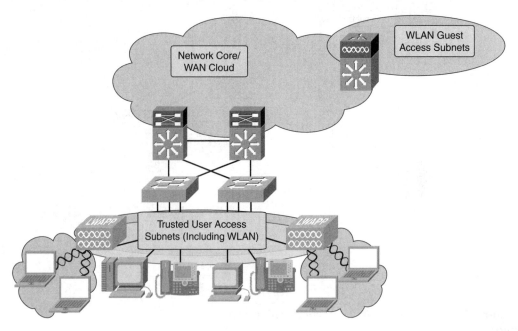

Figure 6-15   *Campus HREAP*

Campus HREAP has some design parameters that should be taken into consideration. For example, Cisco CKM is supported for fast secure Layer 2 roaming, but PKC is not. A Layer 2 roaming domain should not exceed 50 access points. Furthermore, Layer 3 roaming is not supported with locally switched traffic. Call admission control (CAC) is also not supported for locally switched traffic. Note that these design parameters are true at the time of writing, so consult the latest documentation as things might have changed by the time you're reading this chapter.

Campus HREAP is a suitable solution for small satellite sites where the cost of deploying a controller on-site is prohibitive. Campus HREAP is typically not suited for medium to large campuses.

Branch Architectures

The following sections present the following conceptual design ideas for "places in the network" for controllers in distributed, branch networks:

- Distributed branch controller placement

- Centralized controller placement with HREAP

Enterprise architects should select the design that best fits their needs.

Distributed Branch Controller Placement

Figure 6-16 illustrates distributed controller placement for branch deployments.

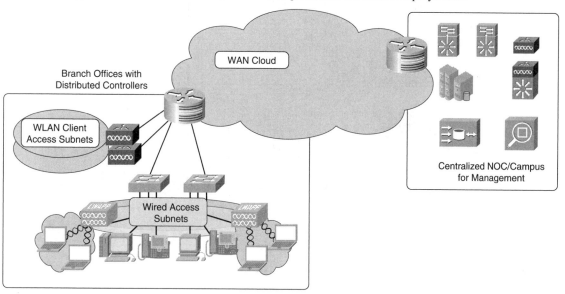

Figure 6-16 *Distributed Branch Controller Placement*

In this deployment, one or more controllers are placed in each branch location. This is a suitable architecture for full services support in the branch. It does incur the costs of deploying more controllers in distributed locations; typically, this architecture makes the most sense for medium- to large-sized branch offices.

Centralized Controller Placement with HREAP

Another approach to branch deployments is to centralize controllers in some head-end location and deploy APs in HREAP mode in the branch locations. Figure 6-17 illustrates this architecture.

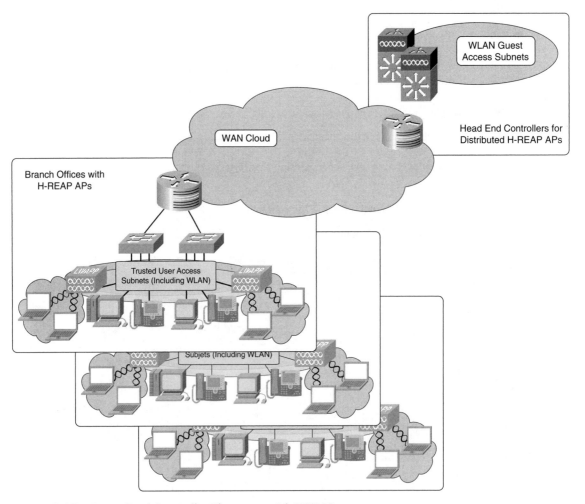

Figure 6-17   *Centralized Controller Placement with HREAP*

This approach to branch deployments is a suitable solution for small satellite sites, where the cost of deploying a controller on-site is prohibitive. Locally switched data traffic can also be optimized with Wide Area Application Services (WAAS) for more efficient core and WAN traversal. As previously noted, there might be some design parameters and trade-offs to using HREAP, so this solution is typically not suited for medium to large branches.

Office Extend AP (OEAP)

With the introduction of CAPWAP, CUWN supports an option for deploying APs in untrusted networks called Office Extend AP (OEAP). In an OEAP deployment, centrally switched data traffic is encrypted between the WLC and AP using DTLS.

OEAP is typically deployed for small offices, home offices, and full-time teleworkers. OEAP requires hardware support on the WLC, so not all WLCs can support the architecture. At press time, only the 5508 has the necessary hardware support for OEAP.

Summary

Hopefully, this chapter helped you appreciate the versatility and power of the Cisco Unified Wireless Network. The CUWN is truly a flexible, scalable, resilient, services-rich approach to building WLAN systems. The CUWN supports a variety of network architectures so that IT architects can select an approach to the WLAN that best suits their needs.

Chapter 7

Troubleshooting

Troubleshooting is an essential skill for all wireless networking professionals.

Wireless networks have become a ubiquitous network access technology in the enterprise as well as the home. A wireless network provides convenience and increase in productivity; however, troubleshooting wireless networks can be vastly more complex than troubleshooting traditional wireless LANs.

Wired Ethernet LANs are inherently easier to troubleshoot from the following perspectives:

- **Client configuration:** Some, if not all, of the client configuration options such as speed/duplex/DHCP are either automatically negotiated or invisible to the user. When using a wired Ethernet connection, the user simply plugs in a patch cable. For the most part, there aren't any additional security configurations, speed/duplex configurations, or QoS configurations necessary.

- **Physical medium:** While cabling issues can occur, they are very rare and easily fixed. Again, because of the maturity of standards and the experience of contractors, the physical medium (the wire) is rarely an issue.

- **Protocol/network:** The protocols used in 802.3 wired LANs are very simple and well implemented.

Consider these same three aspects when examined using a modern wireless LAN:

- **Client configuration:** To effectively implement a secure wireless network, client devices must carry a specific configuration. These configurations must be entered correctly into each client device. If a user misconfigures a network ID or encryption key, the client will not associate to the wireless network. To make matters worse, different manufacturers make different wireless client utilities, meaning there isn't a standard methodology for configuring the wireless client. This chapter will address these issues in detail in the later section, "Client Troubleshooting."

- **Physical medium:** In a wireless network, connections are made using radio frequency (RF) as the physical medium. The RF medium changes by the second and even well-designed wireless networks can experience issues with cochannel interference, physical obstructions, and fading.

- **Protocol/network:** The Cisco Unified Wireless Network (CUWN) introduces additional protocol and network devices into the network. Wireless LAN controllers (WLC), the Lightweight Access Point Protocol (LWAPP), and the Content and Provisioning of Wireless Access Points (CAPWAP) Protocol make wireless networks easier to manage and add important wireless services. It is important to understand these components and protocols to be successful at troubleshooting.

This chapter focuses on fundamental troubleshooting techniques that can help an administrator detect, isolate, and solve common issues in the CUWN.

The first part of the chapter introduces several tools that administrators use to troubleshoot wireless networks. The industry has come a long way since the advent of 802.11 wireless LANs as have the related troubleshooting tools. The tools outlined this chapter are invaluable resources to an administrator debugging a wireless network.

The second part of the chapter focuses on common issues that present themselves in the wireless network. The section provides a framework to quickly detect, isolate, and solve issues within the CUWN. Because wireless networks have very unique and distinct aspects, it is important to isolate problems early in the troubleshooting process.

Finally, the chapter highlights two advanced wireless networking services—location-based services and Voice over WLAN. Both of these areas pose unique challenges in terms of design and troubleshooting.

Tools for Troubleshooting 802.11 Wireless Networks

Troubleshooting WLANs has traditionally been a challenging undertaking. The primary reason for difficulty was the lack of coordination between network elements and the lack of troubleshooting tools. The CUWN was created with both of these issues in mind.

Using the CUWN, coordination between access points (AP), clients, and other network elements becomes possible. Interestingly, by solving the coordination problem, a powerful troubleshooting tool was created. The wireless LAN controller (WLC) and the Wireless Control System (WCS) are the primary tools available to the network administrator to resolve these CUWN issues.

In addition to the embedded features of the CUWN, there are two tools that are important to mention. The wireless protocol analyzer (wireless sniffer) and wireless spectrum analyzer can be powerful tools in the hands of an advanced wireless system administrator.

Wireless LAN Controller Command-Line Interface

In the CUWN, most 802.11 management traffic is processed at the WLC. This makes the WLC an excellent place to collect information during the troubleshooting process. Throughout this chapter, the WLC command-line interface (CLI) is used to identify and solve a variety of issues that you might encounter on the wireless network.

It is helpful to make a distinction between the WLC CLI and the WCS. The WCS uses the Simple Network Management Protocol (SNMP) to poll the WLC and other network elements and collect the information in a centralized control point. While this information is by no means *stale*, it is not real-time because of the nature of the polling system it uses to collect this data from the WLCs. Conversely, the WLC CLI is a source of real-time information, again based on the real-time control channel provided by CAPWAP. The WLC CLI has similar functionality to running **debug** commands in a Cisco IOS router or switch. While the CLI is similar, the command set is very different. Some of the strengths and limitations of the WLC CLI are as follows:

- **Strengths:**

    - Real-time information

    - Familiar interface for troubleshooting for users of the Cisco IOS

- **Limitations:** Information is limited to registered APs and clients, while information about unregistered controllers and APs is not available.

Figure 7-1 is an example of a client **debug** log being run from the WLC CLI.

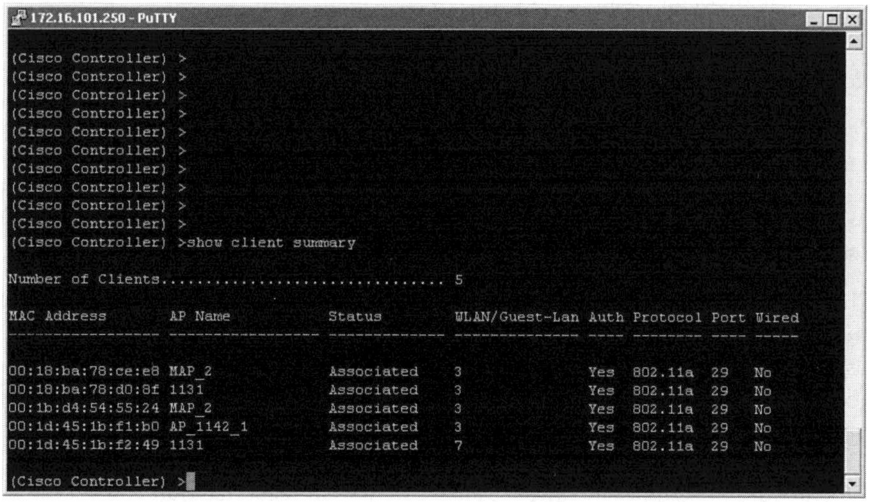

Figure 7-1 *Client Debug Log from the WLC CLI*

For a complete list of WLC CLI commands, visit the following URL:

www.cisco.com/en/US/docs/wireless/controller/6.0/command/reference/cli60.html

Wireless Control System (WCS)

WCS is an optional network component that works in conjunction with Cisco WLCs, Cisco Lightweight Access Points, Cisco Wireless Location Appliances, and/or Mobility Services Engines. WCS offers network administrators a single solution for RF prediction, policy provisioning, network optimization, troubleshooting, user tracking, security monitoring, and wireless LAN systems management. WCS provides an intuitive graphical user interface (GUI) to make deployment, monitoring, and troubleshooting simple. In addition, WCS provides robust reporting capabilities for ongoing system operations.

In most deployments, WCS is the primary tool used by network administrators to troubleshoot the CUWN. WCS is in an excellent position to provide a central repository for information about all aspects of the network. WCS is usually the first tool used in the troubleshooting process. By virtue of its broad network visibility, WCS allows administrators to quickly locate troubled APs and clients in large environments. Some of the strengths and limitations of the WCS are as follows:

- **Strengths:**

    - Visibility: Central view of all network elements makes identification of trouble spots quick and easy

    - Intuitive GUI allows easy, cost-effective operation

- **Limitations:** Information not quite real-time

Note   Chapter 8, "Introduction to WCS," provides an overview of the functionality of WCS.

Figure 7-2 shows the WCS dashboard.

Wireless Protocol Analyzer

The wireless protocol analyzer (also referred to as a wireless sniffer) is an application that runs on a wireless PC, usually a laptop. Much like a traditional sniffer, the wireless analyzer uses the wireless network interface card (NIC) in promiscuous mode to capture traffic. The benefit of a wireless analyzer is that it is capable of capturing all 802.11 management traffic on a particular channel. The wireless analyzer has the intelligence to decode the traffic into a readable format, allowing the user deep insight into the network. Wireless analyzers typically offer the ability to filter the captured traffic by a variety of different parameters, allowing the user to drill down on particular clients and APs.

The wireless analyzer is a recommended tool for any serious wireless professional; however, analysis of 802.11 protocol-level exchanges between clients and APs is an advanced skill.

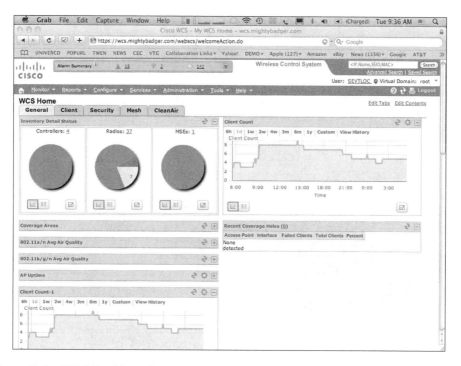

Figure 7-2   *WCS Dashboard*

When debugging complex wireless issues, many vendors' customer support organizations (including Cisco TAC) might request wireless capture files to assist with analysis. A good wireless capture file can reveal significant detail about a particular problem to a trained engineer. For example, 802.11 beacons provide a significant amount of information about how a client and AP are configured. Without a sniffer, much of this information would be impossible to access.

Figure 7-3 depicts a wireless capture file using Wild Packets.

Some of the strengths and limitations of a wireless protocol analyzer are as follows:

- **Strengths:**

    - By examining the protocol exchange between AP and client, an administrator can learn a lot about a network.

    - Wireless capture files allow administrators to troubleshoot wireless issues without being physically on-site.

- **Weaknesses:**

    - Might be difficult to use unless intimately familiar with the 802.11 protocol.

    - Incapable of capturing non-802.11 devices in the area; traffic captured pertains to 802.11 protocols only.

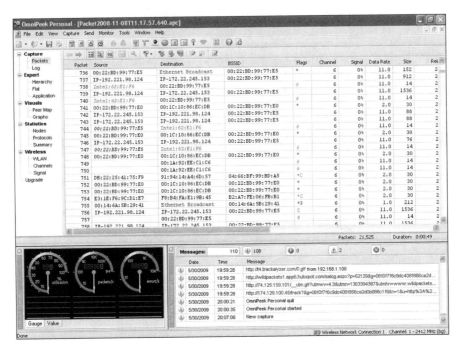

Figure 7-3 *Wireless Analyzer Output*

Spectrum Analyzers

Wireless protocol analyzers do not reveal the entire picture of the wireless network. Wi-Fi operates in the 2.4-GHz and 5-GHz unlicensed spectrum. Wi-Fi devices do not have exclusive use of the spectrum. The purpose of the unlicensed spectrum is to encourage innovation by offering anyone the opportunity to develop wireless devices and applications without obtaining a license. The 2.4-GHz spectrum, where Wi-Fi 802.11b/g/n operates, is notoriously overcrowded. Devices and applications operating in this spectrum generally use proprietary send and receive mechanisms that generally go undetected by Wi-Fi devices. This traffic raises the RF noise floor and might result in harmful interference.

Examples of non-Wi-Fi devices operating in the 2.4-GHz and 5-GHz spectrum are as follows:

- Cordless phones

- Wireless video cameras

- Microwave ovens

- Bluetooth devices

- Medical equipment

The challenge for wireless administrators is to detect interference sources and deal with them. Traditionally, it has been cost-prohibitive to obtain spectrum analyzers to detect harmful interference. These analyzers were generally purpose-built devices that cost upwards of $15,000–$20,000.

In 2007, Cisco acquired a company called Cognio. Cognio created a breakthrough spectrum analysis device in the form of a standard PCMCIA card. These devices work with a standard Windows-based laptop in coordination with the Spectrum Expert software package. Using this device, an administrator can detect Wi-Fi interference sources, categorize the interference source, and even locate the origin of the interference. Prior to these tools, harmful interference frequently went undetected in the wireless network. The Spectrum Expert product is now an integrated part of the CUWN. Spectrum Expert is a powerful tool that empowers network administrators to take control of their wireless spectrum.

Figure 7-4 is a screen shot taken from Cisco Spectrum Expert showing the 2.4-GHz wireless spectrum. It represents a microwave oven interfering with the wireless spectrum. This is something that would go undetected without the use of a spectrum analyzer.

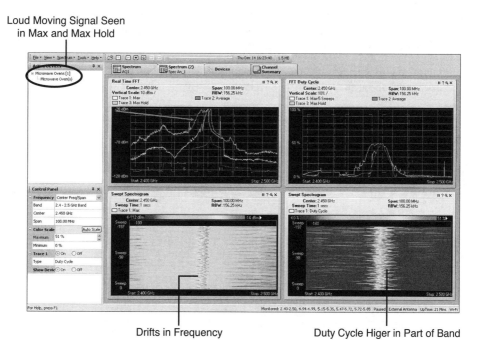

Figure 7-4 *Spectrum Expert Screen Shot*

Isolating Issues on the Cisco Unified Wireless Network

After a brief introduction of some of these tools, it's time to apply the tools to real-world scenarios that occur in wireless networks on a daily basis. Much like any troubleshooting process, when looking at issues on the CUWN, it is important to isolate the problem prior to proceeding.

The wireless network administrator must be able to first detect and then isolate issues into one of these three categories:

1. Protocol/network issues

2. Client configuration

3. Physical medium

After the issue is narrowed down to one of these categories, troubleshooting is much easier and predictable. As a general rule, it is prudent to troubleshoot wireless issues using a top-down approach in the order listed.

The next three sections examine each category in detail, highlight some common issues and solutions, and apply the tools discussed in the previous section.

Protocol/Network Issues

When beginning the troubleshooting process, it is essential to determine the overall health of the CUWN. The WCS is the primary tool used by network administrators to get a system-level view of CUWN health.

Figure 7-5 is an example of the WCS dashboard. The dashboard can reveal a great deal of information about the health of the CUWN.

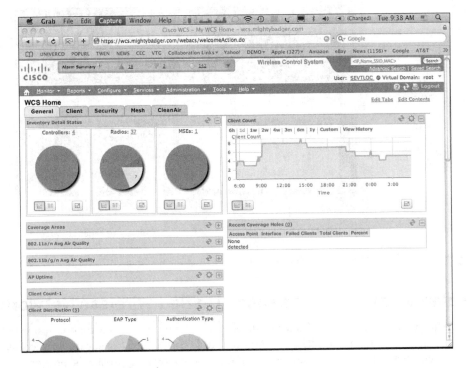

Figure 7-5   *WCS Dashboard*

To determine that WLCs and APs are operational, look at the dashboard's Inventory Detail Status component on the General tab, as shown in Figure 7-5, to ensure that the WLCs and radios (APs) are operational.

If it is determined that radios are inoperable or WLCs are unreachable, there is likely a CAPWAP/Lightweight Access Point Protocol (LWAPP) issue or an issue with network connectivity. The next section describes some of the most common problems related to the protocols and the network.

LWAPP/CAPWAP Discovery Process

A lightweight AP is useless until it joins a WLC. After it is joined to a WLC, all management, monitoring, and troubleshooting can be accomplished using the controller CLI, GUI, or WCS.

A common problem encountered when first deploying the CUWN is the AP–WLC discovery process. The text that follows briefly reviews the discovery process and identifies some troubleshooting techniques.

The following are the steps an AP takes to join a WLC:

1. The AP receives an IP address through DHCP or static assignment.

2. The AP hunts for the IP addresses of a WLC to join.

3. Based on configuration and WLC load, the AP picks the best WLC and joins.

Figure 7-6 illustrates the CAPWAP discovery/join process.

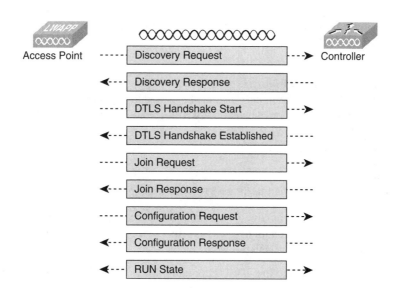

Figure 7-6 *CAPWAP Discovery/Join Process*

The hunting process described in the preceding list is usually where issues can arise. LWAPP and CAPWAP use the same hunting process, but differ slightly between the discovery and join states. Chapter 3, "802.11n," describes the protocols in detail. The following is a brief description of the LWAPP/CAPWAP WLC hunting process:

1. The AP sends a broadcast on the local subnet to identify whether the WLC is on the same subnet. Discovery will work only if the AP is on the same Layer 2 segment as the WLC. If the AP doesn't receive a response, it moves on to the next discovery method.

2. The AP attempts to use the Over-the-Air Provisioning (OTAP) feature. If there are other APs in the area that have joined a WLC and are enabled for OTAP, the AP can learn WLC IP address information using its radio. Note: Because of known vulnerabilities in OTAP, OTAP might be disabled by default or even removed from the CUWN code base at the time this book is published.

3. The AP attempts to utilize a locally stored IP address. It is possible to statically assign WLC information in the APs using a console connection or through the WLC if the AP in question has been associated with a controller in the past.

4. The AP listens for a DHCP assigned address—(DHCP) Vendor Specific Option 43. By setting up the DHCP server to hand out the WLC IP address, the AP can receive its own IP address along with the WLC IP address through DHCP Option 43 reserved for this purpose.

5. The AP utilizes Domain Name System (DNS) resolution to find the WLC. The access point will attempt to resolve "CISCO-LWAP-CONTROLLER.localdomain" or "CISCO-CAPWAP-CONTROLLER.localdomain."

6. If a WLC is not discovered, the process is repeated until a WLC is discovered.

After the AP compiles a list of WLCs, the AP sends a unicast Discovery Request message to each of the WLCs in the list. The WLCs that receive the Discovery Request respond with a Discovery Response.

Note The CAPWAP process differs from LWAPP between the discovery and join process. CAPWAP adds a Datagram Transport Layer Security (DTLS) handshake process to enable control plane encryption, whereas in LWAPP, the controller and the AP use PKI (X.509 certificates) to validate each other.

Based on the contents of the Discovery Response, the AP will send a Join Request to the preferred WLC. The criteria the AP uses to choose the best WLC are as follows:

1. It is possible to configure the AP's preferred primary, secondary, and tertiary WLCs. The AP will always attempt to join these first; these primary/secondary/tertiary assignments are done through the WLC.

2. The AP will attempt to join a WLC configured as a "master" WLC, a setting that might be enabled on a WLC if one is being used to prime APs before deployment.

3. The AP joins the WLAN with the greatest excess AP capacity (least-joined APs).

Note   Each AP maintains a list of controllers. The administrator can assign each AP a primary, secondary, and tertiary controller. Under normal operating conditions, the AP will always register to the primary controller. In the case of a failure of the primary, the AP fails to the secondary controller. In the event of a secondary controller failure, the AP fails over to the tertiary controller, if available.

The AP Join Request contains the AP's signed X.509 certificate for mutual authentication. The WLC will validate the certificate before it accepts the Join Request and send a Join Response. The Join Response contains the signed X.509 certificate. If the AP validates the WLC, the AP will begin downloading its firmware (if different from what the WLC currently runs on) and request its configuration from the WLC.

Troubleshooting the LWAPP CAPWAP Discovery Process

When troubleshooting the AP discovery process, it is important to start at the basics. First, be sure that there is network reachability between the AP and the WLC. The join process will work over a Layer 2 or Layer 3 network. If the AP's IP address is known, use the **ping** function in the WLC to verify connectivity. If the address was assigned through DHCP, check the DHCP server bindings to find the IP address of the AP.

Note   A useful method for verifying network connectivity at the AP is to connect a laptop to the same switchport that the AP was using. Ensure that the laptop receives an IP address, and use the **ping** command to verify reachability to the controller.

When Layer 3 reachability is verified, ensure that the AP is able to discover the WLC using the hunting process. At this point, it is prudent to make sure that your discovery method of choice is functioning properly. Some common problems with the discovery process are DHCP Option 43 and/or DNS misconfiguration. The following is a link to detailed application notes that describe DHCP and DNS configuration in detail (this requires a Cisco.com account):

www.cisco.com/en/US/partner/products/ps6366/tsd_products_support_design_
technotes_list.html

Double-check the discovery method against these application notes to be sure that the AP is receiving valid WLC information.

The next step in the troubleshooting process is to log in to the controller and look at the debug logs. Perhaps the most useful **debug** command available from the WLC is as follows:

```
(WLC_CLI)debug capwap events enable
```

Note In the 3.x and 4.x releases of WLC software, the command was **debug lwapp events enable**. This command was deprecated in the 5.x release.

This command will show the entire sequence of LWAPP/CAPWAP discovery and join events. Using this command, you can confirm that the WLC is receiving the AP Discovery Requests. Figure 7-7 is an output of a CAPWAP Control Message resulting from the **debug capwap events enable** command.

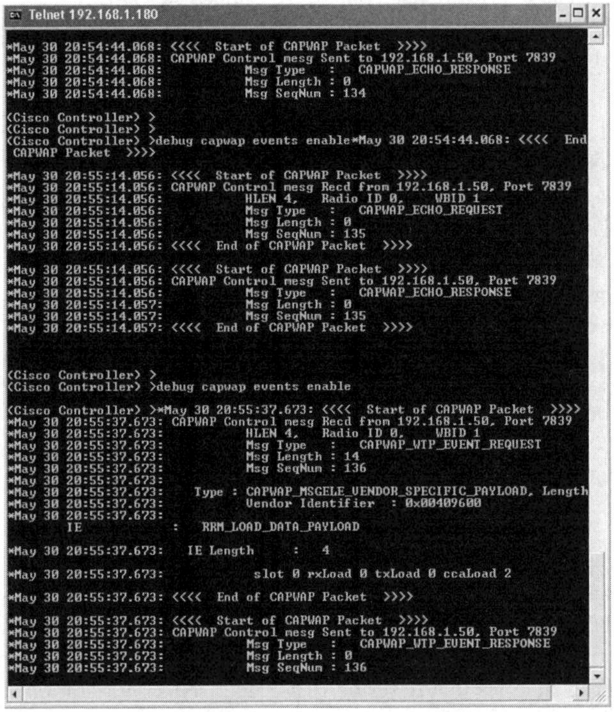

Figure 7-7 *CAPWAP Control Message Output*

Figure 7-7 shows CAPWAP control messages being exchanged between an AP and the WLC. You can see from the output that CAPWAP control messages are being received from an AP with an IP address of 192.168.1.50 and replies are being sent back to the AP from the WLC. This kind of bidirectional communication indicates that the AP has received the IP address of the WLC and is able to send and receive control traffic. The output is truncated, but after the initial registration process, you subsequently see the AP download software from the WLC and become registered. For a complete list of system message outputs, refer to the "Cisco WLAN Controller System Message Guide," which can be found at

www.cisco.com/support

www.cisco.com/en/US/partner/docs/wireless/controller/message/guide/controller_smg.html

If the WLC receives the Discovery Request and Join Request and rejects the AP, the number-one reason for the failure is inaccurate WLC time. The discovery process is dependent upon security handshakes that are dependent upon accurate timestamps. Ensure the time setting on the WLC by using the **show time** command, as demonstrated in Example 7-1.

Example 7-1   *Verifying the WLC Time Setting*

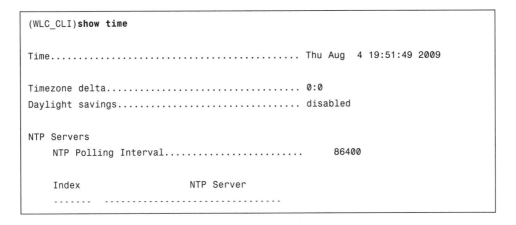

```
(WLC_CLI)show time

Time............................................. Thu Aug  4 19:51:49 2009

Timezone delta................................... 0:0
Daylight savings................................. disabled

NTP Servers
    NTP Polling Interval........................     86400


    Index               NTP Server
    -------   -------------------------------
```

If the time is not accurate, set up Network Time Protocol (NTP) on the WLC or set the time manually.

To set the WLC time and date manually, use the following command:

(WLC_CLI)>**config time manual** *MM/DD/YY HH:MM:SS*

To set the WLC time/date using NTP, use the following commands:

(WLC_CLI)**config time ntp server** *index ip-address*
(WLC_CLI)**config time ntp interval** *3600 - 604800 sec*

APs can be ordered with different regulatory domains based on available unlicensed bandwidth in different countries. Another reason for a join failure could be a regulatory domain mismatch between the AP and WLC. Ensure that the AP was ordered using the correct regulatory domain.

To confirm that all APs have joined the WLC, use the CLI **show ap summary** command and examine the output, as demonstrated in Example 7-2.

Example 7-2   *Verifying That APs Have Joined the WLC*

```
> show ap summary

Number of APs.................................... 2
```

```
Global AP User Name............................ user
Global AP Dot1x User Name...................... Not Configured


Number of APs.................................. 2
Global AP User Name............................ user
Global AP Dot1x User Name...................... Not Configured


AP Name    Slots  AP Model          Ethernet MAC Location   Port Country Priority
--------   -----  ---------------   ------------ --------   ------------- --------
wolverine  2      AIR-LAP1252AG-A-K9 00:1b:d5:13:39:74  Reception  1     US       3
ap:1120    1      AIR-LAP1121G-A-K9  00:1b:d5:a9:ad:08  Hall 235   1     US       1
```

If all the APs show up in the list, you can be confident that your discovery process worked as advertised.

Network Considerations

The CUWN is an extremely flexible solution that can be deployed in a multitude of different network environments; however, there are some general network considerations you must follow to ensure a successful deployment. The following are some rules to adhere to when deploying the CUWN:

- Network round-trip times should be less than 100 ms. While this isn't a hard requirement, the AP-to-WLC control traffic can become unpredictable in a highly latent network. Network round-trip can be tested using a **ping** from a laptop or more accurately using a network-monitoring utility.

- Network bandwidth between the AP and the WLC must be above 128 kbps. This is the minimum bandwidth to accommodate LWAPP/CAPWAP control traffic across a link.

- The network path must not deliver IP fragments over multiple links. The CUWN now has support for Path MTU Discovery, which can help ensure that packets aren't being fragmented in transit by discovering the MTU of the path from host to destination.

When you're confident that the network is not the issue and all CUWN components appear healthy, it is safe to say that the wired network is not the problem.

Client Troubleshooting

Client configuration problems can be difficult to isolate as they are often confused with issues related to the wireless medium. Proper configuration between the client and the WLC is essential for seamless operation. It is a fact that most support calls made to the help desk are a result of client misconfiguration. Unfortunately, because of the advanced security requirements and multivendor solutions on the market, client configuration is not simple or consistent across these different vendors' implementations of 802.11.

The following sections outline common problems and pitfalls experienced by administrators when deploying a WLAN. The goal is to outline a process and provide descriptions of tools that will help administrators quickly and efficiently diagnose wireless client issues.

Troubleshooting Client Issues Using the WLC CLI

The WLC CLI is an excellent source of real-time client information in the wireless network. If a client is having configuration issues, it is likely that the client will show up in the debug logs and offer clues to the administrator.

There are many useful commands that assist an administrator in troubleshooting client problems. The first command, which can help an administrator begin the troubleshooting process, is **show client summary**, the output of which is illustrated in Example 7-3.

Example 7-3   show client summary *Command Output*

```
(WLC_CLI) >show client summary

Number of Clients............................... 5

MAC Address        AP Name          Status        WLAN  Auth  Protocol   Port
-----------------  ---------------  ------------  ----- ----- ---------  ----
00:09:5b:69:f9:5b  AP0014.6a1b.3b88  Probing      N/A   No    802.11b    1
00:11:92:0c:6e:40  AP0014.6a1b.3b88  Probing      N/A   No    802.11b    1
00:13:ce:45:db:4a  AP0014.6a1b.3b88  Probing      N/A   No    802.11a    1
00:13:ce:57:2b:84  AP0014.6a1b.3b88  Associated   1     Yes   802.11g    1
00:40:96:ad:0d:1b  AP0014.6a1b.3b88  Probing      N/A   No    802.11b    1
```

The output from this command lists clients seen by that particular WLC and their status:

- **MAC address:** The physical (MAC) address of the client device

- **AP name:** The name of the AP to which the client is associated

- **Status:** Probing or associated

- **WLAN:** The WLAN to which the client is associated

- **Auth:** Shows whether the client is authenticated

- **Protocol:** 802.11 PHY Protocol—802.11a, 802.11b, 802.11g, or 802.11n

- **Port:** The WLC port that the client traffic is using

After the client MAC is found, you can isolate the client of interest and look at subsequent debugs, as demonstrated here:

```
(WLC_CLI)>debug mac address 00:13:ce:57:2b:84
(WLC_CLI)>debug dot11
```

The client **debug dot11** command can provide valuable information as to what is causing the association problem such as

■   What is causing a controller to reject the client association requests

■   Client is not responding to EAP requests

■   EAP authentication to the RADIUS server is not successful

■   DHCP request from the client is failing

While the WLC CLI is a valuable tool, WCS has some unique capabilities that are not available from the WLC.

Troubleshooting Client Issues Using WCS

WCS includes a number of useful features that facilitate client troubleshooting including

■   Network reports and search capabilities

■   Client troubleshooting tool

■   Client debugging logs

The WCS client search feature will locate a client in the CUWN by MAC address, IP address, or username. Figure 7-8 shows a screen shot of the Client Monitoring page in WCS.

The page displays information regarding clients on the wireless system, including

■   Protocol: 802.11a/b/g/n

■   EAP type: EAP-FAST, EAP-TLS, PEAP, LEAP

■   Most recent client notifications

■   Current client count and historical client count information

■   Manually disabled clients

■   Top-five access points by client count

■   Client Troubleshooting dialog box

An administrator can use the troubleshooting feature to locate a troubled client in the system and begin to perform analysis, or an administrator can choose a client from a list of clients that the system knows about. Figure 7-9 is screen shot of the WCS client list.

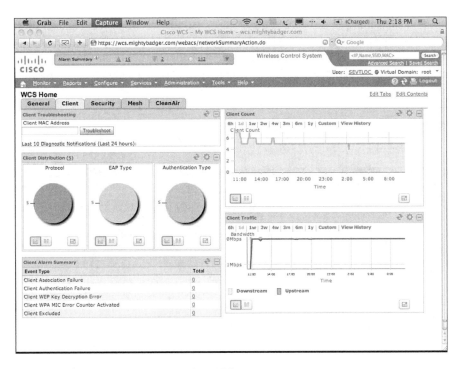

Figure 7-8   *Client Monitoring Page in WCS*

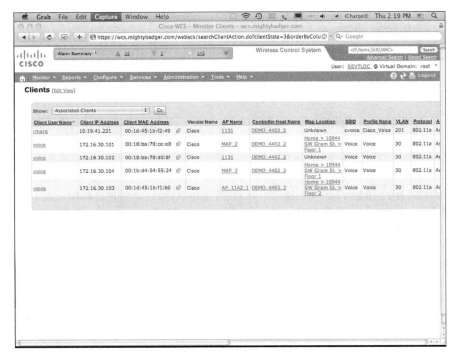

Figure 7-9   *WCS Client List*

If the client is found in the system, the Client Details page is displayed. Figure 7-10 shows the Client Details page in WCS. The administrator can gather valuable information about the status of a particular client from this page. The administrator can also utilize the mapping feature to display the client's location on a map. This can help rule out physical or environmental issues.

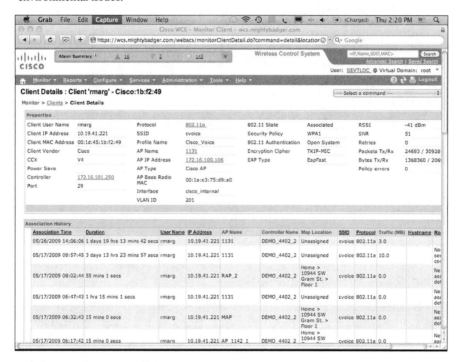

Figure 7-10   *WCS Client Details Page*

In addition to the Client Details page, a Troubleshooting window will open. Figure 7-11 illustrates what a successfully associated client should look like. If the pop-up window indicates a successful association, it is safe to say that client configuration can be ruled out as a root cause of the problem.

If there is a problem with the client, the Log Analysis tab in the client troubleshooting window will provide log data, which could be helpful in debugging the client issue. The Log Analysis tab allows the administrator to begin a capture of all the real-time log data from the WLC. The log data is similar to the output of the **debug** commands on the WLC mentioned earlier. Figure 7-12 shows the output of the Log Analysis tab.

The Cisco Compatible Extensions (CCX) program provides additional features beyond the scope of current 802.11 standards that provide functionality for enterprise wireless networks. In CCX v5, Cisco added advanced client troubleshooting features that enable users to run a variety of diagnostic tests on the client. If the client is CCX v5 compatible, the Troubleshooting tab will display additional tabs including Test Analysis, Messaging, and Event Log. These features are only available on CCX v5–compatible clients.

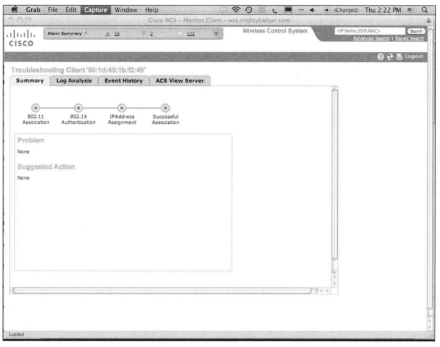

Figure 7-11 *WCS Client Troubleshooting Tab*

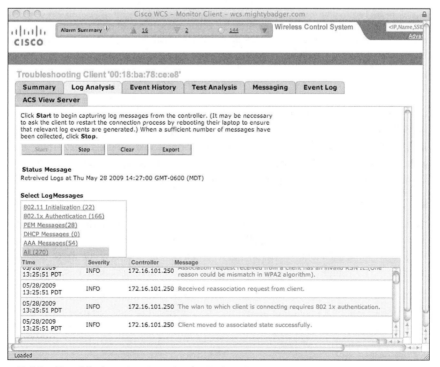

Figure 7-12 *Troubleshooting Log Analysis Output*

Figure 7-13 shows the client troubleshooting window for a CCX v5–compatible client. The figure shows the Test Analysis tab, which makes available a series of tests that can be performed to troubleshoot the client.

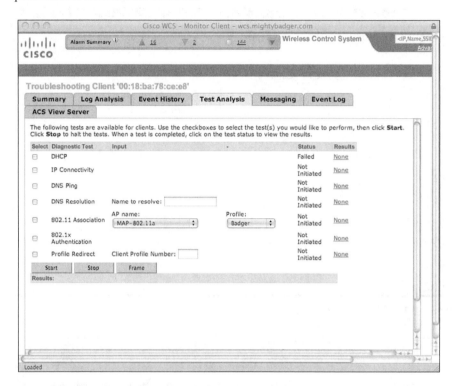

Figure 7-13   *WCS Client Troubleshooting*

Common Client Problems and Solutions

The following sections describe the most common client problem scenarios with solutions. Within each problem, wireless troubleshooting tools are used to diagnose and, if applicable, correct the problem. This list is by no means complete, but it should begin to illustrate a methodology for approaching client troubleshooting.

SSID Mismatch

The first parameter to check when troubleshooting client connectivity is the service set identifier (SSID). Ensure that the SSID parameters match on the client device and the WLAN to which the client is attempting to connect. The SSID can be up to 32 characters long. The SSID usually consists of a string of ASCII characters and is case sensitive.

When troubleshooting client issues, it's important to understand where in the client association process the client is failing. Using the troubleshooting features previously described, you can identify where in the association/authentication process the client is failing.

WEP

Wired Equivalent Privacy (WEP) is an obsolete form of wireless security. It is not secure and should be treated accordingly. However, wireless network administrators might have legacy clients that use WEP for wireless security. WEP can be tricky to configure and troubleshoot because of some unintuitive configuration parameters. The following are some common configuration pitfalls:

■ **WEP key length:** As specified in the original IEEE 802.11, WEP uses a 40-bit encryption key concatenated with a 24-bit initialization vector. Later, a 104-bit WEP key length became available. Ensure that the key length is set consistently between the client and the WLAN to which it's attempting to connect.

■ **WEP key index:** Often, client and infrastructure vendors interpret the specifications differently, causing different implementations in the product. One common example is the choice of using key indices from 0 through 3 versus using key indices from 1 through 4. This can result in a mismatched configuration and therefore failed connection attempts. Pay close attention to the key index configured on the client and WLAN to which it is attempting to connect.

■ **Configured authentication method (open versus shared key):** WEP has two authentication methods that must be configured consistently for the client to authenticate to the WLAN.

WPA-PSK

Wi-Fi Protected Access with Pre-Shared Keys (WPA-PSK) is very similar to WEP in that it requires a static key to be configured on the wireless LAN controller and client. The key is almost always entered as a passphrase containing 8 to 63 ASCII characters. The most frequent client problem related to WEP and WPA-PSK is misconfiguration. Take care that the passphrase is entered consistently between the WLC and the client. Another typical problem is related to WPA versus WPA2. WPA uses Temporal Key Integrity Protocol (TKIP) for encryption, whereas WPA2 uses Advanced Encryption Standard (AES) for encryption. There is a generation of client devices on the market that can support WPA without supporting WPA2. Ensure that the client and WLC are configured consistently for the WPA-versus-WPA2 parameters.

WPA/WPA2 Enterprise with 802.1X

The most pervasively deployed security mechanism is WPA/WPA2 Enterprise. By using 802.1X for client authentication, WPA/WPA2 Enterprise provides significant benefits in terms of security and scalability. Figure 7-14 illustrates the standard WPA/WPA2 Enterprise components of 802.1X authentication, which include the client (supplicant), WLC (authenticator), and authentication, authorization, and accounting (AAA) server.

Describing the details of a full 802.1X transaction is out of scope for this chapter; however, Figure 7-14 illustrates the packet flow of a successful 802.1X authentication process in WPA/WPA2 Enterprise.

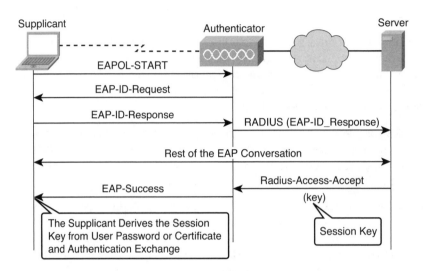

Figure 7-14   *802.1X Authentication Components*

For the purposes of this section, the assumption is that the configuration on the AAA server is valid and operational. The main issues that can occur between the supplicant (client) and the authenticator (AP) are as follows:

■ Wrong EAP type configured on the client

■ Wrong credentials on the client or expired certificates

As discussed in the earlier section, "Tools for Troubleshooting 802.11 Wireless Networks," the WCS client troubleshooting features do an excellent job of identifying *where* the issue might be occurring. Figure 7-14 illustrates a successful 802.11 association. Figure 7-15 shows the client troubleshooting features of WCS.

In addition to the information available on the Summary tab, additional information is available on the Log Analysis tab. As described in the earlier section, "Tools for Troubleshooting 802.11 Wireless Networks," the Log Analysis tab serves as a front end for the WLC CLI debug messages. The same information can be obtained by initiating **debug** commands on the WLC CLI. By using the following commands, an administrator can isolate a particular client's 802.1X-related transaction in real-time:

```
(WLC_CLI)>debug mac address 00:13:ce:57:2b:84
(WLC_CLI)>debug AAA (all)(detail)(events)(packets) enable
```

Alternatively, the following CLI command turns on all client-related debugs at once:

```
(WLC_CLI)>debug client mac-address
```

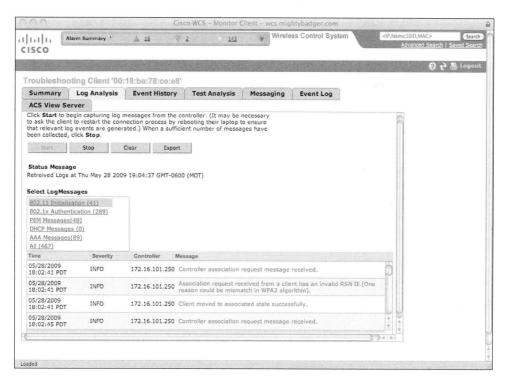

Figure 7-15 *WCS Client Troubleshooting Log Analysis Page*

In the event of an 802.1X authentication failure, ensure that the EAP type configured on the client matches the EAP type configured in the AAA server. If an EAP type mismatch can be ruled out as a cause, the next place to check is user credentials. Ensure that the credentials on the client machine (that is, username/password, X.509 certificate) are valid and correct. It is also possible to check the log data on the AAA server for clues as to why the authentication is failing. If you're using the Cisco Access Control Server (ACS), WCS is capable of automatically displaying log data within the client troubleshooting screen. This feature is called ACS View.

IP Address Assignment

Another common issue on wireless LANs is DCHP problems. Many users of wireless networks are inherently mobile. This means that laptops go home with the users, are used at hotels and hotspots, and so on. It is possible that a laptop user might have assigned a static IP address to his/her machine that might be preventing the laptop from obtaining a valid address from the DHCP server. In addition, IP address assignment problems can be symptoms of an exhausted DHCP scope or a DNS problem. The WCS client troubleshooting tool can help isolate DHCP problems.

As you would imagine, it is also possible to use the WLC to obtain real-time details related to client DHCP assignment using the following command set:

```
(WLC_CLI)>debug mac address 00:13:ce:57:2b:84
(WLC_CLI)>debug dhcp packet (message)(packet) enable
```

Alternatively, the following CLI command turns on all client-related debugs at once.

```
(WLC_CLI)>debug client mac-address
```

To cover all client misconfiguration scenarios would take an entire book. The purpose of this chapter was to introduce the fundamental areas where things can go wrong and provide tools to get to the bottom of the problem. If you're confident that the WLC and client are configured properly and issues are still showing up, the following sections cover issues related to the RF medium.

The Wireless Medium: Troubleshooting Performance-Related Issues

The most common culprit for performance-related issues in a wireless local-area network is the wireless medium itself. In the absence of physical, deterministic connections, the wireless medium can pose complex challenges for administrators. Coverage—too much or too little—and interference are extremely common in 802.11 networks. As with other issues, it's important to first detect the performance problem and isolate its source prior to making changes to the wireless network.

Coverage and Interference Issues

There are three "most likely" causes for coverage and/or interference issues:

■ **Coverage—too much or too little:** Coverage holes in your network will cause poor performance or no connectivity in the affected area. Too much coverage will result in cochannel interference. The 2.4-GHz spectrum only has three nonoverlapping wireless channels (Channel 1, Channel 6, and Channel 11). When an AP on Channel 1 overlaps coverage with another AP on Channel 1, the result is cochannel interference. Cochannel interference causes excessive management overhead, frequent collisions, and poor performance.

■ **Interference from 802.11 devices:** There are a lot of 802.11-compatible devices in service. These devices will interfere with one another and often do.

■ **Interference from non-802.11 devices:** 802.11 devices operate in the 2.4-GHz and 5-GHz unlicensed spectrum. There are many other devices occupying this spectrum that will cause harmful interference.

Detecting, Isolating, and Solving Coverage Issues

The easiest and most proactive way to monitor coverage problems is to pay attention to alarms in WCS and WLCs. These can be your first clues to interference and coverage problems. The CUWN uses advanced algorithms to detect coverage holes and measure signal-to-noise ratio (SNR) and activate alarms at particular thresholds. Figure 7-16 provides a screen shot from WCS showing the event log. The event log is an excellent place to proactively look for clues that your wireless network might be experiencing coverage or interference issues. Be on the lookout for noise, interference, and coverage hole traps.

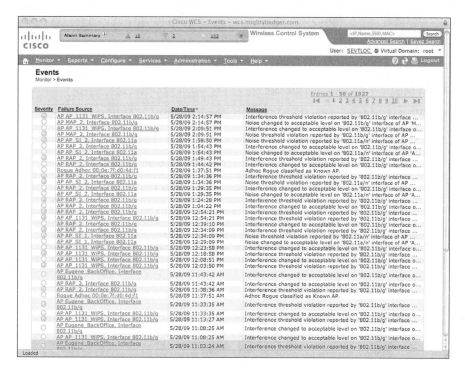

Figure 7-16 *Event Log in WCS*

Note   You can set custom trap thresholds. Check the configuration guide for details.

Make sure to watch for APs with recurring problems. It is common to see noise, interference, and coverage hole alarms for the same APs repeatedly. If this is the case, it is a good idea to investigate before the user complaints start occurring.

While WCS might be useful for proactive monitoring, at times, your users are the eyes and ears. Complaints of intermittent problems from users can be an indication of a problem. The key word here is *intermittent*. If the issue is not predictable and misconfiguration has been ruled out, this is a good tip-off to a coverage or interference issue.

Pay close attention to *where* the problems are occurring. Physical location is important to correct the issues. Train your help desk to catalog important information about trouble tickets associated to wireless, for example:

- Where is the problem occurring? Is it isolated to a particular geographic area?

- When is the problem occurring?

- What is the type of client? Is it a laptop wireless client? Which version? Is it a wireless telephone?

After this information is compiled, it can be useful in cleaning up a problem area. The next step is to physically walk the area and attempt to reproduce the problems. The first step might be to reproduce the problem at the application layer. If a user is complaining of poor performance from a web-based application, ensure that the problem is repeatable.

The next step is to check the wireless coverage. Every organization should have set a benchmark for Received Signal Strength Indication (RSSI). Most Cisco Wireless Advanced Technology Partners will design wireless networks for -70 dBm wireless coverage or better.

Note   The -70 dBm number applies to *data* applications only. If the network is going to support advanced technologies such as *voice* or *location* applications, be sure to consult the design guidelines pertaining to these technologies.

Use a site survey tool such as Airmagnet to walk around the problem area and measure signal strength from the neighboring AP. If the coverage doesn't meet the benchmark, it might be necessary to move or add APs to augment coverage. If the APs are using external antennas, it might be possible to reorient antennas to fix the coverage holes.

Note   Site survey tools can be expensive; however, it is possible to perform a site survey using standard client utilities. Figure 7-17 is a screen shot from the Cisco Aironet Site Survey utility, which comes free with the Cisco CB21AG client adapters.

If coverage appears to be strong throughout the area, the problem might be related to interference.

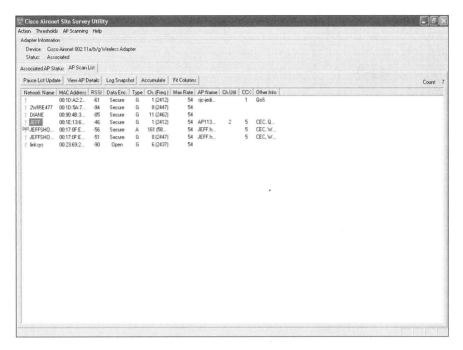

Figure 7-17 *Aironet Site Survey Utility*

Detecting, Isolating, and Solving Interference Issues

Interference is a common problem with 802.11 WLANs. The success of 802.11 has resulted in millions of Wi-Fi radios deployed throughout the world. In a given city block in a major metropolitan area, literally hundreds of 802.11 radios could be detected.

A second problem with 802.11 wireless networks is that they operate in the 2.4-GHz and 5-GHz unlicensed spectrum. Both of these spectrums contain non-802.11 devices operating in some or all of the available spectrum. Non-802.11 interference is much more difficult to detect.

Luckily, the CUWN provides the administrator with a set of tools to detect and isolate interference sources. The WCS trap log will provide the user with proactive alarms when interference and noise thresholds are reached. Analyzing which APs are reporting alarms allows the administrator to know where interference is occurring.

Interference alarms aren't going to detect interference all the time. User complaints of poor performance are another indication that harmful interference is occurring. Be certain that the help desk logs all user complaints with information about location, device, driver information, and so on.

A useful tool for troubleshooting coverage and interference issues caused by the network itself is the Rx Neighbor measurement.

The APs constantly measure the strength of signals heard from neighboring APs. If two APs on the same channel can measure the neighbor's signal at greater than 80 dBm, it is safe to assume that the APs are interfering with one another.

Figure 7-18 is a screen shot from WCS indicating an interference threshold being hit by an AP.

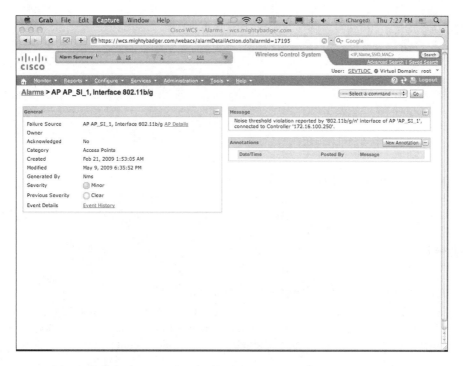

Figure 7-18   *WCS Interference Threshold Alarm*

The Rogue AP detection feature is another way to detect 802.11 interference. Rogue AP detection is known as a security feature, but it also useful for detecting 802.11 devices that might be interfering with the wireless network. The administrator should make a habit of evaluating all rogue AP alarms on a daily or weekly basis. By examining the signal strength at which the CUWN is detecting the rogue, an administrator can determine whether the rogue is producing interference. Figure 7-19 shows a rogue access point detected by WCS. It is also possible to use the location features of the system to locate the approximate location of a rogue AP in the CUWN.

Most of the time, rogue APs do not have malicious intent. Normally, they belong to the neighbor in the office downstairs or to another department. Detecting and mapping these devices are essential, however.

Another type of interference source is a non-802.11 device operating in the 2.4-GHz or 5-GHz unlicensed spectrum. Until recently, spectrum analysis was out of reach to most users. The devices were bulky, expensive, and difficult to use. Cisco Spectrum Expert allows anyone to take advantage of spectrum analysis technology. Spectrum Expert is capable of detecting non-802.11 interference from a variety of sources.

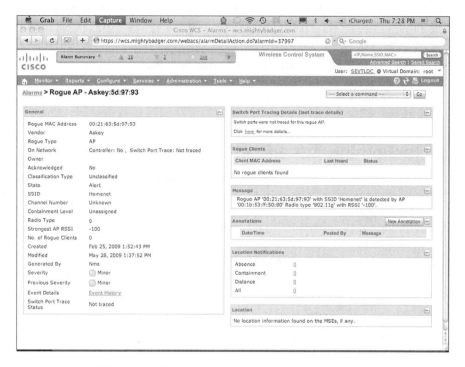

Figure 7-19 *WCS Rogue AP Details*

After it is detected, non-802.11 interference must be dealt with. If the interference source cannot be removed, it might be possible to plan the wireless channels around the interference. A careful analysis is required to do proper channel planning. Another option might be to move the 802.11 clients to the 5-GHz spectrum. This spectrum is significantly less crowded, and there are more available channels to work around interference. The "Voice over WLAN" section, later in this chapter, analyzes the benefits/drawbacks of moving clients to the 5-GHz unlicensed spectrum.

If coverage and interference have been ruled out, you might still see poor performance from one client and good performance from another client in the same location. This is because of discrepancies in wireless card and driver performance. In this case, try these different options:

■ Try upgrading client driver firmware; manufacturers are constantly making improvements to client driver firmware. Make sure to have the latest and greatest.

■ Try different supplicants. Sometimes the supplicants (also known as configuration utilities) used to configure the client adapter have flaws. Cisco offers a free trial of its Cisco Secure Services Client (CSSC). Try using CSSC. CSSC is a wired and wireless supplicant capable of working with almost any wireless radio. CSSC offers enterprise provisioning and security features that other supplicants do not.

■ Experiment with different security types to rule out security problems. Try running different encryption and key management, and if all else fails, try getting it going without security configured.

■ Try disabling CUWN features such as Management Frame Protection (MFP), Aironet Extensions, and Short Preambles. Poorly designed or older legacy clients occasionally have problems with these features. If possible, always ensure that clients are CCX certified.

Troubleshooting Advanced Wireless LAN Services

As WLANs became more advanced and increasingly mainstream, it made sense to use the infrastructure for advanced services beyond simple wireless connectivity. Voice over WLAN and location-based services are the primary advanced services deployed on wireless LANs today. An advanced wireless network administrator will be expected to design and troubleshoot networks with one or both of these services in production. The following sections introduce these services and explore some of the most common troubleshooting scenarios.

Voice over WLAN

Two of the most pervasively deployed advanced technologies in the twenty-first century are Voice over IP and wireless LANs. Over seventy percent of the enterprise phones shipped today are Voice over IP phones.

Most enterprises either have wireless LANs deployed or have plans to deploy in the near term. It stands to reason that these two technologies would converge. Today's Voice over WLAN applications are deployed in one of three flavors:

■ **Voice over WLAN handsets:** First pioneered by SpectraLink Corporation in the late 1990s, Voice over WLAN (VoWLAN) handsets are increasingly more common in enterprises with mobile workforces. Healthcare, retail, and manufacturing often deploy VoWLAN handsets to increase the productivity and customer satisfaction in their workforces.

■ **Software-based phones:** Softphones running on laptops and other mobile devices are more common today than ever before.

■ **Dual-mode handsets:** Cellular phones and smartphones are beginning to ship with Wi-Fi radios in addition to their cellular radio. Some of these handsets have the capability to use VoWLAN technology to make telephone calls.

Today's wireless network must be designed with VoWLAN in mind, even if the application isn't there today. As time goes on, the technologies previously described and others will begin to be deployed. As the next section describes, voice can pose unique challenges to the wireless LAN.

Voice over WLAN Challenges

Most Voice over IP (VoIP) protocols, including Session Initiation Protocol (SIP), Skinny Call Control Protocol (SCCP), and H.323, have similar characteristics that are important to understand. First, they all use the Real-time Transport Protocol (RTP) to transmit audio over the network. RTP implementations are based on the User Datagram Protocol (UDP), meaning that packets are sent unreliably over the network. RTP is also deterministic, sending a packet in 20-ms or 30-ms intervals. Being deterministic makes RTP extremely latency sensitive. Network impairments resulting in latency and jitter (defined in the following list) will result in diminished voice quality:

- **Latency:** The time delay from the transmit of a datagram to the receipt of the datagram

- **Jitter:** The variability of latency between datagram transmissions

Conversely, data traffic is very bursty; users will transmit and receive traffic in bursts as they navigate a web page or download an e-mail attachment. Additionally, most wireless data applications use TCP. TCP is much more tolerant of latency and jitter. TCP packets are sent reliably; if a packet is corrupted or lost, it is simply retransmitted. In most wireless data applications, users rarely even notice a packet retransmission or other problems. Reliable packet transmission is not suitable for real-time applications, because by the time a packet is retransmitted, it's too late because that part of the conversation is already over.

The net effect of introducing Voice over IP into a wireless network is magnification of all the 802.11's design inadequacies. The effect is further magnified by the fact that users of VoWLAN will *hear* network problems. Users will undoubtedly be frustrated if conversations are interrupted by wireless network problems. Deploying VoWLAN on a poorly designed wireless network is an invitation for a string of user complaints.

Another unique aspect of VoWLAN is the mobility of the clients. Wireless clients need to be able to seamlessly roam from AP to AP without degrading service. This is especially true for VoWLAN clients. It is helpful to put clients into one of two categories:

- **Portable clients:** Portable clients access the wireless network from different physical locations but rarely maintain connectivity while moving between locations. The best example of a portable client is a laptop. Users might use their wireless laptop from their cubicle, close the lid, and move to a conference room and reconnect, but wireless connectivity was not required while in motion.

- **Mobile clients:** Mobile clients access the wireless system from different physical locations and require seamless connectivity while moving. The best example of a mobile client is the Voice over Wi-Fi handset. These handsets leverage the wireless network for voice applications and require the wireless network to offer a seamless experience as users are moving throughout a facility.

All Wi-Fi networks should be designed for seamless handoff performance; however, if the network has a requirement for mobile clients, it is crucial to plan for seamless handoff performance.

It is important for a wireless network administrator to keep all these factors in mind when responding to issues related to VoWLAN. The next section explores some of the most common issues related to VoWLAN performance.

Troubleshooting VoWLAN

The most common complaint from a VoWLAN user is going to be choppy audio. Choppy audio is the result of lost packets and/or excessively latent packets. Anytime the VoIP stream is not being delivered deterministically, a packet at every 20–30 ms, audio quality will degrade. Fortunately, jitter buffers in a well-designed wireless device should account for 100 ms of varying delay. Anything above 100 ms is going to cause serious quality issues and result in complaints.

The most common causes for lost packets, latent packets, and jitter have already been discussed in this chapter—coverage holes, interference, and roaming performance.

Identifying and Troubleshooting Coverage Holes

Coverage holes will result in the wireless device having a suboptimal connection to the wireless infrastructure. Keep in mind that by deploying VoWLAN, all deficiencies in your wireless network will now be audible to the world (or your users at least). Utilize the same techniques outlined earlier in the chapter—look proactively at alarms, clean up troubled areas, and test.

One aspect to keep in mind is client design. Most likely, the initial site survey was completed using a laptop and a wireless client card. The client card likely has very different RF properties than the VoWLAN handsets you're about to deploy. Make sure to redo the site survey using the built-in tools of the wireless handset that you plan to deploy. Most if not all wireless handsets will have a site survey tool built in. Make sure that your coverage never strays below -67 dBm. Figure 7-20 shows a Cisco 7921 wireless handset's site survey tool. Pay attention to the dBm readings from all the access points it hears.

Another useful way to test is to initiate a phone call between the wireless IP phone and a wired IP phone. Test the audio quality; Cisco 79xx series wired IP phones have quality-monitoring tools built in. Press the ? on a 79xx handset twice to enable quality monitoring. This is an excellent way to determine whether you have coverage or interference problems in a particular area.

Moving Voice to 5 GHz

Many vendors of VoWLAN products (including Cisco) are recommending moving voice applications to the 5-GHz band. There are two primary reasons for this recommendation:

- **More channels:** The 5-GHz band is larger than the 2.4-GHz band. There are eight nonoverlapping channels as opposed to three in the 2.4-GHz space. More channels can cover up a lot of site survey mistakes and give an administrator more options to fix a troubled area.

■ **Less devices competing for the spectrum:** The 5-GHz band is significantly cleaner than 2.4-GHz band. The noise floor in the 5-GHz band is almost always much lower. There are simply less devices competing for the spectrum.

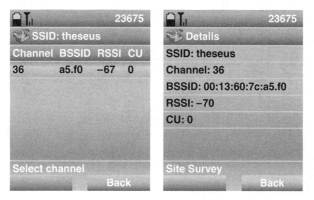

Figure 7-20 *7921 Wireless Phone Site Survey Utility*

Of course, there are some other issues with 5 GHz. The higher the frequency, the less chance the signal has to pass through and around obstructions. When site-surveying for 5 GHz, it is evident that the signals do not propagate as well as at 2.4 GHz. With this said, 5 GHz is a good place for VoWLAN.

Roaming Performance

Roaming performance can be affected by a number of factors, not the least of which is client design. A well-designed wireless client will roam from AP to AP quickly and efficiently. A poorly designed client will likely hang onto an AP for a long period, lose its connection, and then reconnect to a better signal.

Another factor in roaming performance are the security protocols. 802.1X-based authentication has been known to cause roaming problems on VoWLAN devices. The reason behind this problem is that 802.1X forces a client to reauthenticate every time the client moves from one AP to another. Reauthentication requires an exchange between the RADIUS server, AP, and client. This process can take anywhere from 200 ms to 5 seconds. With portable clients, this is usually not an issue. With mobile clients such as VoWLAN phones, this is a huge issue. Imagine a user walking down a hallway engaged in an important phone conversation. In the course of 30 seconds, the user might be required to hand off between APs up to five times. Even a 1-second handoff delay is unacceptable in this user case.

Fortunately, technology is in place in the CUWN to minimize handoff delays. Cisco Centralized Key Management (CCKM) uses the WLC to proxy authentication traffic to eliminate the need for clients to authenticate to the RADIUS server. CCKM authenticates the client without perceptible delay in voice or other time-sensitive applications. To confirm that CCKM is enabled, check on the WLAN template that the VoWLAN devices are using. Figure 7-21 is a WCS screen shot of a WLAN with CCKM enabled.

CCKM must also be supported by the client device. All CCX v4–compatible clients will support CCKM.

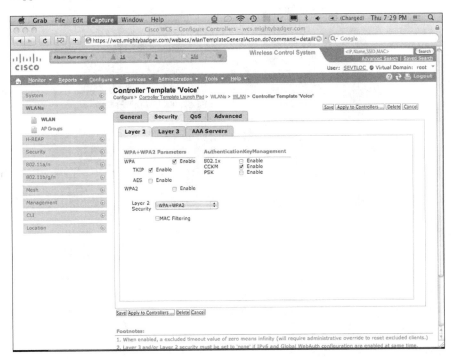

Figure 7-21   *WLAN with CCKM Enabled*

If a network is running into problems with roaming, start with a detailed site survey using the wireless phone, as described previously. Make sure that the wireless phone is able to see at least three wireless APs at all times. The key to roaming is to ensure that the client device has options when RSSI from the current AP begins to degrade. If a client doesn't have an option, there is no way to preserve quality as the user roams.

Beyond simple coverage problems, roaming problems are notoriously difficult to troubleshoot. Interference and client design are the usual culprits. Interference can be detected using a spectrum analyzer such as Cisco Spectrum Expert (described earlier in this chapter). Client design is much more difficult to isolate.

If you suspect that client performance is the issue, first ensure that the device is running the latest version of firmware. Manufacturers are constantly upgrading and improving firmware on their devices; make sure that you have the latest and greatest. Next, try different configurations—change the SSID, change the security settings, disable security, and so on. All or one of these factors could be affecting performance. Finally, contact the manufacturer's support organization; be sure to be armed with troubleshooting data and a detailed description of what is happening. The manufacturer might request wireless analyzer capture files, so be prepared to get these. Sometimes, the only way to debug a roaming issue is to capture simultaneously on multiple channels so that it is possible to see the client as it makes its roaming decision and executes the roam. Capturing on multiple channels should provide a definitive answer to what is happening.

Voice troubleshooting is an essential skill for today's wireless administrator. It is also a multidisciplinary skill that requires a deep understanding of wireless networks and a solid understanding of VoIP.

Location Troubleshooting

Location Services is another useful application for wireless infrastructure. The CUWN supports location monitoring using the Mobility Services Engine (MSE). Both track the location of 802.11 devices using advanced RF fingerprinting technologies. The system can track any Wi-Fi device, including Wi-Fi clients, standards-based Wi-Fi active radio frequency ID (RFID) tags, rogue APs, and clients. Customers can leverage a current investment in wireless infrastructure to provide location services to users. Figure 7-22 illustrates the components of the CUWN with location services enabled.

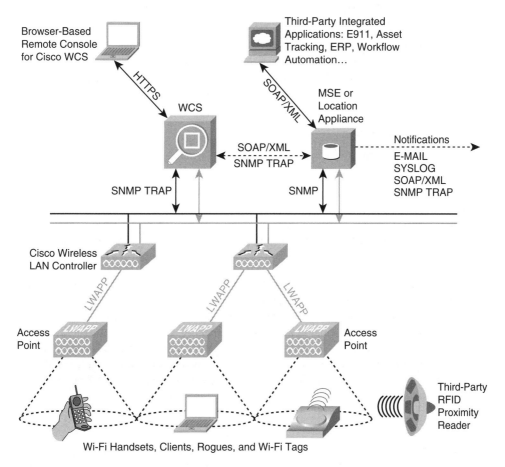

Figure 7-22 *Location Components*

The most common complaint that administrators will hear from users will be related to location accuracy. It is important to set the correct expectations to users when deploying location-based technologies. Cisco says that the location will be within 10 meters 90 percent of the time. This number is probably conservative but can vary based on the implementation and environment. The following section explains what can be done to troubleshoot a wireless location implementation to improve accuracy.

First, it is important to understand how wireless location operates. The MSE calculates the location of traced devices using RF fingerprinting. This technique uses RF characteristics such as reflection, attenuation, and multipath to identify the approximate location of the wireless location. The system also takes environmental variables specific to the environment into account. For this reason, there is an RF calibration process that must take place after the initial wireless installation. During calibration, the system creates a grid. For each point in the grid, many different APs detect devices; each AP detects these devices at different signal strengths.

After calibration is complete, a database is populated within the MSE. The database contains each grid coordinate and describes how each AP views that coordinate from the standpoint of signal strength.

When devices' locations are required by WCS or a third-party system, each WLC replies on behalf of its APs with the signal strength at which they detect the device. The management system then matches the information it gathers from the WLCs against a database of location RF fingerprints. Device locations can then be plotted visually on a floor map.

Troubleshooting Location Accuracy

When troubleshooting location accuracy, there are two main areas to focus on:

- AP density

- AP placement

Both of these factors will have a direct impact on how well location is operating.

AP Density

In terms of density, Cisco recommends placing an AP for every 2500–5000 square feet. For location accuracy, AP density is important. The more APs measuring client signal strength, the more accurate location information will be. However, placing APs extremely close together is likely to result in cochannel interference, especially in the 2.4-GHz spectrum. For this reason, CUWN allows the administrator to run APs in a Monitor mode. In Monitor mode, an AP does not serve client or participate in the Basic Service Set (BSS). It basically runs passively, collecting information and measurements about the network.

If your network is experiencing location accuracy problems, ensure that the deployment is dense enough. It is also possible to use the Location Readiness Tool inside WCS to do an inventory of the network. After running the tool, WCS will make recommendation in terms of density.

Access Point Placement

AP placement is extremely important to location accuracy. Because clients need to be detected by as many APs as possible, it is essential to deploy APs at the perimeter of the building and toward the center. This is very important and might require moving or adding APs. If the facility was surveyed for data and voice coverage, it is possible that APs were not placed at the perimeter. This is a sound design for data/voice; it will not provide good location accuracy. Figure 7-23 illustrates a network designed poorly for location and a network designed well for location.

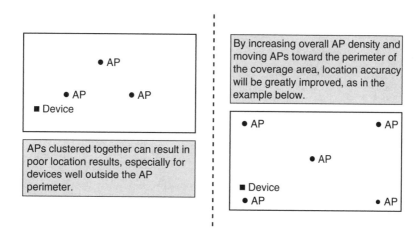

Figure 7-23 *Network Designs for Location: Good Versus Bad*

In the figure on the left, it is evident that the client is not "surrounded" by APs. In the right figure, the client is surrounded by AP coverage and has a much better chance of being located accurately by the system.

The CUWN location services can be a valuable business tool; however, it is important to set the expectations of your users. If users understand the accuracy of the system, they will be happy with the performance; if they're expecting 1-meter accuracy, they will be disappointed.

Summary

Troubleshooting wireless networks can be a daunting task. In fact, it is possible to build a career around troubleshooting wireless issues. This chapter was not intended to be a comprehensive guide to every wireless issue that could be seen in an enterprise. It is intended to provide tools and a process that can be applied to any issue that comes up in your wireless network.

The beginning of the chapter outlined various tools that can be used to assist with the troubleshooting process. Tools are essential to the success of a wireless system administrator. Fundamentally, a good wireless troubleshooter will have a sound understanding of the 802.11 protocol and RF design and, most importantly, an understanding of the tools available. Applying the right tool to the situation is the key to being successful.

Chapter 8

Introduction to WCS

Some of the toughest challenges with any wireless deployment and strategy are determining and finding the right tools to manage it. Cisco has put a tremendous effort into developing and improving the capabilities of the management suite known as the Wireless Control System (WCS). The capability to seamlessly discover, report, troubleshoot, and manage hundreds of controllers, thousands of clients, and thousands of APs has been the cornerstone of the development process and allows a unified way to manage the complete life cycle of a Cisco wireless LAN (WLAN), indoors and outdoors, from anywhere in the world with minimal IT staffing. WCS offers customers the ability to migrate away from the traditional standalone design to a controller design while providing the ability to manage both architectures from end to end from anywhere in the network; WCS also provides tools to facilitate this migration process.

In this chapter, you will understand the best-use cases for WCS, how to implement WCS, when to implement WCS, and any best practices to ensure success from the onset of a wireless deployment. A question you might ask is, "When do I really need to look at WCS and its features?" The answer is, "From the beginning of the project or deployment to the end." There are many features built into the WCS software that simplify the setup and deployment of not just one controller but hundreds of controllers. Imagine having 1 site, 10 sites, or 100 sites with a controller or multiple controllers in each and having to configure each one individually and ensure that the end-user experience is the same at every location. To touch each and every device would take many man-hours, and because we are all human, this process would surely encounter some mistakes along the way, increasing the number of man-hours to troubleshoot and correct. WCS was developed to address this and to ensure that each controller can be managed centrally and each controller looks identical. Consistency of configuration is key when it comes to wireless, especially because of the mission-critical nature of environments in which it's being deployed.

Note that at this point in the design of the wireless network, you have yet to even touch your controllers, and that is because you want to use a centralized tool to deploy all configurations. By using template functions for both controllers as well as access points, you will simplify the overall design and deployment, and in the process, you also gain a centralized backup repository for all configurations that are made to the network. WCS provides a key benefit in that there's no more configuring one box and then configuring another, hoping that you've applied the same rules and configurations. Most Cisco Unified Wireless Network (CUWN) customers will state that one of the key benefits of the WCS is the capability to push out multiple templates to thousands of devices in just a few clicks. This has simplified administrator workflow, as well as reduced the overall hours required to maintain the wireless network and ensure consistent configurations across the design. After you have combed through the different features and functions of the WCS management platform (covered later), you will have the tools to manage and maintain a robust wireless network.

There are many WCS design documents and best practices located at the Cisco Design Zone for Mobility link:

   www.cisco.com/en/US/netsol/ns820/networking_solutions_program_home.html

If all this information were consolidated into a simple cheat sheet, this chapter of the book would not be required. As alluded to earlier in the chapter, WCS has many features and functions that can be used to deploy a unified network, and you will be able to use this chapter to best understand how.

Designing Wireless Networks with WCS

Cisco WCS provides a foundation that provides you, the network administrator, with the ability to design, control, and ultimately monitor the wireless network from any location. Cisco WCS is a graphical user interface (GUI)–based application installed on either a standalone server platform or ESX server from VMware and ties directly into the controller and access point (AP) infrastructure. You can find more information on the product specifications and requirements at www.cisco.com/go/wireless.

Some of the benefits of the WCS include

- Wireless planning and designing

- Wireless monitoring and troubleshooting

- Wireless trending and reporting

- Services management for context-aware Cisco CleanAir and Cisco Adaptive Wireless Intrusion Prevention Service

Other benefits of WCS include, but are not limited to, the configuration and management of the mobility services engine (MSE), which provides wireless intrusion prevention system (wIPS) management and monitoring; location-based management and monitoring of asset tags, clients, and rogues; and RF spectrum intelligence (or CleanAir).

WCS Requirements

You can install WCS on either a Linux-based or a Windows-based system, and either can be deployed on VMware's ESX 3.5 or greater software.

With the migration to centralized management and virtualization, WCS installations on ESX have grown significantly and are becoming the norm. The key to any deployment of WCS is to ensure that you follow the minimum server requirements based on the number of APs you will be supporting. If you install WCS on a system that has less than the minimum requirements, you might run into performance issues.

The server-to-device support matrix for the unified wireless deployment with WCS is as follows:

■ **Cisco WCS high-end server requirements:** 3000 lightweight access points, 1250 standalone access points, 750 wireless LAN controllers

■ **Cisco WCS standard server requirements:** 2000 lightweight access points, 1000 standalone access points, 450 wireless LAN controllers

■ **Cisco WCS low-end server requirements:** 500 lightweight access points, 200 standalone access points, 125 wireless LAN controllers

For further details on the server requirements as well as the new servers supported, see Chapter 2 in the Cisco WCS 7.0 Configuration Guide located here:

www.cisco.com/en/US/docs/wireless/wcs/7.0/configuration/guide/7_0wst.html

It is out of the scope of this chapter to cover the step-by-step installation of WCS; however, the instructions can be found here:

www.cisco.com/en/US/products/ps6305/products_installation_and_configuration_guides_list.html

Based on the version of WCS server software you are running, the instructions in the preceding link will also provide additional server requirements as well as features that are supported in each respective release.

WCS Interface

How many times have you been asked to generate a report based on client activity or AP utilization in the network and not had the tools readily available to provide that information? How many times have you been asked to help troubleshoot or monitor the network and not had a simple tool to provide that information?

If you are new to WCS or a long-time user, you will notice that Cisco has taken great strides in simplifying the way in which network administrators manage the Unified Wireless Network and in answering those previous questions. Throughout the rest of this chapter, you will learn key benefits of each area within WCS and see why WCS is a valuable tool in designing, deploying, and managing a Cisco Unified Wireless Network.

Note   When you use WCS for the first time, the network summary pages show that the controllers, coverage areas, most recent rogue APs, top 5 APs, and most recent coverage holes databases are empty. It also shows that no client devices are connected to the system. After you configure the WCS database with one or more controllers, the WCS home page provides updated information.

Note   The scope of the WCS management tool warrants an entire book, so in the interest of time and paper, the sections that follow will uncover key areas that will allow you to monitor, report, configure, and administer the Cisco Unified Wireless Network.

After completing the preliminary installation steps and logging in to WCS, you will notice the following key menus, as noted in Figure 8-1. Take some time to familiarize yourself with the different options that are available.

Figure 8-1   *Cisco WCS Top-Level View*

■   **Monitor:** The Monitor menu provides you with a top-level description of the devices on your network. You can monitor your network, maps, devices (WLCs, access points, clients, tags, interferes), Radio Resource Management (RRM) alarms, and events.

■   **Reports:** The Reports launch pad provides access to all WCS reports from a single page. From this page, you can view current reports, access specific types of reports, create and save new reports, and manage scheduled run results.

- **Configure:** The Configure menu enables you to configure templates, controllers, access points, Ethernet switches, config groups, autoprovisioning, scheduled configuration tasks, profiles, Access Control Server (ACS) view servers, and TFTP servers on your network.

- **Services:** The Services menu provides the adding, configuring, and managing of mobility services engines and legacy location engines. It also provides key configuration options such as northbound trap receivers, context aware tag, and client configuration.

- **Administration:** The Administration menu enables you to schedule tasks, administer accounts, and configure local and external authentication and authorization. Also, you can set logging options, configure mail servers, and provide data management related to configuring the data retain periods. Information is available about the types of WCS licenses and how to install a license. You also use administration to define and configure virtual domains.

- **Tools:** The Tools menu provides access to the Voice Audit, Location Accuracy Tool, Configuration Audit Summary, and Migration Analysis features of WCS.

- **Help:** The Help menu provides access to online learning modules, submitting feedback, and a help option to send periodic information to help improve the product.

WCS Monitoring

One thing that you might have noticed is the ability to monitor many different devices and services in your wireless network not limited to controllers, APs, tags, alarms, events, and so on. It is here that you will use the WCS to its fullest potential. Covered in more detail in Chapter 7, "Troubleshooting," you find details on client troubleshooting, which is one key feature that will help in simplifying the overall management of the network. Having the ability to define a MAC address and monitor the client association, authentication, and access to the network from one central spot is invaluable. The need to visit the client to troubleshoot access to the wireless medium can be limited or even removed.

The WCS monitor menu provides a great deal of information to help you manage the wireless network. Without centralized monitoring features, you would have to touch possibly hundreds of devices to understand issues and problems in the network. There are many monitoring options; however, you will learn just a few to help you better understand the flexibility and options of monitoring your deployment.

Maps

The Cisco WCS provides the ability for you to add maps and view your managed system on realistic campus, building, and floor maps. Additionally, you can enable location presences in the mobility server to provide expanded civic (city, state, postal code, country) and Geosynchronous Earth Orbit (GEO) (longitude, latitude) location information beyond the Cisco default setting (campus, building, floor, and X,Y coordinates). This information can then be requested by clients on a demand basis for use by location-based services and applications. See Figure 8-2 for an example map within WCS.

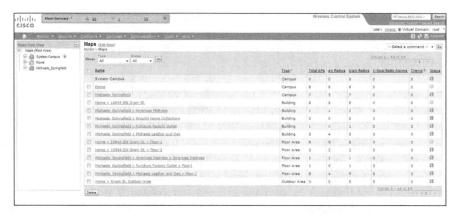

Figure 8-2   *WCS Maps*

Adding maps is so vital to the deployment of the WCS and a Unified Wireless Network because they provide a graphical representation of AP placement, heat maps of the coverage areas, and a visual representation of tracked clients, rogues, tags, and other 802.11 devices such as Bluetooth and other potential causes of interference.

The other key reason to add maps is that they can help in leveraging the planning and site survey tools to reduce deployment times as well as enhance troubleshooting, which you'll discover later in this chapter. The capability to add maps to WCS and then perform modeling scenarios with the built-in tools allows you to design and budget your deployment prior to purchasing additional hardware and software to perform site surveys and modeling. Note that site surveys are still recommended for voice and data deployments to ensure the best AP placement and coverage.

Adding maps to WCS is simple and straightforward. However, you will most likely spend a good deal of time configuring this correctly, so make sure that you allocate the time appropriately for this part of the setup process. Refer to the section "Adding and Using Maps" in Chapter 5 of the Wireless Control System Guide 7.0:

www.cisco.com/en/US/docs/wireless/wcs/7.0/configuration/guide/WCS70cg.html

Recall that the maps functionality in WCS is designed to give you a visual representation of the wireless network. WCS also provides monitoring capabilities for day-2 postimplementation support and provides tremendous value in the planning and site survey process.

You can access the maps from the **Monitor > Maps** menu option in the WCS, which in turn provides you with a list of all the campuses, buildings, and respective floors. Figure 8-3 shows a typical map that you would find in WCS.

The maps begin in the context of a campus. To create a new campus, use the drop-down menu from **Monitor > Maps** and select **New Campus**. Then click Go. This brings you to a page where you enter the campus name, contact, and browse to the image file. After the campus is created, it will appear in the list of map hierarchy. You can now add a building to the campus. However, buildings don't necessarily need to be added to a campus; they can be standalone buildings. Add a building by selecting **New Building** from the **Monitor > Maps** drop-down menu, as shown in Figure 8-4.

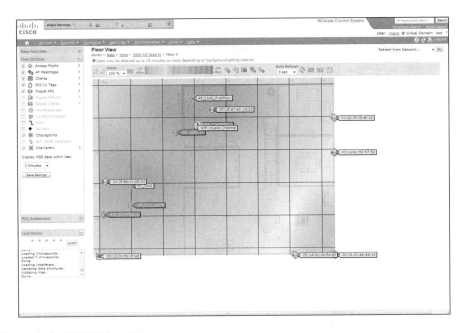

Figure 8-3   *WCS Floor Map*

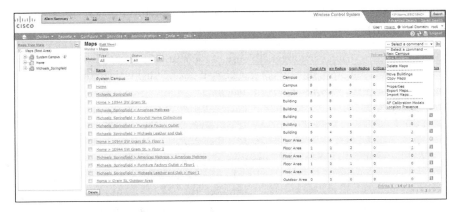

Figure 8-4   *WCS Adding a Building*

By selecting the drop-down menu from the **Monitor > Maps > Building** list, you can add a new floor area, which gives you a good view of the environment. This lets you add valuable information such as the floor type, height, and image file. Figure 8-5 provides a visual representation of floors already added to the building and the drop-down option to configure a new floor area. Once you have selected the new floor area option, you will notice that the floor type options include Cubes and Walled Offices, Drywall Office Only, and Outdoor Open Space. This is important because it assists WCS with RF modeling that you will do later.

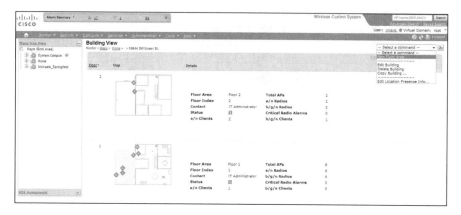

Figure 8-5   *WCS Adding a Floor Area*

After the floor area is created, you can add APs to the floor area. However, because no controller has been added to the WCS configuration, you will not be able to place APs on the floor. As you can tell, each element is layered on top of the prior, for example, **Campus > Building > Floor Area > AP**.

Using the map editor functionality, you have the ability to edit the map for walls, windows, and doors as well as provide additional attenuation or path loss values as a part of the RF predictive model. The key here is that radio waves impacted by walls, columns, shelves, and so on can cause the RF radiation patterns to be irregular and unpredictable, resulting in maps that are incorrect. The use of the heat map created by the RF prediction model helps improve display coverage based on an individual AP or a combination of APs. Figure 8-6 shows a sample of a heat map.

To better explain the difference between a site survey and the WCS RF prediction model, you first need to understand what a site survey is. A wireless site survey, sometimes called an RF site survey or wireless survey, is the process of planning and designing a wireless network, in particular an 802.11 Wi-Fi wireless network, to provide a wireless solution that will deliver the required wireless coverage, data rates, network capacity, roaming capability, and quality of service (QoS). The survey usually involves a site visit to run tests to determine the presence of RF interference and identify optimum installation locations for access points. This requires analysis of building floor plans, visual inspection of the facility, and usage of site survey tools. The WCS RF predictive modeling is simply that—a predictive model based on the map and map editor information that you defined earlier to pick the overall AP coverage in that environment. The WCS modeling can provide 80 to 90 percent accuracy in the overall AP placement based on both voice and data design and is often used by network administrators to formulate a suitable bill of materials.

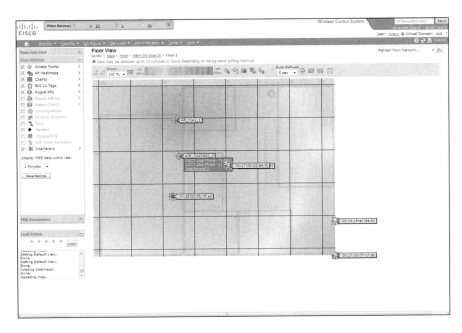

Figure 8-6 *Heat Maps in WCS*

Using the drop-down list or using the radial map editor button on the floor view you created, you can gain access to the map editor functionality. See Figure 8-7 for the drop-down option on a floor map.

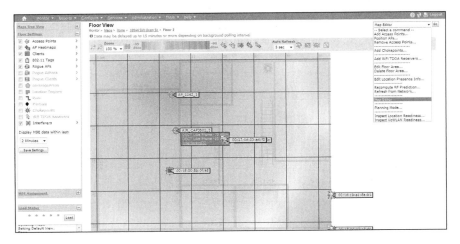

Figure 8-7 *Accessing Map Editor*

The Map Editor provides the ability to add a parameter or walls or other attenuation points on that floor. See Figure 8-8 for a view of perimeter functionality.

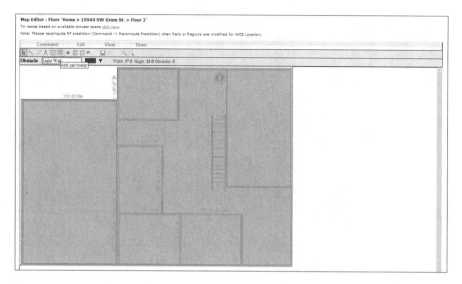

Figure 8-8   *Creating a Floor Perimeter Using the MAP Editor*

You have barely scratched the surface with maps, but for now, let's continue the discussion of the monitoring options within the WCS Monitoring heading. You will come back to maps after the discussion of the Configuration tab within WCS later in this chapter.

Controllers and AP Monitor

The Controllers and AP submenu of Monitor provides a detailed view into the health and configuration of your deployment. Within the Controllers submenu, you can see the list of controllers, names, IP addresses, code version, audit status, and so on. This simplified view allows you to see a snapshot of your controller deployment, as shown in Figure 8-9.

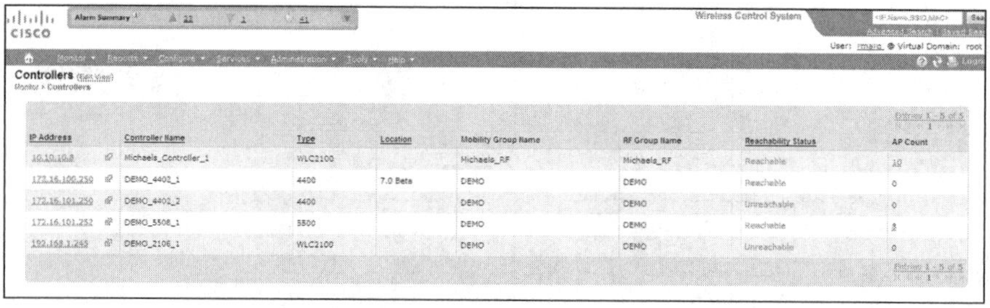

Figure 8-9   *Controller Monitoring*

Note   The WCS Monitor menu provides you with the ability to modify each submenu as you see fit. The flexibility to add and remove fields can simply the management of the system.

Built into the WCS is the ability to launch the controller directly from the Monitor page. You will notice an icon next to the IP address of each controller, and by clicking the controller web UI, you can launch into a separate browser session. Later in this chapter, you will learn how using controller templates can simplify the network deployment. However, if you are interested in making minimal modifications to the controller, this provides a simple launch pad from one central location.

Monitoring APs is critical to the overall health of the network. Being able to sort and identify the APs in your network and to seamlessly delve into the configuration and events of that AP is invaluable. The WCS allows you the flexibility of viewing operational status, client count, MAC address information, Cisco Discovery Protocol (CDP), channel, transmit power, and many more options to help in monitoring the network. From the moment you access the monitoring access point view, you can dive right into generating reports based on load, interference, VoIP call tables, and so on.

To monitor AP configuration, up/down status, model information, map location, and so on, you will use the Monitor Access Points submenu. As you can see from Figure 8-10, you get very important data about each AP in the network. You can also edit the view of this page to suit your business requirement or preference. The views that you define are used only during your login session and are saved to your login so that each time you come back, you get the same look and feel. Any administrator of the WCS will see his or her own view.

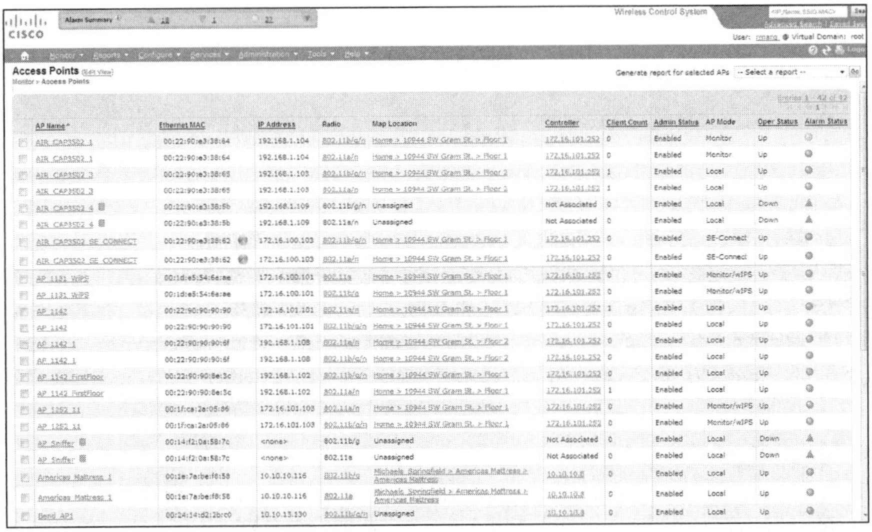

Figure 8-10 *AP Monitoring*

One of the key features of the Monitor Access Points submenu is being able to see detailed information about the specific radios and the health of each one. The system has the capability to classify interference sources with the Cisco 3500 CleanAir AP, and those interference devices will show up in graphical format. More importantly, the

Monitor Access Points submenu can provide radio statistics based on RF energy, Control and Provisioning of Wireless Access Points/Lightweight Access Point Protocol (CAP-WAP/LWAPP) uptimes, controller information, location, CDP neighbor information, and so on. As you have noticed, there is a great deal of information gathered that can help you make the appropriate adjustments in the network.

Figure 8-11 provides an example view of specific radio statistics.

Figure 8-11   *802.11b/g/n Radio Information*

Client Monitoring

The Monitor Clients option will provide you with better insight about the number of clients, the types of clients, session information, associated AP, client IP address, and so on. You have the flexibility of editing this view to match your needs and requirements. Looking at Figure 8-12, you will notice the vast client details as well as provided association history, map locations, and Received Signal Strength Indication (RSSI) and signal-to-noise ratio (SNR) data, giving you a one-stop shop for monitoring your clients. From this view, you can also get additional information about the client from the drop-down menu.

It's very important to be able to see client information in a concise, consolidated manner.

Figure 8-12   *Client Details*

You can look at the client's association history and statistical information in several ways on the Cisco WCS GUI. With WCS 7.0, you can view client session–related information and determine client presence, usage patterns, and historical session data. You can also use these tools to analyze and troubleshoot client issues. The information can be used in addition to maps to assess which areas experience inconsistent coverage and which areas have the potential to drop coverage.

One feature that will come in very handy is the built-in troubleshooting tool to help the Help desk or Network Operations Center (NOC) determine client connectivity issues. In the past, you might have had to walk or even fly to a location where a client is having troubleshooting issues. Leveraging the WCS Client Troubleshooting tool, as shown in Figure 8-13, you can add the MAC address of the client that is experiencing difficulties and run a series of tests to determine the problem.

Information such as failed association, failed authentication, and so on is provided in a graphical representation and in a workflow manner. If the client fails any step in the flow, the system will identify the probable cause of failure and allow you to streamline the next course of action.

Not limited to just monitoring clients, access points, and controllers, the WCS server provides an elegant and easy approach to detecting rogues, intrusion detection system/intrusion prevention system (IDS/IPS) attacks, and other malicious behaviors. You, the network administrator, need the capability to access a flexible and dynamic interface to manage malicious events and activities impacting your network. This is where the WCS also shines by providing over 100 severity alerts that can be categorized based on severity, alarm condition, and alarm category for determining attacks and events in your network, as illustrated in Figure 8-14.

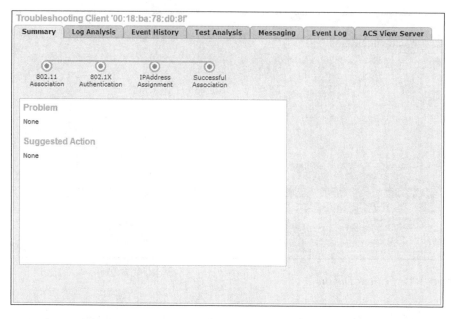

Figure 8-13 *Client Troubleshooting*

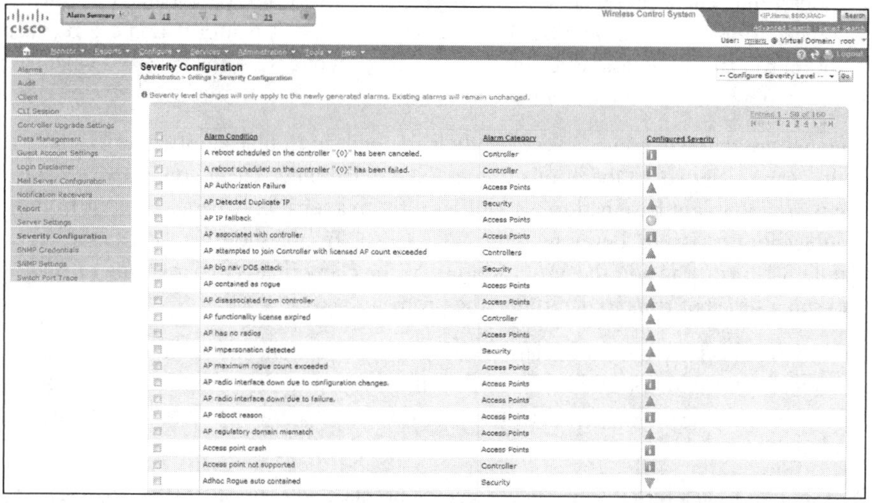

Figure 8-14 *Administrative Settings: Severity Configuration*

A part of the troubleshooting process is understanding what outside influences are causing your client issues. Malicious activities such as denial of service (DoS) attacks against the AP, against the infrastructure, or against the station; an 802.11 video camera occupying a particular channel; or even possibly a non-802.11 interfering source could be the source of client issues. Figure 8-15 shows an example view of the Security alarm page in action.

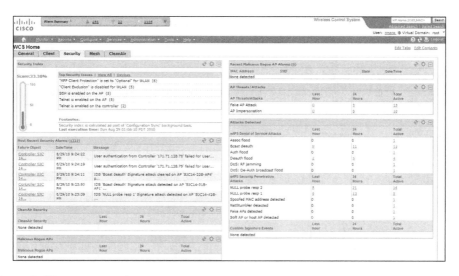

Figure 8-15 *Security Alarm Page*

WCS Reporting

You might have purchased the WCS because management has asked for reports on utilization of their investment. The WCS provides extensive customizable reports that allow you to monitor network activity; monitor system information including inventory, performance, security, access points, clients, radio utilization, 802.11 counters, RF management, and configuration history; and see granular, flexible reports. The WCS reporting functionality also offers the ability to generate reports and have them e-mailed on a set schedule and to the appropriate individuals. As of WCS version 6.0, Cisco introduced the Report Launch Pad, which provides a more granular, configurable, intuitive view. Figure 8-16 shows the WCS Report Launch Pad.

All reports can be saved and run at later dates or scheduled based on the needs of the organization. If your organization requires a Payment Card Industry (PCI) compliance report, the WCS has one prebuilt into the reporting tool. Looking deeper at the PCI reporting option, you'll notice that you will define a report title, indicate when you want the report to generate the information, and have the ability to schedule the report and e-mail or export and customize the report format, depending on the needed fields. Figures 8-17 and 8-18 show views of PCI report output.

A key takeaway of the PCI reporting functionality is the ability to determine whether you need to add a firewall, provide additional rogue detection and mitigation solutions, configure wireless IDS/IPS services, and determine whether you are in compliance.

There are many more customizable reports that can provide CEOs, CIOs, CFOs, and other key decision makers with valuable feedback on the health and utilization of the system. The reports also provide detailed information on the performance, components, security alarms, and threats, and each can be customized to meet the needs of the organization. After they are set, these reports can be pushed on demand or run as a part of a daily, weekly, or monthly schedule.

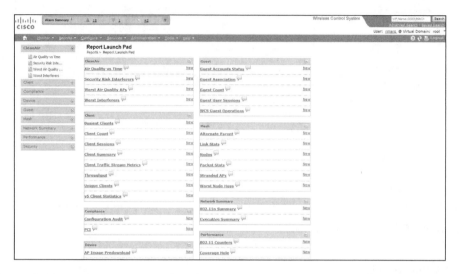

Figure 8-16 *WCS Report Launch Pad*

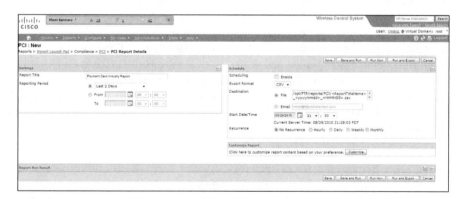

Figure 8-17 *PCI Report Configuration*

WCS Configuration

The WCS Configure menu provides network administrators and others with a central location to configure each device in your network through either a single change or through the Configuration Template Launch Pad, which can push hundreds of changes. Each mode has it benefits, and you will spend most of your time in this section covering the Controller Template Launch Pad.

At this point, however, you can't truly reap the key benefits and features of the WCS until you add a wireless LAN controller (WLC). One key reason for waiting to configure the WLC is to ensure that you understand the network management tool that will be used in postinstallation as well as the tool that will help in the overall predeployment. The controller is quite easy and straightforward because Cisco has provided a setup script to run through the basic installation.

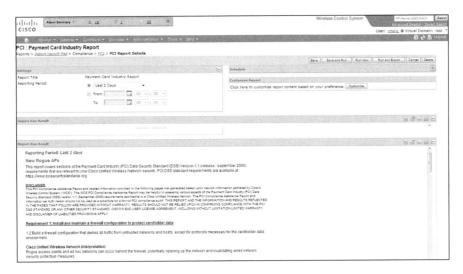

Figure 8-18 *PCI Report Output*

Three key fields that are required during the installation are as follows:

■ The configuration of the management interface, which is used to manage the controllers and is also as a part of the AP discovery process

■ The AP manager interface, which is used to terminate the LWAPP or CAPWAP tunnels in the controller

■ The virtual IP address that is used as part of the internal processes of the controller

Note The Cisco 5500 Series controller removed the requirement for the AP-Manager and, as such, the termination of the LWAPP or CAPWAP tunnels on that interface. The management interface now handles both the process of configuring and AP termination.

The other features and configurations of the WLC are out of the scope of this chapter. However, review the following links for definitions and configuration best practices for the controller, switches, and other network services:

■ **Cisco Enterprise Mobility Design Guide:** www.cisco.com/en/US/docs/solutions/Enterprise/Mobility/emob41dg/ch3_WLAN. html

■ **Wireless LAN Controller (WLC) Configuration Best Practices:**
www.cisco.com/en/US/tech/tk722/tk809/technologies_tech_note09186a0080810880.
shtml

■ **Cisco 4400 Series Wireless LAN Controllers (Configuration Examples and TechNotes):**
www.cisco.com/en/US/products/ps6366/prod_configuration_examples_list.html

After the basic configuration of the controller is done, you need to reboot the controller and then manage the controller through the built-in GUI or by adding it to the WCS to make your global configurations. Either method is approved. However, one step that you might find to be helpful is to configure the controller as a standalone controller with the appropriate gold-standard configurations. Such configurations include, but are not limited to, interfaces; WLANs (service set identifiers [SSID]); any QoS or security policies; any 802.11 wireless features such as transmit power control, dynamic channel assignment, or voice call admission control; and so on. The goal of this process is to generate a controller configuration that will be the gold standard for all controllers in your network based on the required applications and services. The only differences between the controllers will be based on templates generated for that specific site or location. This controller configuration will then be replicated across one, ten, or hundreds of controllers in your deployment.

Upon defining your global configuration in the standalone controller, add that controller to the WCS and use the discover templates from the Controller Command option on the **Configure > Controllers** menu. The goal here is to pull in that global configuration template defined earlier and apply it to future controllers added to WCS, once again assuring that you have consistent configurations across the network. Any APs that were actually joined to that controller will also be pulled in, and you will use the WCS Maps feature to place the respected floors in your design.

Now that the WLC has been added and you are starting to notice that WCS has considerable features and benefits to help deploy and manage your wireless network, you need to understand a key feature within the configuration menu—the Controller Template Launch Pad. There is no better way to manage a large or even small deployment than to leverage the WCS's controller and AP template's functionality. Continuing where you left off adding the controller to the network and pulling in the golden template, you will now take advantage of the WCS's controller template functionality.

Controller Configuration Templates

The WCS Launch Pad feature was introduced in version 6.0 and has been a time savior for many engineers like yourself. Reviewing the template options, there are numerous centralized options for configuring multiple controllers in your network, as well as multiple APs on those controllers. The recommended best practice after you've pulled in your golden configuration template is to rename those templates to a more meaningful option that others will be able to use as a part of a global configuration policy. You will use the general system template as the basis of your starting point. As you'll see in Figure 8-19, the general template name is not as obvious as you would like (Switching 21715 really means nothing to you as an administrator). If you change the name by selecting the field and deleting the entry, you can change the name to Gold Global Template, and that should allow you and others to understand the importance of this template, as shown in Figure 8-20.

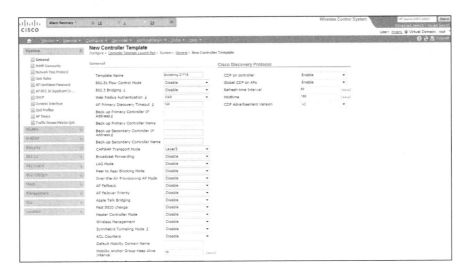

Figure 8-19 *General Template Configuration (Switching 21715)*

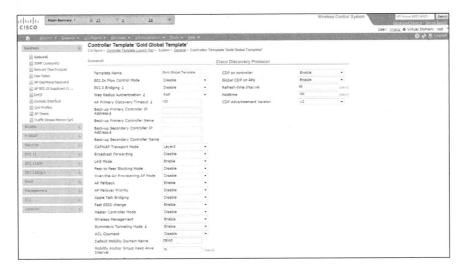

Figure 8-20 *Gold Global Template Configuration*

Note   The default length for renaming templates is 32 characters with release 7.0, including all letters, numbers, and spaces. Prior to the release of version 7.0, a maximum of 21 characters could be used.

At this point, you also configure any of the other general advanced features that you will want to apply across all controllers in your network, which might include, but is not limited to, mobility domain name, aggressive load balancing, wireless management, and so on. After all changes have been made, don't forget to click Save. After you feel comfortable with the template defined, you will select Apply to Controllers, and in your situation, you'll have one controller or maybe many controllers already defined. Figure 8-21 shows the controllers that you can choose from when applying the template.

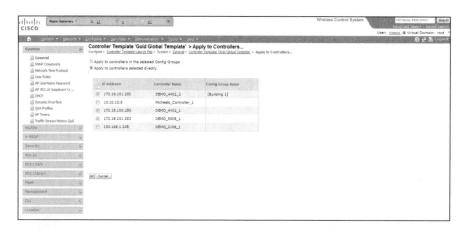

Figure 8-21   *Available Controllers*

In the preceding example, there is only one controller. However, you are probably reading this book to better understand best practices for many controllers and leveraging WCS to manage them. If you already installed a WCS infrastructure and controllers, don't worry, because the WCS template options will still help you simplify and manage your overall deployment.

The key here is that if you have controllers already defined in the WCS, you can leverage the discover templates from the controller option to generate a global golden configuration. After you discover that template and modify the name and settings, you can apply that template to all controllers in your network.

After you have completed the discover template task and applied the appropriate changes, apply the new templates to the WLCs.

WLAN Template

A template you will commonly use in WCS is the WLAN template. You will use this template often in part because WLANs are the cornerstone of your deployment and provide the connectivity to the network. You will be required to change, add, or delete WLANs based on the application needs of your organization. Refer to Figure 8-22 for an example of this template. It is within the WLAN template that you can define whether you have multiple client authentication types (for example, Wi-Fi Protected Access/Temporal Key Integrity Protocol [WPA/TKIP] or WPAv2/Advanced Encryption Standard [WPAv2/AES]) as well as define security, QoS, and advanced features. The key to this template is that if you have multiple controllers in your network and you were to configure each individual controller's WLANs, you might end up making a configuration mistake that will prevent clients from seamlessly roaming or being able to visit another site and seamlessly connecting. The WCS template prevents that problem by ensuring that all controllers have the same configuration, ensuring that mobility and site-to-site travel work seamlessly for the end user.

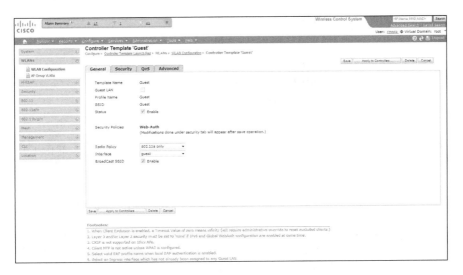

Figure 8-22   *WLAN Template*

802.11a/n and 802.11b/g/n Template

Another template that is often modified is the 802.11a/n and/or the 802.11b/g/n controller template, as illustrated in Figure 8-23. These templates are often modified in part because of the applications running in the network. You might want to disable certain data rates because of AP placement or application requirements, or change various thresholds and parameters based on other application characteristics. Imagine how long it would take without the WCS templates to configure thousands of access points individually or even scripting configuration management and the challenges of applying that across many APs. The WCS templates allow you the flexibility to make these configurations consistently, easily, and at any time.

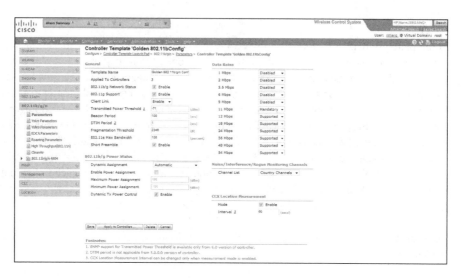

Figure 8-23   *802.11b/g/n Global Template*

WCS Configuration and Template Auditing

Since the release of WCS 6.0, Cisco has offered an adaptive interface to the Controller Template Launch Pad as well as access point launch pads to simplify the overall deployment and configuration of the controllers and access points in your network. It is these modifications and improvements that will allow you to work on other activities besides hand-holding your wireless network deployment. The adaptability of WCS also provides an intuitive interface for monitoring and troubleshooting your network when needed, as in the monitoring of controllers, APs, and clients.

You now know how to use the WCS as a configuration and monitoring tool; however, what about the changes that you have made? How do you know that those changes have been applied to the controller or better yet applied to all controllers? How do you know whether another coworker has made modifications to the controller, not through WCS, and now the template doesn't match? The Cisco WCS has a key feature called *controller auditing* to track those changes and to be very granular (down to a specific setting on an SSID, for example). The goal is to ensure that the controllers are consistent and synchronized with each other as well as the WCS. How many times have you configured something, only to find that it has been modified and you have no trail or you lost the baseline configuration?

You have probably stopped and started making changes to your network already after reading through eight chapters of this book, but it is imperative that you spend time on this section and understand how auditing works. As shown in Figure 8-24, you will notice a column for controller audits that you will learn more about in a moment. The takeaway here is that if the audit status fails to say Identical, you need to determine why.

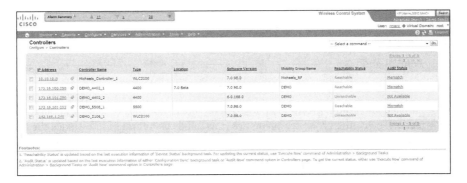

Figure 8-24 *Controller Configuration Audit*

Delving into the auditing functions of the WCS management tool, on the **Administration > Settings > Audit** submenu, as shown in Figure 8-25, you will notice that two auditing options are defined in WCS:

■ **Basic Audit:** Audits the configuration objects in the WCS database against current WLC device values

■ **Template Based Audit:** Audits on the applied templates, config group templates (which have been selected for the background audit), and configuration audits (for which corresponding templates do not exist) against current WLC device values

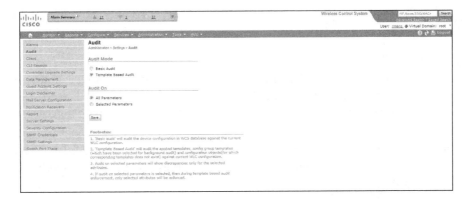

Figure 8-25 *WCS Audit Options*

A configuration audit includes the following sections: Audit Summary, Applied Templates and Config Group Template Discrepancies, Enforced Values, Failed Enforcements, and WCS Config Discrepancies. After an audit is performed, a report will be generated with the following pieces of information if any part of the policy fails.

The audit report displays the following:

- **Device name**

- **Time of audit**

- **Audit status**

- **Applied and config group template discrepancies:** Occur because of applied templates. The config group templates are listed, and the information includes the following:

  - Template type (template name)

  - Template application method

  - Audit status (such as mismatch, identical)

  - Template attribute

  - Value in WCS

  - Value in controller

- **Config WCS discrepancies:** Occur because of configuration objects in the WCS database. The current WLC configuration is listed, and the information includes the following:

  - Configuration type (name)

  - Audit status (for example, mismatch, identical)

  - Attribute

  - Value in WCS

  - Value in controller

- **Total enforcements for config groups with background audit enabled:** If discrepancies are found during the audit in regard to the config groups enabled for background audit and if the enforcement is enabled, this section lists the enforcements made during the controller audit.

- **Failed enforcements for config groups with background audit enabled:** Click the link to view a list of failure details (including the reason for the failure) returned by the device.

Note   The following sections are displayed if the audit selected is a template-based audit:

- Applied and config group template discrepancies

- Total enforcements for config groups with background audit enabled

- Failed enforcements for config groups with background audit enabled

- Config WCS discrepancies

The Config WCS discrepancies section is displayed if the audit is selected to be a basic audit.

■ **Restore WCS Values to Controller** or **Refresh Config from Controller:** If the audit reveals configuration differences, you can either restore WCS values on the controller or refresh controller values. Choose Restore WCS Values to Controller or Refresh Config from Controller.

If you choose Restore WCS Values to Controller, all the WCS values are enforced on the controller in an attempt to resolve the discrepancies on the device. All the applied templates and the templates that are part of the config group are applied to this controller (for a template-based audit). If the audit is a basic audit, the configuration objects in the WCS database are enforced on the controller.

If you choose Refresh Config from Controller, a Refresh Config page opens and shows the following message: "Configuration is present on WCS but not on device, do you want to:" Choose one of the following options, and click Go to confirm your selection.

You should choose Refresh Config from Controller after an upgrade of software to ensure that the AP timer's configuration is visible.

■ **Retain:** The WCS refreshes the configuration from the controller but will not delete any devices or configurations that no longer exist in the controller configuration. For example, if the WCS database shows an AP1, but that access point is no longer present in the controller configuration, the WCS will not delete AP1 from its database.

■ **Delete:** The WCS deletes the configuration of the controller from its database and retrieves a new configuration from the controller. Delete is the recommended option so that the WCS matches the most recent configuration you are refreshing from the WLC.

Note   On the Refresh Config page, only the configuration objects for this controller in the WCS database are updated. Upon refresh, the WCS templates are not updated.

The text that follows provides a walk-through example of the auditing process for a controller that indicates a mismatch under the audit status, as shown in Figures 8-26 through 8-28. At the end of the audit process, you will be asked to either retain the values in the WCS or use the configuration on the controller. In the example, you will select the **Use the configuration on the controller currently** radio button, and then choose the appropriate option to either delete or retain the template association. It is important to understand the distinction of both, so be sure to review the previous notes before making your decision. In your example, you are going to retain template association for this controller and click Go. The controller will state that there is an audit mismatch because the audit is against the templates and not the base configuration. If you want the audit value to be identical, change the audit option under **Administration > Settings > Audit** to Basic Audit and perform the audit steps.

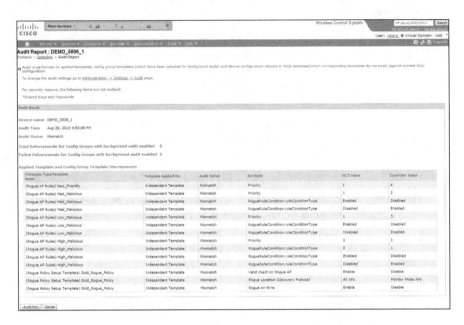

Figure 8-26   *Preaudit Report*

On the **Configure > Controllers** menu, there is also a Config Group submenu, and you should become familiar with the options because you can apply templates and perform audits seamlessly across controllers that have the same configuration. (An example would be a WLC providing the same services to the same location and providing redundancy to another set of WLCs.)

AP Configuration Templates

Imagine if you were running autonomous mode APs and you didn't have the wireless LAN solutions engine or you hadn't scripted configuration management. Was that a groan? Anyone that has deployed APs prior to the centralized WLC model has been down this rocky road. If the tools you had in-house didn't work, you had to purchase new ones, and oftentimes those tools didn't provide for all your needs.

Since the first release of a Cisco-branded WCS over five years ago, Cisco has continued to innovate and improve both WLC management and AP management. We briefly covered the controller management flexibility of the tool earlier; however, what is just as useful are the AP management tools.

Figure 8-27 *Postaudit Report*

Figure 8-28 *Refresh Config Options from Postaudit Report*

Imagine that you have a few hundred lightweight access points deployed as Hybrid Remote Edge Access Points (HREAP) and you need to modify the HREAP VLAN mappings. You can surely do this through the controller and touch every AP, or you can define an AP template, make the appropriate modifications, and push the template to the APs that needed the change. Instead of touching each one and wasting valuable time, the WCS allowed you to change all values in one spot and push out to all APs at once. Figures 8-29 through 8-31 step through the process of modifying settings for a group of access points, selecting the APs, and applying the template.

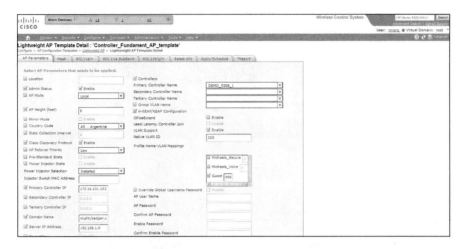

Figure 8-29 *Modifying AP Settings*

Figure 8-30 *Selecting APs*

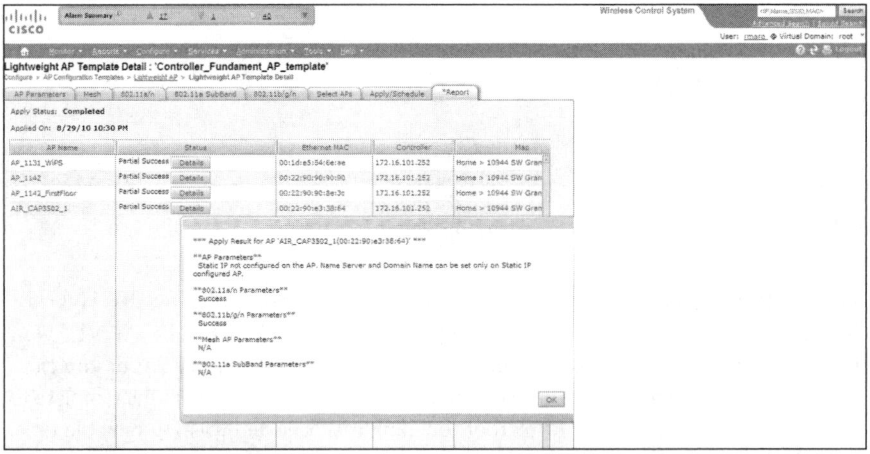

Figure 8-31 *Applying Template*

There are many key submenus of the Configure menu that you should familiarize your-self with including, but not limited to, the scheduling of tasks, wIPS profiles, and so on. For further information on these features and how to configure each option, refer to the URLs provided earlier that cover Enterprise Mobility 4.1 Designs and the Cisco WCS 7.0 Configuration Guide.

WCS Services

A key component to the overall Cisco Unified Wireless Network is the mobility services engine (MSE). This section will briefly describe the Context Aware Services (CAS) and wIPS services that the Cisco WCS supports.

Note   Starting with MSE Release 6.0, you can enable multiple services (Context Aware and wIPS) to run concurrently. Prior to version 6.0, mobility services engines could only support one active service at a time.

You will use the WCS Services menu to add/delete/upgrade/configure the MSE or the 2710 location engine. There are many key features of the MSE; however, a few that should be noted are as follows:

■   Provides longer historical reporting

■   Provides context aware client and tag tracking configuration and management

■   Provides advanced wIPS configuration and management

■   Provides third-party API/SOAP/XML integration

The two key features currently supported on the MSE are as follows:

■   **Context Aware Services (CAS):** Allows a mobility services engine to simultaneously track thousands of mobile assets and clients by retrieving contextual information such as location, temperature, and availability from Cisco access points.

■   **Cisco Adaptive Wireless IPS (wIPS):** An advanced approach to wireless threat detec-tion and performance management. Cisco Adaptive wIPS combines network traffic analysis, network device and topology information, signature-based techniques, and anomaly detection to deliver highly accurate and complete wireless threat prevention.

For the features to work, the MSE needs to be added to the WCS. After adding an MSE to the Cisco WCS, you can synchronize network designs (campus, building, floor, and outdoor maps), controllers (name and IP address), specific Catalyst Series 3000 and 4000 switches, and event groups with the MSE. The list that follows describes these capabilities:

■ **Network design:** A logical mapping of the physical placement of access points throughout facilities. A hierarchy of a single campus, the buildings that comprise that campus, and the floors of each building constitute a single network design.

■ **Controller:** A selected controller that is associated and regularly exchanges location information with a mobility services engine. Regular synchronization ensures location accuracy.

■ **Switches (wired):** Wired Catalyst switches that provide an interface to wired clients on the network. Regular synchronization ensures that location tracking of wired clients in the network is accurate.

  ■ The mobility services engine can be synchronized with Catalyst stackable switches (3750, 3750-E, 3560, 2960, IE-3000 switches), switch blades (3110, 3120, 3130, 3040, 3030, 3020), and switch ports.

  ■ The mobility services engine can also be synchronized with the following Catalyst 4000 series: WS-C4948, WS-C4948-10GE, ME-4924-10GE, WS-4928-10GE, WS-C4900M, WS-X4515, WS-X4516, WS-X4013+, WS-X4013+TS, WS-X4516-10GE, WS-X4013+10GE, WS-X45-SUP6-E, and WS-X45-SUP6-LE.

■ **Event groups:** A group of predefined events that define triggers that generate an event. Regular synchronization ensures that the latest defined events are tracked.

Note   Network Time Protocol (NTP) is mandatory in the Cisco Unified Wireless Network. NTP ensures that time is synchronized among the WCS, controller, APs, and MSE, making sure that events, trusted or not trusted, are provided in real time and updated accordingly.

Refer to the following references for additional CAS and wIPS configuration and management details:

■ **Cisco Context Aware Services Configuration Guide Release 7.0:** www.cisco.com/en/US/docs/wireless/mse/3350/7.0/CAS/configuration/guide/CAS_70.html

■ **Cisco Adaptive Wireless Intrusion Prevention System, Configuration Guide Release 7.0:** www.cisco.com/en/US/docs/wireless/mse/3350/7.0/wIPS/configuration/guide/wips_70.html

WCS Administration

The Administration menu provides granular control for background tasks; authentication, authorization, and accounting (AAA) services; auditing; virtual domains; logging; and so on. As Figure 8-32 illustrates, under Administration, there are just a few submenus; however, under those submenus you will uncover the vast options available to you to ensure that the WCS is performing as intended.

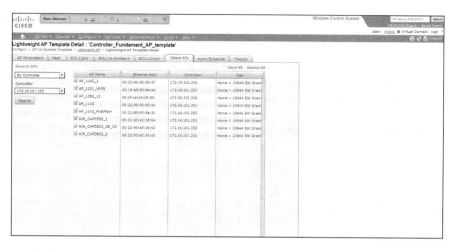

Figure 8-32 *Administration Options*

Administration is critical to the control and provision of services within the WCS and what allows you to configure role-based access control, add appropriate licenses, and provide logical portioning through virtual domains. The following sections will highlight three key features, and after completing this chapter, you should be well on your way to designing a robust, secure, and scalable network.

Three key areas covered under WCS administration are as follows:

- **Role-based access control:** Provides granular access to WCS management based on authorized access through AAA or built-in roles

- **Virtual domains:** Provide logical partitioning of devices, maps, and role-based access control

- **Licensing:** Provides interface to license AP quantities, CAS, and wIPS services

Role-Based Access Control (RBAC)

RBAC determines whether you can be granted a specific type of access to a resource. In an RBAC system, you are granted or denied access to a device or service based on the role that you have as part of an organization. You can assign and are assigned roles and access rights that are defined in an organizational structure. Privileges or access rights are then associated with these roles based on the tasks that you assign to a user in that position. In this case, you can define a user policy that allows full access to the Monitor menu while denying access to the Configure and Administration menus. By leveraging Cisco ACS or a third-party RADIUS server, you can tie your RBAC policies to your active directory users in the organization, which helps to reduce the operational costs and operational errors. Most organizations already perform this activity for access to network and security resources to main tight control on the configurations and log who makes changes.

To implement RBAC, you only need to have a RADIUS or TACACS+ server (Cisco ACS 4.2, in this case) and a good understanding of the groups to which you are going to assign policies. The task for which a user is entitled is configured in the TACACS+ (ACS) server using the custom Attribute-Value (AV) pairs. The user can be authorized for one or multiple tasks. The minimum authorization is MONITOR only, and the maximum is ALL (authorized to perform all seven tabs). If a user is not entitled for a particular task within the WCS, a corresponding Permission Denied message will be presented. If authentication is enabled and the authentication server becomes unreachable or unable to authorize, the user will only be allowed access if the corresponding Enable Fallback on Local option is selected in the AAA mode submenu of the Administration menu.

Note   WCS RBAC is supported through third-party RADIUS solutions; however, those solutions will not be covered in this section.

Note   Authentication can be performed using a local database, RADIUS, or TACACS+ server that uses a username and a password. The implementation is not fully modular. Authentication and authorization services are tied to each other. For example, if authentication is performed using RADIUS/local database, authorization is not performed with TACACS+. It would use the permissions associated for the user in the local or RADIUS database, such as read-only or read-write, whereas when authentication is performed with TACACS+, authorization is tied to TACACS+.

In Figure 8-33, you will notice the fixed as well as customizable AAA groups for access to the WCS. Each respective group has a specific set of tasks that the group can perform, and you will use this information as you set up your RBAC.

The text that follows walks you through an example of setting up RBAC for a Help desk team. It is essential that the Help desk gain access to the Monitor and Reporting menus to perform day-2 support.

You will need to define, add, and modify the following attributes in the WCS with root access for this to work properly:

■   RADIUS or TACACS+ server

■   AAA group tasks list

In this example, you will use the Cisco Access Control Server (ACS) to perform TACACS+ authentication and provide the authorization level for the group by defining the appropriate AV-Pair that maps to the AAA group task list.

You add the TACACS+ server from the **Administration > AAA > TACACS+ > TACACS+ Server Detail** subconfiguration menu. Figure 8-34 shows the configuration of the TACACS+ server.

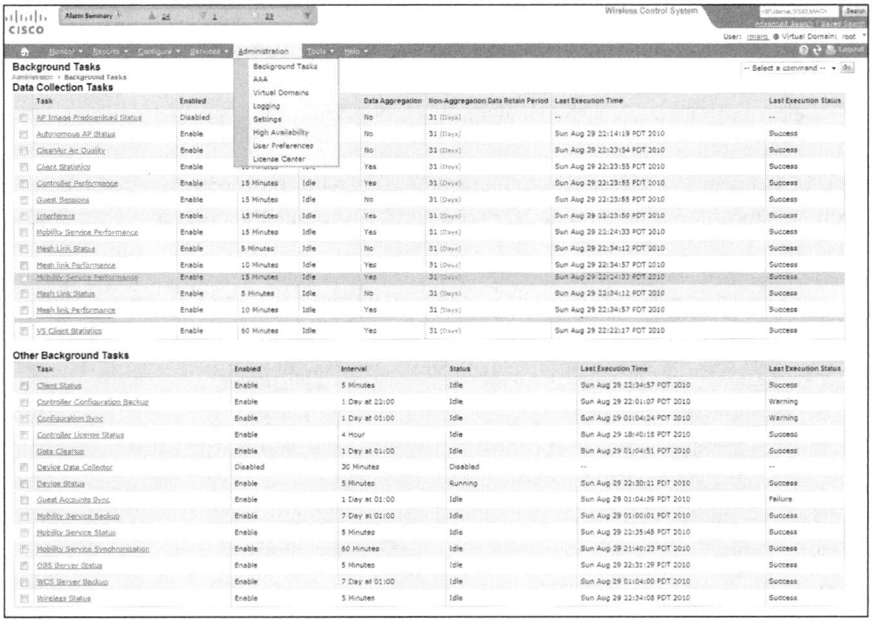

Figure 8-33 *AAA Roles*

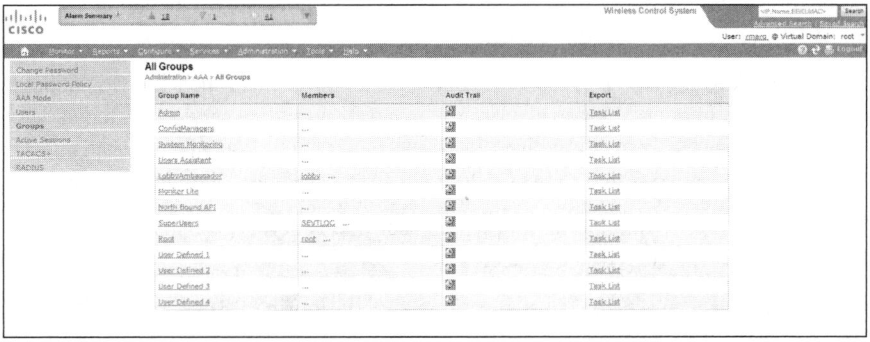

Figure 8-34 *TACACS+ Server*

After the TACACS+ server is defined in the WCS, you need to ensure that the AAA mode is set to TACACS+ and that Fallback on Local is selected.

Now proceed to configure the ACS server for the attributes to allow AAA to work. You need to add the WCS server's IP address and secret key and modify the Authenticate Using field to be TACACS+ (Cisco IOS). After the WCS server is added, navigate to **Interface Configuration** > **TACACS+(Cisco)** and add the following new service:

- Service = Wireless-WCS

- Protocol = HTTP (Note: Protocol field is case sensitive.)

- Select both User and Group and apply the configuration

At this point, the WCS has been added to the ACS with the appropriate communication protocols to process login requests. Figure 8-35 represents the properly configured attributes.

Figure 8-35   *ACS Interface Configuration*

You will now utilize either a defined user or group within the ACS to map the appropriate Help desk controls. Go back to the WCS server and use the System Monitoring AAA group to export the task list. Select the task list to see the list of TACACS+ and radius custom attributes, and copy all entries under the TACACS+ Attribute list, as noted in Figure 8-36.

Now go back to the ACS server and select the group or user to which you would like to apply the system monitoring attributes. You will notice that the service created earlier now shows up under the Custom Attribute field, and this is where you will copy the information selected in the previous step to the Custom Attributes field, as shown in Figure 8-37.

Log out of the WCS and log back in with a user that is in this group, and you will notice the menus that the Help desk has access to.

For details on the exact step-by-step process for configuring RBAC on the WLC and WCS, refer to the document Cisco Unified Wireless Network TACACS+, located at the following link:

> www.cisco.com/en/US/tech/tk722/tk809/technologies_tech_note09186a0080851f7c.shtml

WCS Virtual Domains

Virtual Domain is a new feature introduced with WCS version 5.1. A WCS virtual domain consists of a set of devices and maps and restricts a user's view to information relevant to these devices and maps. Through a virtual domain, you can ensure that users can only view the devices and maps for which they are responsible. In addition, because of the virtual domain's filters, users can configure, view alarms, and generate reports for only their assigned part of the network. You will specify a set of allowed virtual domains for each user. Only one of these can be active for that user at login. The user can change the current virtual domain by selecting a different allowed virtual domain from the Virtual Domain drop-down menu at the top of the screen. All reports, alarms, and other functionality are now filtered by that virtual domain.

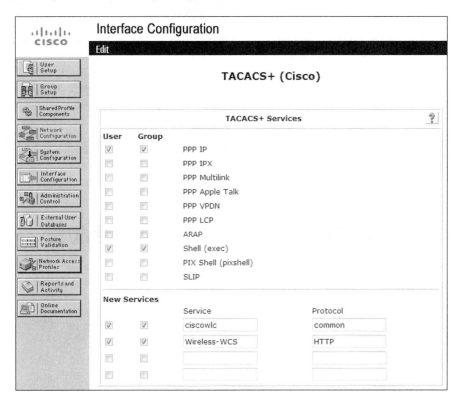

Figure 8-36   *WCS System Monitoring TACACS+ Custom Attribute List*

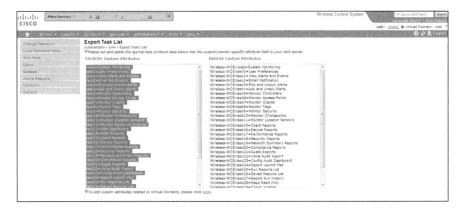

Figure 8-37   *ACS User/Group Custom Attributes*

If there is only one virtual domain defined (root) in the system and the user does not have any virtual domains in the custom attributes fields in the TACACS+/RADIUS server, the user is assigned the root virtual domain by default.

If there is more than one virtual domain, and the user does not have any specified attributes, the user is blocked from logging in. To allow the user to log in, the virtual domain custom attributes must be exported to the RADIUS/TACACS+ server.

The Virtual Domain Custom Attributes window allows you to indicate the appropriate protocol-specific data for each virtual domain. The Export button on the Virtual Domain Hierarchy sidebar preformats the virtual domain's RADIUS and TACACS+ attributes. You can copy and paste these attributes into the ACS server. This allows you to copy only the applicable virtual domains to the ACS server and ensures that the users only have access to these virtual domains.

Figure 8-38 shows the export output for the virtual domain attributes for a user logged in with root access.

Figure 8-38   *Root-Level Virtual Domain Attributes*

You will notice that the root user has the ability modify the following attributes:

- **Maps:** View maps
- **Controllers:** View controllers
- **Access points:** View APs

- **Controller Template Launch Pad:** View controller templates

- **Config groups:** View config groups

- **Access point templates:** View AP templates

Under each respective tab, you will see the maps, WLCs, and access points that the root user has access to. Let's walk through an example of a Help desk user having access to only a specific set of maps, WLCs, and access points. The reason for this type of example is that you might be a global organization and you have partitioned your maps, WLCs, and access points for specific areas around the globe. No need for a Help desk user to view devices in Europe if he is only responsible for helping users in North America.

First you need to define a virtual domain under the **Administration > Virtual Domains** submenu; you will use NorthAmerica as the name. You will now notice that under each tab for that virtual domain, all maps, WLCs, and access points are available for that new virtual group.

At this point, you will select the appropriate maps, WLCs, and access points the virtual domain will have access to, and in the example, you will choose Home for the maps, DEMO_5508_1 for the WLC, and the following APs (AIR_CAP3502_1, AIR_CAP3502_3, and AIR_CAP3502_SE_CONNECT). Figures 8-39 through 8-41 show the graphical view of the NorthAmerica virtual domain selections as previously listed.

After you complete those steps, you will need to export the TACACS+ virtual domain

Figure 8-39 *Maps for Virtual Domain NorthAmerica*

attributes from the Export option. You will select only virtual-domain1=NorthAmerica and copy that value to the ACS Help desk group created earlier. See Figure 8-42 for the new attributes values in the ACS.

Now that you have defined the virtual domain, submitted the changes, and completed the tasks for WCS RBAC, log out of WCS and log back in with user Help desk defined in the ACS Help desk group.

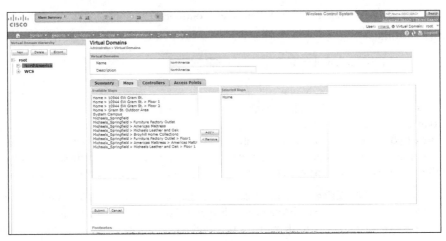

Figure 8-40 *WLCs for Virtual Domain NorthAmerica*

Figure 8-41 *Access Points for Virtual Domain NorthAmerica*

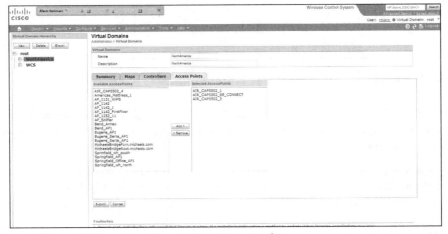

Figure 8-42 *ACS Help Desk Group TACACS+ Attributes*

Based on the custom attributes assigned earlier and the addition of the virtual domain NorthAmerica, you will have access to the Monitor and Reports menus, and you only have access to the maps, WLCs, and access points based on the NorthAmerica attributes. You will also notice that when you select one of the other WCS menus, a warning appears stating that you don't have privileges for the requested operation. Figures 8-43 Figure 8-45 show the screens that the Help desk group will see when they log in. The Help desk user will have access to the Monitor and Reporting menus based on the RBAC policy and will get a Permission Denied message for selecting any other menu.

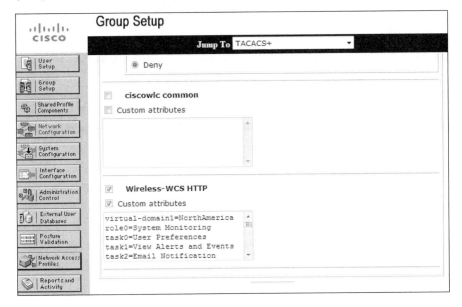

Figure 8-43   *Monitor Menu Allowed for Virtual Domain NorthAmerica*

As you can see, the Virtual Domain feature provides organizations with the flexibility to

- Define the areas of the wireless network that individual IT administrators (users) can manage

- Customize virtual domain names by geographical regions, customer names, building, campus, or other customized parameters to meet each organization's individual needs

- Create up to 128 distinct hierarchical virtual domains

- Maintain tight control of the wireless network infrastructure that is managed by each IT administrator

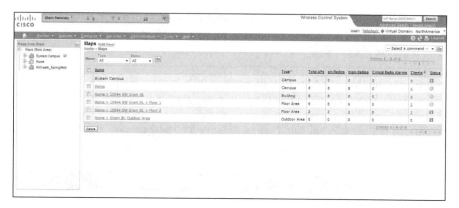

Figure 8-44 *Reporting Menu Allowed for Virtual Domain NorthAmerica*

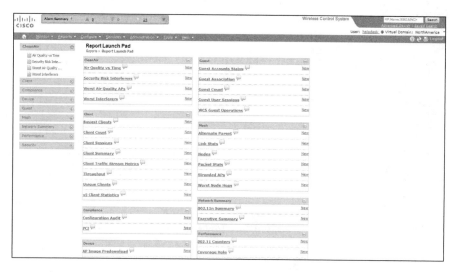

Figure 8-45 *Configure Menu Permission Denied for Virtual Domain NorthAmerica*

Cisco WCS virtual domains also deliver the following benefits:

- Enhanced access control that allows organizations to limit an individual IT administrator's access to only those wireless network segments that are under the IT administrator's individual responsibility.

- Reduced operational costs through the use of a single, centralized Cisco WCS platform to support multiple IT administrators, each of whom has access to only those domains to which they have been assigned.

- Operational cost savings through error reductions because each IT administrator can only make changes to the areas assigned to him or her.

■ Improved productivity because each IT administrator is notified about only the alerts and alarms within his assigned virtual domains.

■ Scalable, simplified WLAN management of all local, remote, and worldwide locations from an easily accessible, centralized management console.

■ Managed service providers can easily manage multiple customer WLANs from a single Cisco WCS platform.

WCS License Center

At this point, you should have realized the tremendous benefits that the WCS and the Cisco Unified Wireless Network approach provides you. You have successfully installed the WCS, but you might have realized the alert that your WCS server is not licensed.

Note   Until you license WCS, you will continue to receive an error that you have exceeded the AP count limit or that you do not have a valid WCS license.

Note that licensing screens have changed with WCS version 6.0 and later. Under the WCS Administration heading, there is a License Center option to license the Context Aware Services for the mobility service engine, WCS, and wIPS services. When licensing the services in WCS, it is important to provide the correct host name because the WCS license is tied to the server host name. Failure to provide the accurate host name will result in the WCS not recognizing the license.

Note   Go to https://tools.cisco.com/SWIFT/Licensing/PrivateRegistrationServlet to generate the license file for each of the services based on the Product Activation Key (PAK) key providing during the purchase.

Figure 8-46 shows the License Center and the appropriate licenses that have been applied.

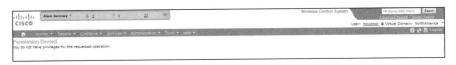

Figure 8-46   *WCS License Center*

Additional Benefits of WCS: Planning and Calibration Tools

You have completed the basic necessary configurations in the WCS to allow the additional tools to be utilized. The sections that follow take a peek into the planning, calibration, and survey tools within WCS.

WCS Planning

Earlier you defined your maps as well as utilized the map editor functionality defining the perimeter, walls, windows, and obstacles. You'll now begin to use the planning tool to formulate an overall AP placement and design. The WCS Planning mode helps you determine how many APs are needed for a given coverage area based on key criteria such as voice, location, or 802.11n coverage. Based on the map editor values, APs are dynamically placed on the map, providing a hypothetical AP deployment.

From the Floor Maps view on the **Monitor > Maps** menu, you can select the planning tool shortcut. See Figure 8-47 for a visual representation of the shortcut.

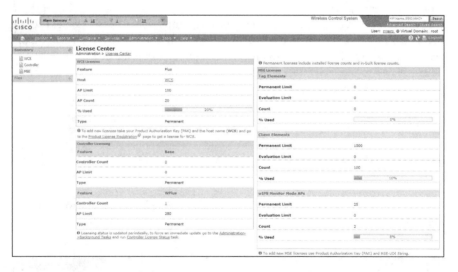

Figure 8-47 *Planning Tool Shortcut Icon*

After you've opened the planning tool, click the Add APs option to view the AP planning mode option for adding APs. You will notice a new set of configurable values such as AP name, AP type, and antenna options and services. Select the parameters that you would like to model for your deployment, and also select the perimeter placement at the top of the screen. You will want to choose Perimeter from the map editor modification performed earlier because this will give you the best overall coverage model for that floor. After selecting the AP type and service, you can calculate the number of recommended AP counts based on the services selected (data, voice, and location-based services) by selecting the Calculate radio button. Figures 8-48 and 8-49 show a configuration example for an 802.11n, voice, and location-based design before and after.

Figure 8-48 *Configuration Example in Planning Mode*

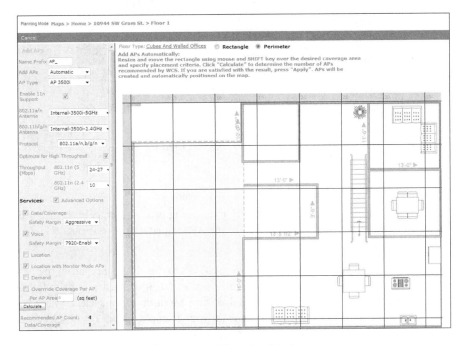

Figure 8-49 *Resulting AP Placement in Planning Mode*

You'll notice that it appears that you have quite a few APs for such a small area, but one of the criteria was that you wanted location-based services, which necessitates APs placed in the perimeter of the floor plan supplied. At this point, you can generate a proposal choosing both 802.11a/n and 802.11b/g/n radios that can be provided as a basis for your deployment. This creates the proposal shown in Figure 8-50.

Once again, remember that this is simply a proposal or predictive model for AP placement, and after you have actually configured the wireless LAN controller, added it to the WCS server, and placed APs accordingly, you or a qualified partner might need to perform an on-site survey with a third-party tool to ensure that coverage is met based on the applications.

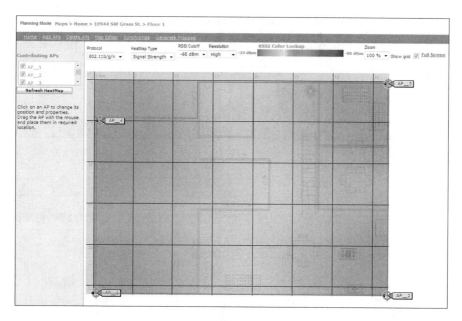

Figure 8-50   *Generated WLAN Proposal for the Specified Floor Plan*

WCS Calibration

To better understand what the RF calibration modeling provides, start by configuring a primary controller that will be the basis for the AP templates and controller templates in the WCS.

You defined your maps, added the controller and APs to the WCS, and placed the APs on the respective map, and you are now ready to leverage the other predeployment functionalities of the WCS server. Revisiting the global maps Monitor option, select a floor by selecting the check box in front of the name (in your example, Floor_1) and select the RF Calibration Models option, as illustrated in Figure 8-51.

It is within this RF Calibration Models option that you can choose from three predefined autocreated models, or you can create your own based on data points taken. You will now add your own calibration model and provide a name. In the example, you will add WCS fundamental calibration and then select the model to begin the process of calibrating. See Figure 8-52 for information on the new model created.

Notice from the drop-down menu on the right side the options that can be performed; choose Add Data Points, as shown in Figure 8-53, to continue the calibration.

Note   For the calibration tool to work properly, your device (laptop, handheld device, and so on) needs to be seen by at least one of the APs in the network.

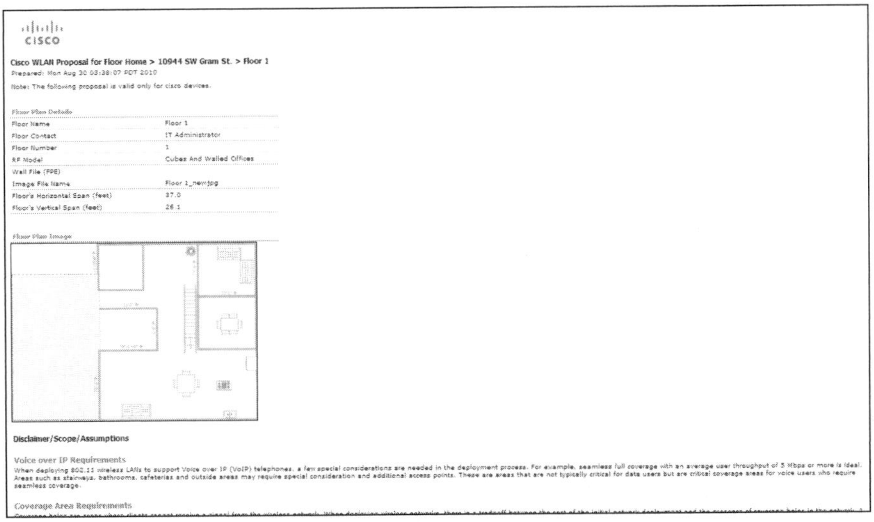

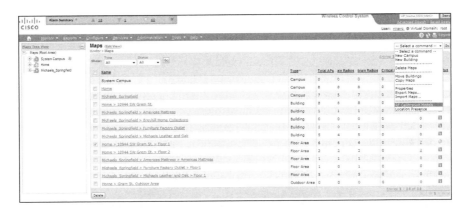

Figure 8-51   *Calibration Models Option*

Figure 8-52   *WCS Fundamental Calibration Properties*

In the next task, you will be asked to select what campus, building, and floor area you want to calibrate. In this example, as shown in Figure 8-54, you will choose the Home campus, the building 10944 SW Gram St, and the floor Floor_1 to begin gathering the data points. Click Next to continue.

Note   For calibration, automatic power assignment should be turned off. This can be done by making sure that the Tx Power assignment mode for the Radios (802.11a/n and 802.11b/g/n) on the selected floor is set to Custom *or* the controllers' Dynamic Power Assignment is set to Disable. After you complete the calibration, you can turn on the automatic power assignment.

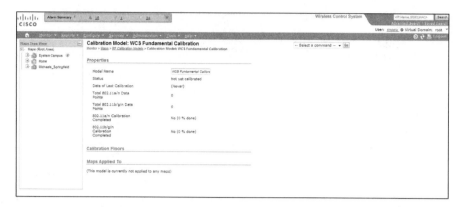

Figure 8-53   *WCS Fundamental Calibration Add Data Points*

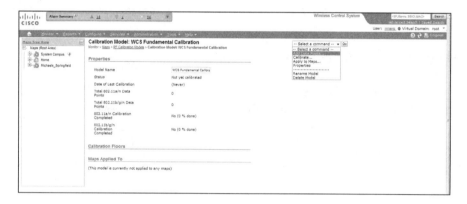

Figure 8-54   *Add Data Points*

At this point, you are now offered two calibration models:

■ **Point calibration:** Use this method to collect data at a single point. This method is best suited for small, enclosed spaces such as office cubicles, private offices, or conference rooms.

   Select Point Calibration from the drop-down menu. A marker will appear on the map. Use the mouse to drag the marker to a location suggested by one of the + signs on the map. While standing in that location with your laptop, click Go to start the data collection. Hold the laptop in various directions and orientations until the data collection is complete.

■ **Linear calibration:** Use this method to collect data along a straight path. This method is best suited for covering large open spaces such as corridors, auditoriums, warehouses, or outdoor areas.

   Select Linear Calibration from the drop-down menu. A pair of markers will appear on the map. Use the mouse to drag the markers so that the line joining the markers coincides with the path you are planning to walk. While standing at the Start location with your laptop, click Go to the start data collection. Walk at a steady pace along the path until you reach the Finish point and immediately click Done.

In the example shown in Figure 8-55, a point calibration is being performed, and upon collecting enough calibration points for both 802.11a/n and 802.11b/g/n, you can apply the calibration to the floor or any other floor that has similar characteristics.

Figure 8-55 *Point Calibration*

The reason for creating your own RF calibration model is that you might have an environment that does not meet the default calibrated models as predefined or you're trying to improve the overall accuracy of location services in your network. By taking specific data points on the floor and generating a calibration based on those data points, you will increase the overall location fidelity of the devices in your network.

By utilizing the map editor, planning mode, and RF calibration tools in the WCS, combined with third-party site survey tools, you can ensure that your AP placement and deployment will be the best it can be for the applications in your network.

Summary

As the comprehensive life cycle management platform for the Cisco Unified Wireless Network, the Cisco Wireless Control System (WCS) accomplishes the following:

■ Reduces operational costs with built-in tools, guides, and templates

■ Improves IT efficiency through an intuitive GUI and flexible ease of use

■ Minimizes staffing requirements through centralized control

■ Scales to support local or remote wireless LANs of any size

■ Protects the performance of 802.11n by mitigating RF interference with Cisco CleanAir technology

As you have just noticed, the Cisco WCS delivers full visibility and control of Cisco access points, Cisco WLCs, and the Cisco mobility services engine (MSE), with built-in support for Cisco adaptive wireless intrusion prevention systems (wIPS) and Cisco Context Aware Services (CAS). This robust platform helps you reduce the total cost of ownership and maintain a business-ready wireless network.

In Chapter 9, you will understand the value of the Cisco unified approach to multicast and see how Cisco can deliver the best-of-breed multicast solution for your network without compromising the switching and routing infrastructure that you have worked hard to protect.

Chapter 9

Next-Generation Advanced Topics: Multicast

As mentioned in Chapter 2, "Wireless LAN Protocols," the demand for higher-performance wireless local-area networks (WLAN) drove the development of the IEEE 802.11n standard, which has also had another impact on wireless designs and deployments—application development. Engineers that have implemented wireless in the past were most concerned with connectivity and mobility; however, because of the proliferation of devices and the requirement for increased bandwidth and reliability, applications now drive the need for intelligence in the network. Educational institutions, manufacturing, health care, and banking—to name a few—are leveraging applications that require high-speed connections without sacrificing quality, mobility, and security on the wired infrastructure. To help improve the efficiency of these transmissions, customers have often relied on the application developer to ensure that there are mechanisms for acknowledgment of the transferred data using TCP at Layer 4.

Therefore, the concept of using multicast to push content to the edge of the network for multiple users requiring the same data has blossomed over the years. The idea that multicast would be developed *just* on your wired infrastructure to watch audio/video multimedia or to ensure end-to-end voice quality across the WAN is no longer because the application boom is requiring information to be passed over the air. To accommodate the ever-increasing payload of these applications and the latency sensitivity, Cisco has developed services that will allow network engineers to seamlessly deploy and support audio and video services without impacting the network as a whole.

Cisco CEO John Chambers was quoted in Computerworld at the annual 2010 International CES show as saying, "Who would have thought a decade ago that Cisco would be here talking about consumer products and video? It is video that changes everything." The full story can be found here: http://tinyurl.com/y977hg5. It's no wonder why Cisco has put much R&D into the development and evolution of multicast in wireless!

Indicated by the chart in Figure 9-1, multicast has been around for years, and the wide adoption of it for the numerous applications continues to grow.

This chapter covers the fundamentals of multicast, the key items that you must understand when building a multicast network, and finally how to best configure and deploy each to ensure that your network is reliable, efficient, and easy to manage.

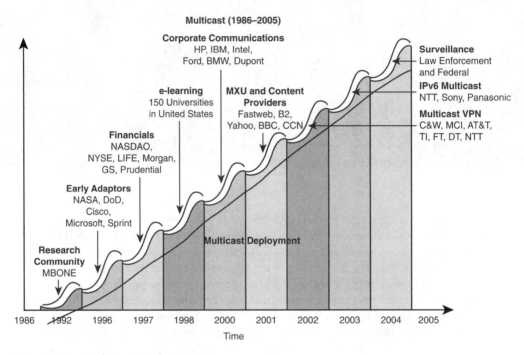

Figure 9-1 *Multicast Deployments*

Multicast

The proliferation of multimedia-enabled devices, such as desktops, laptops, handheld games, and so on, has spawned a new class of multimedia applications that operate in network environments. These network multimedia applications leverage the existing network infrastructure to deliver video and audio applications to end users, such as videoconferencing and video server applications. Table 9-1 shows a brief list of common applications that leverage the use of multicast.

To best understand how to configure and deploy multicast on your wired/wireless network, it is important to understand the principles behind it, namely, the following three key elements:

■   Bandwidth (How much bandwidth does the application need?)

■   Quality of service (QoS) (How are you going to guarantee delivery of that application across the network?)

■   Multicast (Does that application leverage bandwidth-saving techniques?)

Table 9-1   *Applications That Use Multicast*

	Real-Time	Non-Real-Time
Multimedia	IPTV Live video Videoconferencing Live Internet audio	Replication (video, web servers, kiosks) Content delivery
Data-Only	Stock quotes News feeds Whiteboarding Interactive gaming	Information delivery Server-to-server, server-to- desktop Database replication Software distribution

The rest of this chapter focuses on multicast and best practices in the Cisco Unified Wireless Network (CUWN).

IP multicast enables network engineers to deploy a streamlined approach to audio and video delivery when multiple users need the same data at the same time. The challenge for wireless is that not all clients are connected at the same speed and there are no acknowledgements of multicast packets over the air.

Unfortunately there isn't enough time to discuss all the details of multicast routing in this section; however, there are Cisco Press books and RFC 1112 (that could possibly put an insomniac to sleep) to help elaborate on the topics discussed in the sections that follow. The following sections cover the important factors of configuring the Cisco wireless LAN controller (WLC), Cisco switches, and Cisco routers in your network to provide reliable video services without compromising bandwidth on your wired links.

Multicast Definition

At the edge of both IP spectrums is unicast and broadcast, and in the middle sits multicast. Both unicast and broadcast means of communication have their place and needs; however, both can be very inefficient for clients needing access to the same information from multiple locations. To best understand, let's review unicast, which sits at one end of the IP communications where a source IP host sends packets to a specific destination IP host. In this case, the destination address of the packet is the address of a single, unique host in an IP network. IP packets are forwarded across a network from the source host to the destination host by routers. The routers at each point along the path between the source and destination use unicast routing information base to make unicast forwarding decisions based on the IP destination address in the packet.

At the other end of the IP spectrum, IP broadcasts, the source host sends packets to all IP hosts on a network segment. The destination address of an IP broadcast packet has the host portion of the destination IP address set to all 1s and the network portion set to the address of the subnet. IP hosts (including routers) understand that packets, which contain the IP broadcast address as the destination address, are addressed to all IP hosts on that subnet. Unless specifically configured otherwise, routers do not forward IP broadcast packets, and therefore IP broadcast communication is normally limited to the local subnet. If your objective is to get audio or multimedia to a number of users across your network from one source, IP broadcasting becomes completely inefficient.

As a result of this inefficiency, IP multicast is used to send IP packets from one source to many across the routed network. The IEEE 802.11 Multicast/Broadcast Protocol is based on the basic access procedure of carrier sense multiple access with collision avoidance (CSMA/CA). This protocol does not provide any MAC layer recovery on multicast/broadcast frames. 802.11 has ACKs for unicast packets; however, for multicast and broadcast packets, there is no ACK, and packet delivery is on a best-effort basis.

There are two major challenges for transmitting data over wireless LANs:

- Fluctuations in channel quality

- High bit-error rates compared to wired links

In addition to wireless channel–related challenges, when there are multiple clients, you have the problem of heterogeneity among receivers, because each user will have different channel conditions, power limitations, and processing capabilities. With a single multicast wireless stream, it is not possible to transfer the multicast data reliably to all the clients because channel conditions are different for each client.

The challenge then is that the application must accept loss and be prepared to accept the drop or find another means of handling it much like a unicast packet would, utilizing higher layers of the Open Systems Interconnection (OSI) stack. Another means of providing reliable multicast transmission is to leverage the network to classify, queue, and provision by means of QoS. QoS can substantially reduce the issue of unreliability by eliminating dropped packets and delay of the packets to the host. Figure 9-2 shows how packets are transmitted through unicast and multicast.

As a network engineer developing your multicast network for audio and video applications, it is important to understand some additional basics before simply turning on multicast on the CUWN.

Multicast Addressing

The Internet Assigned Numbers Authority (IANA) provides a list of available, used, and reserved addresses that can be implemented by customers. IP multicast uses the Class D range of IP addresses (224.0.0.0 through 239.255.255.255). IANA has specifically reserved Class D addresses for well-known multicast protocols and applications such as router hellos. As a network administrator, it is important that you do not use these reserved addresses in your wireless configuration because destructive consequences can occur within your routed network.

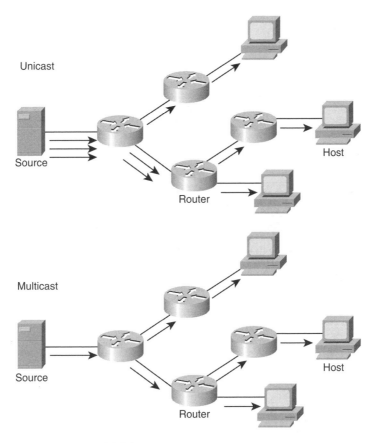

Figure 9-2   *Unicast Versus Multicast*

There are two types of multicast address ranges that you need to be familiar with:

■   Link-local

■   Administratively scoped

Link-local multicast addresses have the reserved range of 224.0.0.0 through 224.0.0.255 for use by network protocols and should not be used. Addresses in this range are locally scoped and are not forwarded, regardless of their time to live (TTL) values. Some well-known link-local multicast addresses that you might have encountered are 224.0.0.5 and 224.0.0.6, which are used in Open Shortest Path First (OSPF), or 224.0.0.10, which is used by Internet Gateway Routing Protocol (IGRP) routers. Table 9-2 lists a few of the well-known link-local addresses.

The second type of multicast address is the administratively scoped address, which you will see later in this chapter in the design of a wireless multicast-enabled network. Administratively scoped addresses provide network administrators with the flexibility to deploy multicast without impacting critical services used by link-local addresses.

Table 9-2 *Link-Local Multicast Addresses*

Link-Local Multicast Address	Usage
224.0.0.0	Base address (reserved)
224.0.0.1	All systems on this subnet
224.0.0.2	All routers on this subnet
224.0.0.3	Unassigned
224.0.0.4	DVMRP routers
224.0.0.5	OSPFIGP: All routers
224.0.0.6	OSPFIGP: Designated routers
224.0.0.7	ST routers
224.0.0.8	ST hosts
224.0.0.9	RIP2 routers
224.0.0.10	IGRP routers
224.0.0.11	Mobile-agents
224.0.0.12	DHCP server/relay agent
224.0.0.13	All PIM routers
224.0.0.14	RSVP-ENCAPSULATION
224.0.0.15	All CBT Routers

Administratively scoped addresses should be constrained to the local group or organization to which they are intended and are used for private multicast domains. For demonstration purposes here, the administratively scoped address will be constrained to the Cisco Unified Controller and access points; however, as you deploy multicast, you as the administrator must ensure that your multicast-enabled routers do not allow this range to cross in and out of your multicast domain. As defined in RFC 2365, the administratively scoped addresses that you can use for your deployment fall in the range of 239.000.000.000 through 239.255.255.255.

Within this scope of address, there are two subcategories:

- Organization-local (239.192.0.0–239.251.255.255)
- Site-local (239.255.0.0–239.255.255.255)

For simplicity, we will use the first. Now that you have an address range to use, you need to examine how the network is going to be configured to support the Cisco next-generation wireless multicast model.

Multicast Forwarding

The design requirements and restrictions of the wired network in which you want your application to traverse are extremely important to understanding the application. Although the details of the IP multicast model are out of the scope of this chapter, we must still highlight the importance and understanding of multicast distribution trees, the multicast protocol we are going to use, and the Internet Group Management Protocol (IGMP) that will be enabled in your network. For simplicity, we will highlight multicast distribution trees, Protocol Independent Multicasting (PIM) mode for routing, and IGMPv2 used by multicast hosts to join a session.

Multicast Distribution Trees

With multicast distribution trees, two modes of trees can be built. Described in the sections that follow are the two trees used to send IP multicast traffic across your network.

Shortest Path Tree

Shortest Path Tree (SPT) has one multicast source as the root of the tree whose branches form a path through the network to the receivers.

As shown in Figure 9-3, the special notation of (S,G) is pronounced *S comma G*, where the source *S* is the IP address of the source and *G* is the multicast group address that a client will want to join. If the network has many sources, you will see in your routers an (S,G) for each of the source IP address and multicast group addresses.

Shared Tree

In a Shared Tree deployment, there is typically a single common root placed in the network to which all multicast traffic is parsed. The root in this case is often called the rendezvous point (RP), depending on the multicast routing protocol used. In Figure 9-4 you can see that although there are multiple sources, they must all send their information to the RP first before sending down the tree to the receivers.

As a result of this method, a notation (*,G) is used, pronounced *star comma G*, where the * represents all sources and the *G* represents the multicast group address. You will notice later how this is represented with the controller and APs as part of the next-generation multicast feature.

With a basic understanding of the two methods used to build and forward multicast packets, you need to understand the mechanics of how these operations transpire. Most multicast implementations leverage some form of multicast routing and, within that, leverage Reverse Path Forwarding (RPF) to determine whether to forward or drop a multicast packet on the network. How does RPF know what do with the packet, and how does the multicast routing protocol work together? The next section discusses one of the multicast routing protocols used to send traffic.

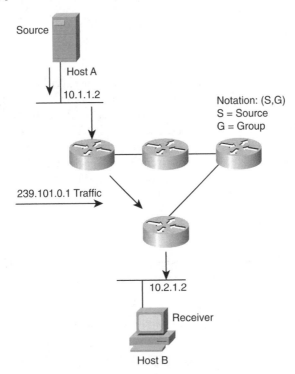

Figure 9-3   *Shortest Path Tree*

Protocol Independent Multicasting (PIM)

Reverse Path Forwarding (RPF) determines whether to drop or forward the packet, and it is PIM (PIM is just one of the methods for routing multicast packets) that is utilized by the multicast router to forward packets between network devices. PIM can utilize the unicast routing table to determine the next-hop interface for the multicast packet, and that is where the RPF check is implemented. RPF works in the following manner as traffic is flowing away from the source down the tree:

1. The router examines the source address of the arriving multicast packet to determine whether the packet is on the reverse path back to the source. If it is on a non-RPF interface, the packet is automatically dropped.

2. If the packet arrives on the interface leading back to the source, is it passed because the RPF check is successful.

There are two modes of PIM routing:

- PIM Sparse

- PIM Dense

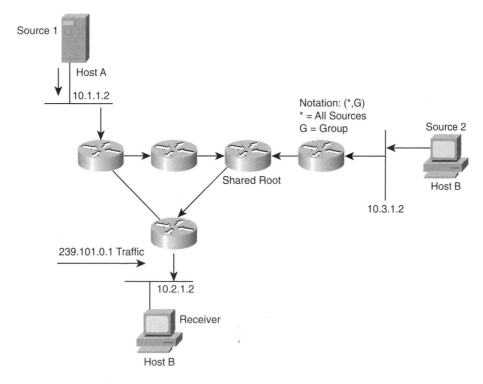

Figure 9-4 *Shared Path Tree*

In your deployments, you will most likely leverage PIM Sparse mode because PIM Dense mode floods multicast packets out all PIM-enabled interfaces on every router on the network. This is both taxing and inefficient to the router's CPU, especially as more multicast applications are added to the network. PIM Sparse mode is more efficient because it assumes that no one device on the network wants the multicast packet unless specifically requested through IGMP. The beauty of this is that the need to flood the multicast packet to all interfaces is removed, the need to send duplicate copies of the same data that can clog the network is removed, and packets are replicated at each point in the downward flow of the tree until the packets reach the receiver.

Note Cisco recommends that you use Protocol Independent Multicast (PIM) Sparse mode, particularly Auto-RP, where possible and especially for new deployments.

Auto-RP automates the distribution of group-to-RP mappings in a network supporting Sparse mode PIM. It supports the use of multiple RPs within a network to serve different group ranges and allows configurations of redundant RPs for reliability purposes. In comparison, manual configuration of RP information is prone to inconsistency, which can cause connectivity problems. In summary, the automatic distribution of group-to-RP mappings simplifies configuration tasks and guarantees consistency.

In a nutshell, the Auto-RP mechanism operates on two basic components, the candidate RPs and the RP mapping agents:

■ All candidate RPs advertise their willingness to be an RP through *RP-announcement* messages.

These messages are periodically sent to a reserved well-known group 224.0.1.39 (CISCO-RP-ANNOUNCE). The default interval is 60 seconds (tunable through the CLI).

■ The RP mapping agents join group 224.0.1.39 and consistently select an RP for each group address range. The pair (group range = RP) is called an *RP-mapping*.

The RP mapping agents advertise the authoritative RP-mappings to another well-known group address 224.0.1.40 (CISCO-RP-DISCOVERY). All PIM routers join 224.0.1.40 and store the RP-mappings in their private cache.

Note As of Cisco IOS Software Release 11.1, you can configure the interface commands **ip pim dense-mode** and **ip pim sparse-mode** simultaneously with the **ip pim sparse-dense-mode** command. In this mode, the interface is treated as Dense mode if the group is in Dense mode. If the group is in Sparse mode (for example, if an RP is known), the interface is treated as Sparse mode.

To enable PIM routing on your network, you must first enable multicast routing globally on your router or L3 switch and then issue the appropriate IP PIM command on the interfaces that you want multicast to participate on:

```
BadgerSwitch01(config)# ip multicast-routing distributed
BadgerSwitch01(config-if)# ip pim passive
```

or

```
BadgerSwitch01(config-if)# ip pim sparse-dense-mode
```

Note Depending on the type of Cisco router or Cisco switch, you might or might not be able to use the preceding command syntax. For example, the Cisco 3750 and 3560 series switches allow both **ip pim passive** or **ip pim sparse-dense-mode** commands, depending on the interface you are configuring.

To enable multicast and PIM on a Cisco 3750 switch, enter the following:

```
BadgerSwitch01(config)# ip multicast-routing distributed
```

The last part of the multicast forwarding equation is the implementation of IGMP.

IGMP

IGMPv1 is defined by RFC 1112 as a means of specifying how the host should inform the network that it is a member of a particular multicast group. IGMP is part of the IP layer and uses IP datagrams to transmit information about the multicast group. It is IGMP that determines whether a tree should be built based on the source of the multicast packet. If there are no hosts attempting an IGMP join, there is no need to transmit the multicast packet out the interface of the upstream router. IGMPv1 and IGMPv2 are both widely deployed, and depending on the OS you are running, you might only have IGMPv1. It is worth noting that a great deal of large enterprises are beginning or have begun to implement IGMPv3 as a means of minimizing the amount of traffic that it sent across the network. IGMPv3 adds support for source filtering, that is, the capability for a system to report interest in receiving packets only from specific source addresses, or from all but specific source addresses, sent to a particular multicast address. This information can be used by multicast routing protocols to avoid delivering multicast packets from specific sources to networks where there are no interested receivers.

The concept of joining a multicast group on a given host interface is fundamental to multicast. Membership in a multicast group on a given interface is dynamic (that is, it changes over time as processes join and leave the group). This means that end users can dynamically join multicast groups based on the applications they execute. Multicast routers use IGMP messages to keep track of group membership on each of the networks that are physically attached to the router.

By default, all Cisco routers and switches support IGMP natively, and IGMP features can be changed to meet the needs of your environment. For simplicity, leave the default IGMP features that came with the IOS release you are running.

IGMP Snooping

An additional aspect of IGMP is the concept of IGMP snooping. *IGMP snooping* is an IP multicast constraining mechanism that runs on a Layer 2 LAN switch. Without IGMP snooping enabled, all multicast traffic will be forwarded to all hosts connected to the switch. IGMP snooping will ensure that only hosts that are interested in the data stream will receive it.

For IGMP snooping to operate correctly, there needs to be an IGMP querier sending out periodic IGMP queries so that the receivers will respond and send out IGMP membership reports. The IGMP membership reports control which switch ports will receive the multicast traffic for a particular multicast group. See Figure 9-5 for a sample multicast-enabled network with IGMP snooping.

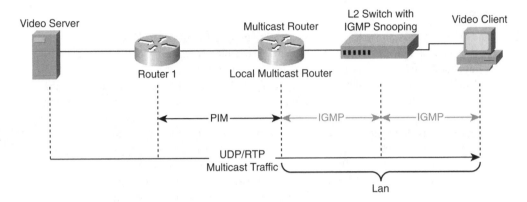

Figure 9-5   *Multicast IGMP*

IGMP snooping is enabled by default on Cisco switches, as displayed in the output in Example 9-1.

Example 9-1   show ip igmp snooping *Command Output*

```
BadgerSwitch01# sh ip igmp snooping

Global IGMP Snooping configuration
-----------------------------------------------------------
IGMP snooping                 : Enabled
IGMPv3 snooping (minimal)     : Enabled
Report suppression            : Enabled
TCN solicit query             : Disabled
TCN flood query count         : 2
Robustness variable           : 2
Last member query count       : 2
Last membery query interval   : 1000


Vlan 1:
-----------------------------------------------------------
IGMP snooping                 : Enabled
IGMPv3 immediate leave        : Disabled
Multicast router learning mode : pim-dvmrp
CGMP interoperability mode    : IGMP_ONLY
Robustness variable           : 2
Last member query count       : 2
Last member query interval    : 1000
```

The following examines the steps of how the CUWN would handle multicast traffic with and without IGMP snooping enabled.

With IGMP snooping disabled:

1.   AP downloads CAPWAP multicast group address during normal join process and issues IGMP join to the controller CAPWAP multicast group.

2.   The IGMP packets from clients are bridged to the router.

     The router IGMP table is updated with the IP address of the client as the last reporter.

3.   The WLC forwards the packet to the CAPWAP multicast group address using its management interface at the lowest QoS level.

4.   APs in the multicast group receive the packet and forward it to *all* the Basic Service Set Identifiers (BSSID) mapped to the interface on which clients receive multicast.

     APs can receive other multicast packets but process only multicast packets that come from their controller. Any other copies are discarded.

     If the service set identifier (SSID) is on both radios, both radios transmit the multicast packet on the WLAN SSID if there are clients associated with it, even if those clients did not request the multicast traffic.

5.   From an AP perspective, the multicast appears to be a *broadcast to all SSIDs*.

With IGMP snooping enabled:

1.   The controller acts as an *IGMP proxy* by sending out IGMP join using its WLAN-assigned interface on behalf of the actual WLAN client.

2.   The controller *facilitates roaming* by providing an IGMP membership report query to the new AP the client roamed to and supports IGMPv2 *fast leave*.

3.   The controller periodically sends *IGMP queries* to its clients and updates its database.

     The WLC gets all multicast groups on a particular VLAN and sends an IGMP report per group when queried by an upstream router. The source IP of the report is the interface IP of that VLAN. The router sees the dynamic interface (of that VLAN) IP in its IGMP database.

     The WLC also creates unique Multicast Group IDs (MGID) from the IGMP reports after checking the Layer 3 multicast address and the VLAN number. The WLC updates the AP MGID with the client MAC address.

4.   When the WLC receives multicast for a particular group, it forwards it to all the APs, but only those APs that have active clients subscribed to that multicast group send multicast traffic on that *particular WLAN*.

As you can see, IGMP snooping reduces the amount of traffic on your network and moves the process of replication to the edge.

Now that you have a brief understanding of three key portions of multicast forwarding, the next section delves into how this is deployed in the Cisco Unified Wireless Network (CUWN).

Multicast Configuration in the CUWN

One of the challenges in a wireless environment is that traditionally multicast and broadcast packets were sent as best effort and at the lowest data rate. The problem is that there is no one to acknowledge receipt of the packet, and as such, the transmission cannot be assured. Applications that leverage the use of multicast, such as Push-to-Talk, Vocera's Broadcast, e-learning, corporate video presentations, and patient-monitoring systems, will be subject to this limitation if it is not the one generating the upstream transmission.

Two scenarios—AP-to-client delivery and client-to-AP delivery—must be covered to understand the issues concerning multicast over wireless and to see how Cisco has implemented VideoStream to minimize them.

Access Point–to–Client Delivery

An understanding of multicast delivery within the 802.11 standard might help in understanding why broadcasts and multicast are considered best effort. Although this is true within the wired space as well, the collision avoidance mechanism combined with a switched network allows far fewer dropped packets than can be said of the shared (data as well as nondata devices) medium of the wireless physical layer.

When an access point receives a multicast packet, the packet is put into a separate queue from unicast packets, because these packets are not transmitted until the *Delivery Traffic Indication Message (DTIM)* timer expires. This is done to permit power-save clients the opportunity to turn on their radio and receive both multicast and broadcast messages as well as receive their queued unicast traffic. Again, by default, the access point does not track individual clients who want to receive this traffic, so these packets are sent out at the lowest configured data rate, which by default on the CUWN is 1 Mbps. This gives the administrator the upward limit of multicast throughput in the wireless spectrum. These packets are sent into the medium at this rate, and regardless of what happens, after the radio sends the packet, it is flushed from memory, with *no* acknowledgment that the packet was received by the intended recipient(s).

Client–to–Access Point Delivery

Many of today's applications, such as Push-to-Talk voice over IP (VoIP) applications, patient-monitoring systems, and others, have the source of the multicast traffic on the wireless segment. Although there is no way to assure delivery of multicast from the infrastructure to the client, there is a way from the client back into the infrastructure. In the wired medium, the MAC address is used to identify the intended recipient. Within the 802.11 medium, the same MAC address is used both at Layer 2 as well as at the physical layer within the 802.11 header. When a client sends a multicast packet toward the infrastructure, it address this packet at Layer 2 with the Ethernet multicast MAC address, while within the 802.11 header, the MAC address used is the BSSID of the access point the client is associated to. If the access point either gets corrupted or misses the entire transmission of this packet, it will not respond with an acknowledgment to the client, and the client will again attempt to transmit this packet upstream to the access point. This process allows the same level of guarantee of delivery to the infrastructure that is given to the unicast packets, making upstream multicast much more reliable.

However, the key to all this is the AP-to-client mechanism, and that is where the Cisco next-generation multicast technology (VideoStream) improves the over-the-air quality and prevents the wireless system from being consumed by video packets. In essence, Cisco has taken what it has learned from years of wired multicast deployments and experience and moved it to the CUWN.

Before Cisco Unified Wireless Network Software Release 3.2, when IP multicast was enabled, the controller delivered multicast packets to wireless LAN clients by making copies of the multicast packets, then forwarding the packets through a unicast Lightweight Access Point Protocol (LWAPP) tunnel to each access point connected to the controller. Each multicast frame received by the controller from a VLAN on the first-hop router was copied and sent over the LWAPP tunnel to each of the APs connected to it. This method is called *multicast-unicast delivery mode* in the CUWN.

Unicast delivery places a heavy burden on the AP, as well as the controller's network processing unit, because of the deluge of packets that need to be replicated down to the AP.

Note   The Cisco multicast-unicast delivery method is commonly used by customers that only want to provide multicast over their wireless network or when the network doesn't support multicast.

Note   Cisco recommends that customers avoid using the multicast-unicast method of delivery because every multicast packet must be replicated to all APs that have joined the Cisco WLAN controller, regardless of whether there is a client requesting the multicast group address. This method can be processor intensive, depending on the number of multicast streams needing support, and can possibly take away network resources for forwarding unicast traffic.

In Figure 9-6, you can see how the CUWN forwards multicast packets when multicast-unicast delivery mode is enabled.

In CUWN Software Releases 3.2 and later, the multicast performance has been optimized with the introduction of multicast-multicast mode. Instead of using unicast to deliver each multicast packet over the LWAPP tunnel to each AP, an LWAPP multicast group is used to deliver the multicast packet to each AP. This allows the routers in the network to use standard multicast techniques to replicate and deliver multicast packets to the APs. For the LWAPP multicast group, the controller becomes the multicast source and the APs become the multicast receivers. For the multicast performance feature, the APs accept IGMP queries only from the router and multicast packets with a source IP address of the controller with which they are currently associated. Figure 9-7 illustrates the multicast delivery method deployed by the CUWN.

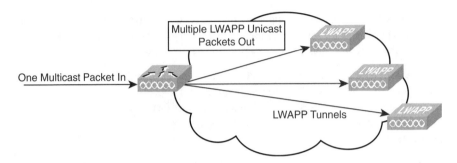

Figure 9-6   *Unicast Delivery Method*

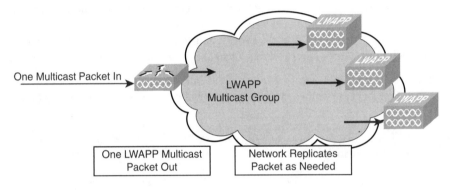

Figure 9-7   *Multicast Delivery Method*

It is important to understand how multicast traffic is handled in the CUWN as of version 3.2. The multicast traffic is either sourced from the wired network or it is sourced from the client. Both scenarios work differently and are explained in the text that follows.

Note   The following explanation is based on CUWN version 5.2 and CAPWAP; however, you can substitute LWAPP for versions prior to 5.2 that support multicast-multicast delivery mode.

When the source of the multicast group is on the wired LAN:

■   When the controller receives a multicast packet from any of the client VLANs on the first-hop router, it transmits the packet to the CAPWAP multicast group through the management interface at the best-effort QoS classification. The QoS bits for the CAPWAP multicast packet are hard-coded at the lowest level and are not user changeable.

■   The multicast-enabled network delivers the CAPWAP multicast packet to each of the access points that have joined the CAPWAP multicast group, using the normal multicast mechanisms in the routers to replicate the packet along the way as needed so that the multicast packet reaches all APs. This relieves the controller from replicating the multicast packets.

■ Access points can receive other multicast packets but will only process the multicast packets that are sourced from the controller to which they are currently joined; any other copies are discarded. If more than one WLAN is associated to the VLAN interface where the original multicast packet was sourced, the AP transmits the multicast packet over each WLAN (following the WLAN bitmap in the CAPWAP header). Additionally, if that WLAN is on both radios (802.11g and 802.11a), both radios transmit the multicast packet on the WLAN if there are clients associated, even if those clients did not request the multicast traffic.

When the source of the multicast group is a wireless client:

■ The multicast packet is unicast (CAPWAP encapsulated) from the AP to the controller, similarly to standard wireless client traffic.

■ The controller makes two copies of the multicast packet. One copy is sent out the VLAN associated with the WLAN it came on, enabling receivers on the wired LAN to receive the multicast stream and the router to learn about the new multicast group. The second copy of the packet is CAPWAP encapsulated and is sent to the CAPWAP multicast group so that wireless clients can receive the multicast stream.

Prior to CUWN Software Release 5.2, the protocol port used to establish this multicast group was LWAPP UDP port 12224. Release 5.2 and later utilized CAPWAP UDP port 5248 to establish the multicast group. The ports used for CAPWAP and CAPWAP multicast groups are as follows:

■ CAPWAP control port: 5246

■ CAPWAP data port: 5247

■ CAPWAP multicast group port: 5248

As an administrator, ensure that no multicast applications on your network use these ports because the controller will, by default, block any traffic that is destined for them.

Enabling Multicast on a Cisco WLAN Controller

To enable multicast on your WLC, you need to configure multicast-multicast because it is disabled by default. To do so, you will choose multicast from the drop-down options and then set the multicast address to an administratively scoped address, as noted earlier in the chapter. Figure 9-8 shows that the multicast address of 239.192.1.141 is the source of multicast packets for the APs to join.

To enable the multicast address through the command line on the WLC, issue the following commands:

```
<Cisco Controller> config network multicast global enable
<Cisco Controller> config network multicast mode multicast 239.192.1.141
```

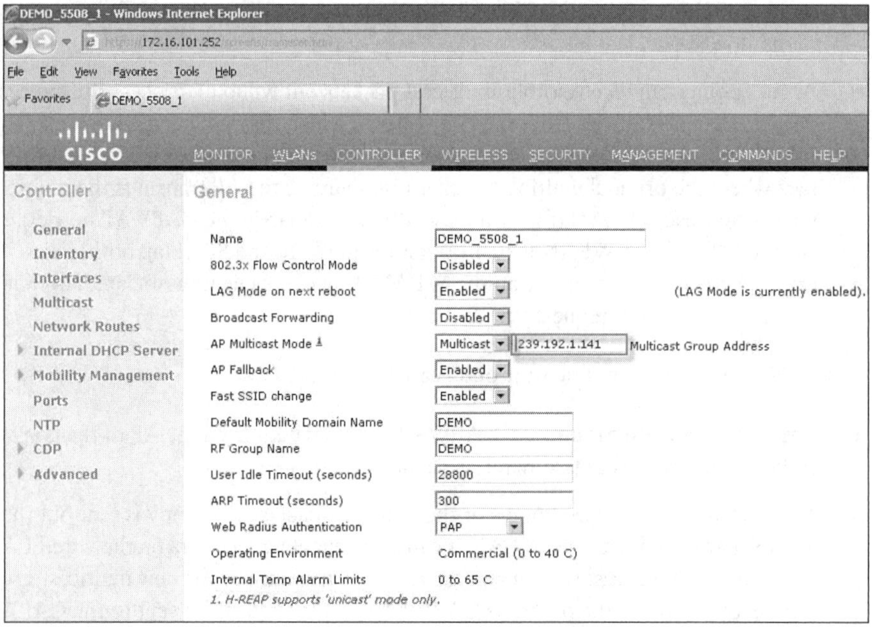

Figure 9-8   *Enabling Multicast on the Cisco WLAN Controller*

Depending on your deployment, each WLC will have its own individually scoped multi-cast address, which we will discuss later as a part of the best practices setup.

The last important feature that you need to enable to take full advantage of multicast on the WLC is to enable IGMP snooping (see Figure 9-9). The purpose of enabling IGMP snooping on the WLC is to gather IGMP reports from the hosts and then send each AP a list of hosts that are listening to any multicast group. The AP then forwards multicast packets only to those hosts.

To configure IGMP snooping on the WLC through the CLI, issue the following commands:

```
<Cisco Controller> config network multicast igmp snooping enable
<Cisco Controller> config network multicat timeout value time-range-from-30-300
```

After you have configured the multicast and IGMP snooping features, you can issue the following commands from the WLC CLI to validate the configuration:

```
<Cisco Controller> show network summary
 <Cisco Controller> show network multicast mgid summary
 <Access Point> show capwap mcast
```

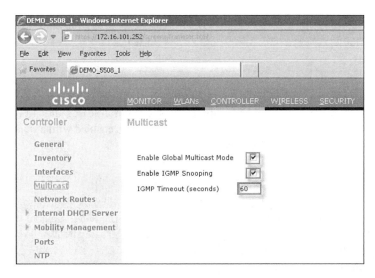

Figure 9-9   *Enabling IGMP Snooping on the WLC*

From the CLI, Example 9-2 shows the multicast and IGMP status, and Example 9-3 shows the AP multicast status. Figure 9-14 shows the multicast MGIDs from the monitor-multicast GUI.

You can enable SSH or Telnet for access into your AP to validate the status.

Note   You need to globally configure a username and password through the WLC GUI or CLI or through the specific AP's configuration to gain access into the AP from a remote client such as Putty or SecureCRT.

Example 9-2   *Multicast and IGMP Status*

```
(Cisco Controller)> show network summary


show network summary


RF-Network Name                          DEMO
Web Mode                                 Disable
Secure Web Mode                          Enable
Secure Web Mode Cipher-Option High       Disable
Secure Web Mode Cipher-Option SSLv2      Enable
Secure Shell (ssh)                       Enable
Telnet                                   Enable
Ethernet Multicast Mode                  Enable        Mode: Mcast 239.192.1.141
Ethernet Broadcast Mode                  Disable
```

```
AP Multicast Mode               Enable      Address: 239.192.1.141
IGMP snooping                   Enabled
IGMP timeout                    60 seconds
```

From the **show network summary** output, you see that multicast-multicast is enabled with IP address 239.192.1.141 and that IGMP snooping is enabled with a timeout value of 60 seconds with a range of 30–600.

Note   If the controller does not receive a response through an IGMP report from the client, the controller times out the client entry from the MGID table. When no clients are left for a particular multicast group, the controller waits for the IGMP timeout value to expire and then deletes the MGID entry from the controller. The controller always generates a general IGMP query (that is, to destination address 224.0.0.1) and sends it on all WLANs with an MGID value of 1.

Example 9-3   *AP Multicast Status*

```
AP_1142# show capwap mcast

CAPWAP MULTICAST
    Multicast Group: 239.192.1.141, Source: 172.16.101.252
V1 Rpt Sent:              0; V2 Rpt Sent:          15435
V3 Rpt Sent:              0; Leave Sent:               1
V1 Query Rcvd:            0; V2 Query Rcvd:        15437
V3 Query Rcvd:            0; V1 Rpt Rcvd:              0
V2 Rpt Rcvd:              0; V3 Rpt Rcvd:              0
```

From the AP multicast status output, you will notice that the AP has joined the source address of 172.16.101.252 (which is the WLAN controller's management interface) and the multicast group 239.192.1.141.

As shown in Figure 9-10, the MGID output displays the details of the L3 and L2 multicast groups and their corresponding MGID value. The Multicast Group ID (MGID) is the combination of a multicast group address and a VLAN on which the multicast traffic is received. The MGID is created when the WLC receives the first IGMP join request for the particular multicast address. The next section goes into more detail about the concept of MGIDs.

MGIDs

Recall that when you enable multicast mode and the WLC receives a multicast packet from the wired LAN, the WLC encapsulates the packet using CAPWAP and forwards the packet to the CAPWAP multicast group address. The WLC always uses the management interface for sending multicast packets. APs in the multicast group receive the packet and forward it to all the BSSIDs mapped to the interface on which clients receive multicast traffic. From the AP's perspective, the multicast appears to be a broadcast to all SSIDs.

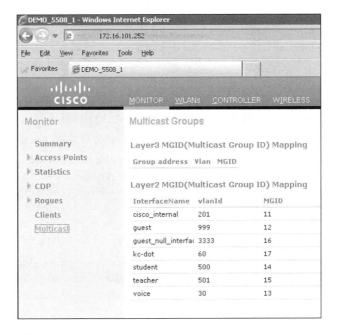

Figure 9-10 *Multicast MGIDs*

With the introduction of IGMP snooping in the WLC software, the WLC gathers IGMP reports from the clients, processes them, creates unique Multicast Group IDs (MGID) from the IGMP reports after checking the Layer 3 multicast address and the VLAN number, and sends the IGMP reports to the infrastructure switch. The WLC sends these reports with the source address as the interface address on which it received the reports from the clients. The WLC then updates the AP MGID table on the AP with the client MAC address.

When the WLC receives multicast traffic for a particular multicast group, it forwards it to all the APs, but only those APs that have active clients listening or subscribed to that multicast group send multicast traffic on that particular WLAN. IP packets are forwarded with an MGID that is unique for an ingress VLAN and the destination multicast group. Layer 2 multicast packets are forwarded with an MGID that is unique for the ingress interface.

When IGMP snooping is disabled, the following hold true:

■ The WLC always uses Layer 2 MGIDs when it sends multicast data to the access point. Every interface created is assigned one Layer 2 MGID. For example, the management interface has an MGID of 0, and the first dynamic interface created is assigned an MGID of 8, which increments as each dynamic interface is created.

- The IGMP packets from clients are forwarded to the router. As a result, the router IGMP table is updated with the IP address of the clients as the last reporter.

When IGMP snooping is enabled, the following is true:

- The WLC always uses Layer 3 MGIDs for all Layer 3 multicast traffic sent to the access point. For all Layer 2 multicast traffic, it continues to use Layer 2 MGIDs.

- IGMP report packets from wireless clients are consumed or absorbed by the WLC, which generates a query for the clients. After the router sends the IGMP query, the WLC sends the IGMP reports with its interface IP address as the listener IP address for the multicast group. As a result, the router IGMP table is updated with the WLC IP address as the multicast listener.

- When the client that is listening to the multicast groups roams from one WLC to another, the first WLC transmits all the multicast group information for the listening client to the second WLC. As a result, the second WLC can immediately create the multicast group information for the client. The second WLC sends the IGMP reports to the network for all multicast groups to which the client was listening. This process aids in the seamless transfer of multicast data to the client.

- If the listening client roams to a WLC in a different subnet, the multicast packets are tunneled to the anchor controller of the client to avoid the Reverse Path Filtering (RPF) check. The anchor then forwards the multicast packets to the infrastructure switch.

Note   The MGIDs are WLC specific. The same multicast group packets coming from the same VLAN in two different WLCs can be mapped to two different MGIDs.

Note   If Layer 2 multicast is enabled, a single MGID is assigned to all the multicast addresses coming from an interface.

Multicast Mobility Messaging

To help improve the efficiency of mobility messages between controllers in your domain, you can enable multicast messaging. The Cisco WLC provides intersubnet mobility for clients by sending mobility messages to other member WLCs. Because there can be up to 72 WLCs in the mobility domain, each WLC will receive a Mobile Announce message each time a new client associates to it. This can create unnecessary network traffic because each WLC will get a copy for each client that associates, even though it might not require the information.

When multicast messaging is enabled on the WLC, the WLC uses the multicast network to send the Mobile Announce messages to corresponding WLCs in the mobility domain. This behavior allows the WLC to send only one copy of the message to the network, which is the new multicast group that you have defined on each. Note that this is not the same multicast address used by the WLC and the APs as a part of forwarding multicast traffic but is used only to pass Mobility Announce messages. Each WLC in the group will have the same mobility multicast messaging address unlike the recommended configuration for each WLC's global multicast address. Figure 9-11 shows multicast mobility messaging.

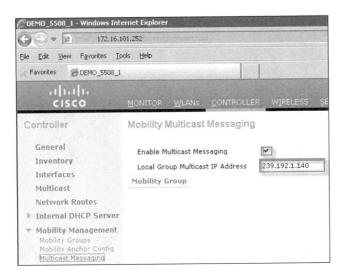

Figure 9-11   *Multicast Mobility Messaging*

All WLCs in the mobility domain should either be enabled or disabled for multicast messaging to take advantage of this feature. If there is a WLC in the mobility domain that is not configured for multicast messaging, it will revert to unicast messaging.

Enabling Multicast on a Cisco Router or Layer 3 Switch

To complete the setup, you must enable PIM on the Layer 3 interfaces of the upstream router or switch on which the WLC and APs reside. In the case of the WLC, PIM needs to be enabled on the management VLAN, and for the APs, any VLAN for which an AP is configured needs to have its corresponding Layer 3 VLAN interface enabled for PIM. Example 9-4 shows a Cisco switch configuration with multicast and PIM enabled.

Example 9-4   *Multicast and PIM Configuration*

```
BadgerSwitch01# ip multicast-routing distributed

interface Vlan100
 description ***VLAN Management for AP***
 ip address 172.16.100.1 255.255.255.0
 ip helper-address 192.168.1.9
 ip pim passive
 ntp broadcast
```

```
interface Vlan101
 description ***VLAN Management for Controller***
 ip address 172.16.101.1 255.255.255.0
 ip helper-address 192.168.1.9
 ip pim passive
 ntp broadcast
```

Issue the **show ip mroute** command on your router or Layer 3 switch to ensure that a tree has been built for your WLC's multicast group and the corresponding interface, as demonstrated in Example 9-5.

Example 9-5   show ip mroute *Command Output*

```
BadgerSwitch01# show ip mroute

IP Multicast Routing Table
! Output omitted for brevity
 (*, 239.192.1.140), 5w5d/00:02::48, RP 0.0.0.0, flags: SJC
 Incoming interface: Null, RPF nbr 0.0.0.0
 Outing interface list:
   Vlan100, Forward/Sparse-Dense, 1w3d/00:02:45
   Vlan101, Forward/Sparse-Dense, 1w3d/00:02:48

(*, 239.192.1.141), 5w5d/00:02::49, RP 0.0.0.0, flags: SJC
 Incoming interface: Null, RPF nbr 0.0.0.0
 Outing interface list:
   Vlan101, Forward/Sparse-Dense, 1w3d/00:02:49

(*, 239.255.255.254), 3d16h/00:02::48, RP 0.0.0.0, flags: SJC
 Incoming interface: Null, RPF nbr 0.0.0.0
 Outing interface list:
   Vlan100, Forward/Sparse-Dense, 1d02h/00:02:48
```

Notice from the output that a (*,239.192.1.141) (a representation of "star comma G," as explained earlier) is represented for the multicast group configured on the controller and that the only interface allowed is the management VLAN for the controller's management IP address.

If you do not see your WLC's multicast group in the output, you have not configured IP PIM on the interface for your WLC's management IP address.

At this point, you have completed the configuration of multicast-multicast on your WLC, your APs will have joined the multicast group (if IP PIM is enabled on the AP's IP subnet), and you can begin enabling VideoStream on your WLC.

VideoStream

Cisco introduced VideoStream as part of the 7.0.98 software feature set for the WLC. Prior to this release, the preceding information held true for all broadcast, unicast, and multicast packets. You can see that as more unicast and multicast clients join an AP, resources will become restricted to the point where all communications can be impacted.

VideoStream provides efficient bandwidth utilization by removing the need to broadcast multicast packets to all WLANs on the AP, regardless of whether there is a client joined to a multicast group. To get around this limitation, the AP needs to be able to send multicast traffic to the host through unicast forwarding, only on the WLAN the client is joined to, and do so at the data rate at which the client is joined. By implementing VideoStream, you are no longer limiting the transmission of multicast packets to 1 Mbps, so if you are using 802.11n, you are getting those multicast packets at the connected speed of the client. Before configuring VideoStream, you need to understand (at a high level) how it differs from the normal multicast deployment (multicast/broadcast).

VideoStream, for the first time in a wireless system, provides a seamless approach for engineers to design and implement a multicast solution without destroying the bandwidth between the WLC and the upstream switch or router. See Figures 9-12 and 9-13 for a comparison of existing WLC multicast deployments versus the Cisco VideoStream technology.

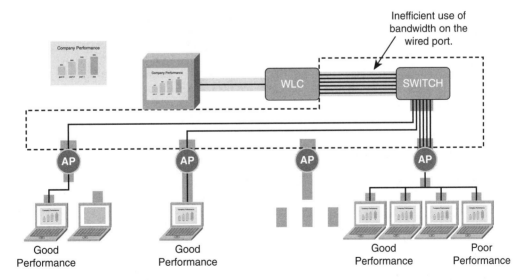

Figure 9-12 *Traditional Wireless Multicast Deployment*

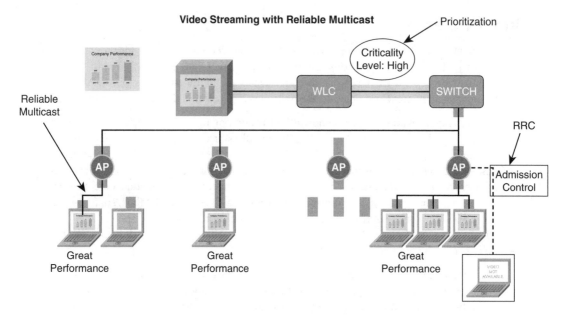

Figure 9-13   *Cisco VideoStream Multicast Deployment*

As you can see in the traditional deployment model, the more multicast traffic and the more clients that are added to the network, the more the wired bandwidth is severely impacted.

In the preceding model, you notice that the wired network is not impacted by the increased number of clients or APs in the network, because the processing and replication of packets are done by the AP and leverage the multicast-enabled network to efficiently route traffic.

Principles of VideoStream

Two key areas are addressed by VideoStream:

- Multicast reliability

- QoS

Multicast Reliability

As previously mentioned, the IEEE 802.11 wireless multicast delivery mechanism is not reliable, because there is no ACK mechanism for clients to acknowledge whether they have received multicast frames sent by the access point. Wireless networks typically operate with a Packet Error Rate (PER) of 1–10 percent (because of collisions, fading, and interference), and without acknowledgments/retransmissions, this results in a multicast Packet Loss Rate (PLR) of 1–10 percent. Video applications, on the other hand, typically require a PLR on the order of 0.1–0.5 percent. Because of this PLR mismatch, using traditional 802.11 multicast delivery mechanisms will often cause an IP multicast video stream to be unviewable.

Converting the multicast transmission at the AP and not at the WLC enables the AP to receive ACKs from the clients, and determines when frames need to be retransmitted (in the case of lost or corrupted frames).

QoS

With 802.11e, Wireless Multimedia (WMM) provides a mechanism for video traffic to be sent in a queue that has a higher priority than best-effort traffic (but lower than voice).

As illustrated in Figure 9-14, there are four queues within the 802.11 specification that map to four access categories with WMM on the client or AP: bronze, silver, gold, and platinum.

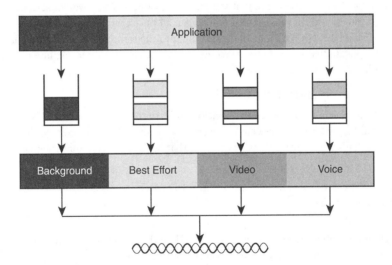

Figure 9-14 *802.11 QoS Access Categories*

Each of these queues contends for the wireless channel in a similar manner to the Distributed Coordinated Function (DCF) mechanism, with each of the queues using different Interframe Space, CWmin, and CWmax values. See the Cisco "Wireless Quality of Service" document at www.cisco.com/en/US/products/hw/wireless/ps430/prod_technical_reference 09186a0080144498.html for a brief description of DCF.

If more than one frame from different access categories collides internally, the frame with the higher priority is sent, and the lower-priority frame adjusts its backoff parameters as though it had collided with a frame external to the queuing mechanism.

In addition to the queuing mechanism illustrated in Figure 9-14, multiple input, multiple output (MIMO) APs and clients receive additional benefits:

- MIMO antenna technology provides a higher SNR.

  - A high SNR allows increased data rates (more throughput) and link reliability (less retransmissions because of fading and rate selection).

  - Benefits legacy 802.11a/g clients in the uplink direction, but not in the downlink direction.

- ClientLink technology (downlink beamforming) provides a significant benefit for downlink video traffic on legacy clients.

Refer to Chapter 3, "802.11n," for further explanation on MIMO and ClientLink.

With VideoStream, Cisco introduced new features to address the queuing of voice and video traffic traversing the network. First is the ability to apply resource reservation and admission mechanisms to ensure that the wireless medium is not oversubscribed, and that voice, video, and BE (best-effort) traffic can all be accommodated. The key here is that you could have two or more clients listening to the same multicast stream, and the AP must replicate that unicast stream to the clients. Without proper queuing mechanisms, those replicated streams could starve other traffic.

Resource Reservation and Control

The implementation of Resource Reservation and Control (RRC) within the WLC provides a health check to prevent channel oversubscription. This is done in conjunction with Call Admission Control (CAC) functions that have long been implemented on voice networks.

RRC provides three key enhanced capabilities to manage admission and policy controls of the wireless system:

- Admission and policy decisions made based on the RF measurements, statistics measurement of the traffic, and system configurations.

- Provides bandwidth protection for video clients by denying requests that would cause oversubscription (SAP messages to clients on drop).

- Channel utilization is used as a metric to determine capacity and perform admission control.

Information gathered from the radio is used to make intelligent decisions on whether traffic can be passed along to additional clients. If the WLC determines, after gathering the preceding statistical measurements from the APs, that there is enough available bandwidth, it will pass the traffic down to the clients. If not, the information is dropped.

The steps for VideoStream in the CUWN would be as follows:

- **Reliable multicast:**

    - Monitors IGMP join results from clients for the configured streams

    - Signals the AP to put the video packet in the correct TX queue

    - Video and voice measurements are considered from the AP

    - RRC engine approved stream will be admitted with the join response

- **Direct Memory Access (DMA) on the AP:**

    - On-the-fly copying of video streams at the AP

    - Packet header modification to unicast

    - Achieves greater throughput

    - AP CPU cycles available for other tasks

- **Admission control:**

    - Implicit admission control with IGMP snooping

    - Radio bandwidth and channel utilization based

    - Integration with Voice CAC

- **Auto QoS:**

    - Reduces Ethernet overrun for 802.11n APs

    - Reduces the probability of drop for high-priority video frames

    - Provides a much better end user experience for multimedia

- **Real-time SAP/SDP denial message: Immediate feedback to client**

Figure 9-15 indicates the steps of VideoStream. After the WLC and AP determine there is enough available resources, the forwarding module on the AP will unicast the stream to the client.

The benefits of VideoStream on the WLC can be summarized with the following points:

- Transmissions adapt to the individual client data rate.

- Reliable retransmission minimizes loss.

- Ensures QoS priority and quality.

- Configurable and manageable bandwidth usage.

- Coexistence with voice.

- Fast and efficient video packet copying.

- Pushing multicast replication out to the very edge of the network reduces the amount of traffic that flows over the wired network.

■ Because unicast requires an ACK from each client, multicast direct makes intelligent decisions about where video shouldn't go to conserve bandwidth.

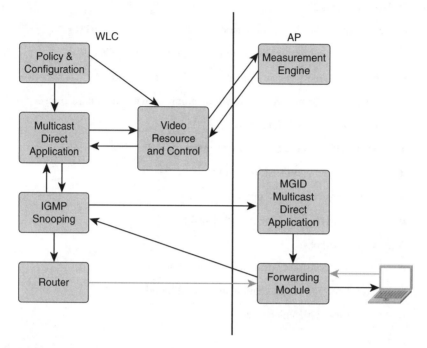

Figure 9-15   *VideoStream Process Flow*

Configuring VideoStream on the WLC

The configuration of VideoStream in the WLC release 7.0.98 is done through the graphical user interface (GUI).

Because VideoStream is going to use statistics and information from the APs and the WLCs, you need to ensure that CAC is reconfigured for "load-based" so that you don't allow multicast joins that might starve voice clients as well as those clients already participating in a multicast session.

Now that you have enabled VideoStream, you will now use the WLC GUI to configure a video stream, the multicast group that you will mark for priority, and any required policies.

From the Wireless menu, you will see a new option called Media Stream. The setup in Figure 9-16 configures the name VideoLan with the appropriate multicast start and ending IP addresses and also configures the Resource Reservation Controls for the appropriate parameters for that session. You can configure the following:

■ Priority from 1 to 8, which in this case is 1 (the lowest priority given)

■ Violation threshold (best-effort or drop), which allows the stream to continue if there is just enough bandwidth or to drop the stream if there isn't

■ Admit or deny the policy

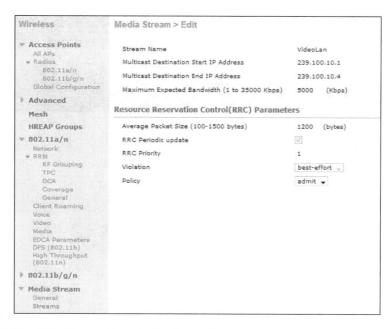

Figure 9-16 *VideoStream Sample Configuration*

In the case of the start and ending IP address, this will correspond to the multicast group stream address range for the source of the video.

After the stream has been defined, you need to configure the media stream QoS parameters on both 802.11a/n as well as 802.11b/g/n, as shown in Figure 9-17. It is here that you need to pay special attention to the amount of bandwidth that you will give to each radio for video traffic. The maximum bandwidth cannot exceed the cumulative bandwidth provided to your voice traffic and video traffic, which is set to 85 percent. You will need to determine, based on your applications, the amount of RF bandwidth you will provision to each service. The configuration shown in Figure 9-18 gives 50 percent CAC to the voice traffic and 35 percent CAC to the video traffic. Information gathered from the AP based on clients connected, the services that are requested, and radio measurements will determine whether a call or another video stream can be made.

At this point, you need to configure the WLAN on which you want to provide VideoStream services. In this case, you simply select the check box under the QoS parameters for your WLAN, as illustrated in Figure 9-19.

At this point, the VideoStream configuration is complete. Multicast traffic will now be unicast only to clients that have joined the configured multicast group. Corresponding MGIDs will be created based on the VLAN, and if the session is properly using VideoStream, the client session will show up under the L3 multicast group mappings with a Multicast Direct status as enabled. If the client is joined to a multicast group that doesn't have a corresponding WLAN with VideoStream enabled, the session will show as Normal status. Figure 9-20 through 9-22 show the output values of the MGIDs and multicast status.

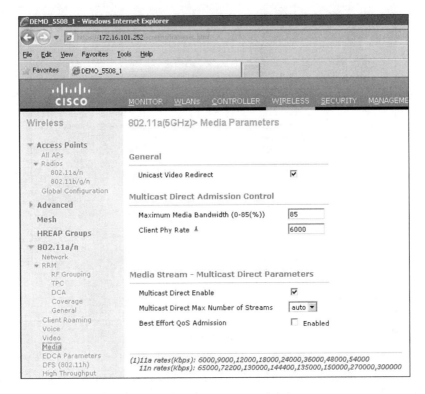

Figure 9-17   *Voice and Video CAC Configuration*

Figure 9-18   *Media Stream Configuration*

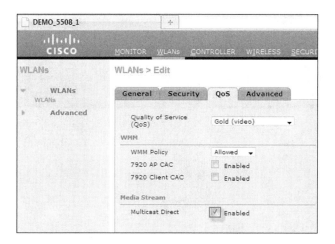

Figure 9-19   *Enabling VideoStream on a WLAN*

Additional Design Recommendations

With any design, you will always want to follow the documented best practices; with multicast, there is no exception. If you do not understand the design constraints or pitfalls of both the wired and wireless multicast implementations, your network might not work or worse yet will cause other issues that are unforeseen. Multicast enablement on the CUWN is no exception. The following sections attempt to identify issues or concerns that you might encounter and address them with best practices.

Wireless Multicast Roaming

A major challenge for a multicast client in a wireless environment is maintaining its multicast group membership when moving about the WLAN. Drops in the wireless connection moving from AP to AP can cause a disruption in a client's multicast session. Knowing what you learned about IGMP earlier, you know that it plays an important role in the maintenance of dynamic group membership information across the WLC.

In a Layer 2 roaming situation, sessions are maintained simply because the foreign AP (the AP the client has roamed to), if configured properly, already belongs to the multicast group, and traffic is not tunneled to a different anchor point on the network. In a Layer 3 roaming environment (L2 WLC with WLANs on different VLANs) where the client is roaming, IGMP messages sent from wireless clients might be affected because the default mobility tunneling mode on a WLC prior to 5.2 is asymmetrical. See the "Cisco Unified Wireless Technology and Architecture" section of the "Enterprise Mobility 4.1 Design Guide" for further clarification on L2 and L3 mobility tunneling: http://tinyurl.com/ybgkd3y.

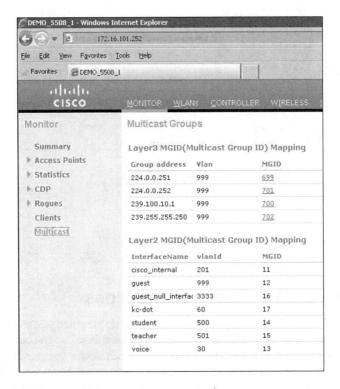

Figure 9-20   *MGIDs*

Figure 9-21   *Multicast-Direct*

As a result of asymmetrical tunneling, the return traffic to the client is sent to the anchor WLC and then forwarded to the foreign WLC, where the associated client connection resides. Outbound packets are forwarded out the foreign WLC's interface.

In symmetrical mobility tunneling mode (introduced in 5.2 and default in 6.0 and later), both inbound and outbound traffic is tunneled to the anchor controller. See the "Cisco Unified Wireless Technology and Architecture" section of the "Enterprise Mobility 4.1 Design Guide" for further clarification: http://tinyurl.com/ybgkd3y.

Symmetric Mobility Tunneling mode should be used in all cases because this allows you to enable security best-practice features like Unicast-RPF.

Figure 9-22 *Normal Multicast*

Wireless CAPWAP Fragmentation

When a WLC receives a multicast packet, it encapsulates it inside of CAPWAP using the CAPWAP multicast group as a destination address and forwards it to the APs through the management interface (source address). If the packet exceeds the maximum transmission unit (MTU) of the link, the WLC fragments the packet and sends out both packets to the CAPWAP multicast group. If another WLC were to receive this CAPWAP-encapsulated multicast packet through the wired network, it would reencapsulate it, treating it as a normal multicast packet and forwarding it to its APs.

Two methods can be applied to prevent this from happening:

■ You can assign all WLCs to the same CAPWAP multicast group address.

■ You can configure each WLC with its own multicast group address and then apply standard multicast filtering techniques to ensure that CAPWAP-encapsulated multicast packets do not reach any other controller.

Table 9-3 lists the pros and cons of these two techniques.

Table 9-3 *Pros and Cons of Using the Same Multicast Group or Different Groups*

	Pros	Cons
All WLCs have the same CAPWAP multicast group address.	No need to take any additional fragmentation-protection measures.	Each WLC's multicast traffic is flooded throughout the network (APs will drop multicast packets that don't have a source IP address equal to their WLC management interface).
All WLCs have an individual multicast group address, and standard multicast techniques are used to block CAPWAP multicast fragments.	Can use a range of addresses, thus preventing flooding throughout the network.	ACL filtering must be applied on the first-hop router on all VLANs configured on the multicast-enabled WLC.

All WLCs Have the Same CAPWAP Multicast Group Address

To prevent the second WLC from retransmitting these CAPWAP-encapsulated packets, the WLC blocks incoming multicast packets to the CAPWAP multicast group and the CAPWAP-reserved ports. By blocking the reserved ports, the WLC blocks the first part of a fragmented packet in an encapsulated CAPWAP multicast packet. However, the second packet does not contain port numbers and can only be blocked by filtering it on the multicast group address (destination address). The WLC blocks any packets where the destination address is equal to the CAPWAP multicast group address assigned to the WLC.

However, assigning every WLC to the same CAPWAP multicast group creates other problems. IGMP versions 1 and 2 used by the APs to join the CAPWAP multicast group use Any Source Multicast (ASM), and the APs will receive multicast traffic from all sources of the multicast group in the network. This means that the APs will receive multicast packets from all controllers on the network if the WLCs are configured with the same multicast group address, and no multicast boundaries have been applied. One WLC's multicast traffic will flood out to all the APs across the network, and every AP receives (and drops it if the source address is not equal to its WLC's management address) the multicast traffic that is being received from any wireless multicast client in the entire network.

The right choice of implementation is going to depend on the size of your network, the number of clients, and the amount of multicast traffic traversing the WLCs. The current recommendation is to define a unique multicast group address per WLC in the mobility domain because this limits the amount of traffic that has to be sent to each WLC in the network.

WLC Placement

This section looks at two different deployments (distributed and centralized) and describes how they impact roaming with multicast clients. In a centralized deployment, WLC WLAN interfaces are attached to the same VLANs/subnets; the multicast stream is uninterrupted when a multicast client roams from APs on one controller to an AP on another controller. The centralized deployment creates a flat client multicast network. Centralized WLCs do not affect multicast roaming because after the multicast stream is requested from a single multicast client on a WLAN, it streams out all APs on that WLAN, on all radios (802.11g and 802.11a), on all WLCs, even if that AP WLAN has no clients associated requesting the multicast traffic. If you have more than one WLAN associated to the VLAN, the AP transmits the multicast packet over each WLAN. Both the unicast-mode CAPWAP packet and the multicast-mode CAPWAP packet contain a WLAN bitmap that tells the receiving AP over which WLAN it must forward the packet.

The distributed deployment does not have this problem because while the WLANs are the same, the WLCs are attached to different VLANs. This means that when the multicast client roams to a new WLC, the WLC will first query the client for its multicast group memberships. At this point, the client responds with its group membership report, and the WLC forwards this message to the appropriate multicast group address through the VLAN associated with its local VLAN. This allows the client to resume its multicast session through the foreign WLC.

The distributed deployment reduces the amount of multicast traffic on the APs because, although the WLAN SSIDs are the same, the WLCs are attached to different VLANs. WLAN multicast traffic depends on a client request on the VLAN of that WLC. Table 9-4 lists the advantages and disadvantages of distributed and centralized deployments.

Table 9-4 *Pros and Cons of Centralized WLCs and Distributed WLCs*

	Pros	Cons
All centralized WLCs connected to the same VLANs (subnets)	Multicast traffic started on any client VLAN will be transmitted to all APs, so clients roaming to any AP will receive a multicast stream.	If only one client requests multicast traffic, all APs attached to all WLCs will receive the stream and transmit it if they have any clients associated, even if those clients did not request the multicast stream.
Distributed WLCs on different VLANs and subnet	Multicast streams are isolated to APs attached to a WLC.	Possible client disruptions caused by multicast stream establishments after client roam.

In case of L3 roaming, you can see that the multicast stream could be dropped or disrupted. This is because the multicast router could possibly drop the IGMP response packet from the clients because those packets are coming from an interface that is in a different subnet than the originating address of the client. To solve this problem, the IGMP responses from the clients by the controller and the source IP address are changed to the dynamic interface of the controller where the client has joined. The upstream network switch receives the IGMP response message from the WLC of the client. If any packet with this multicast address reaches the network switch from anywhere, the network forwards the multicast stream to the foreign WLC and the foreign WLC forwards the packet to the clients.

Summary

As you have learned, Cisco has really changed the way you can approach implementing multicast solutions across your wireless infrastructure. John Chambers wasn't misquoted when he stated "Who would have thought a decade ago that Cisco would be here talking about consumer products and video?" The evolution of multicast on the wired network has now made its way into the 802.11 world by the implementation of key features such as VideoStream.

You should have learned that Cisco provides many key features, such as IGMP, PIM routing, and multicast, in the IOS-based routing and switching platforms that will allow you to build a robust and secure multicast network. It is those principal features found in Cisco IOS Software that have been ported over to the CUWN. You demand features to support critical business solutions, and VideoStream is one feature that will allow you to do just that.

Throughout this book, you should have become familiar with the fundamentals of controller-based networks and the features that will allow you to design, implement, and support your wireless requirements.

Index

U

V

W

cisco

ciscopress.com: Your Cisco Certification and Networking Learning Resource

Subscribe to the monthly Cisco Press newsletter to be the first to learn about new releases and special promotions.

Visit **ciscopress.com/newsletters.**

While you are visiting, check out the offerings available at your finger tips.

–Free Podcasts from experts:
- OnNetworking
- OnCertification
- OnSecurity

Podcasts

View them at **ciscopress.com/podcasts.**

–Read the latest author **articles** and **sample chapters** at ciscopress.com/articles.

–Bookmark the Certification Reference Guide available through our partner site at **informit.com/certguide.**

Connect with Cisco Press authors and editors via Facebook and Twitter, visit **informit.com/socialconnect.**

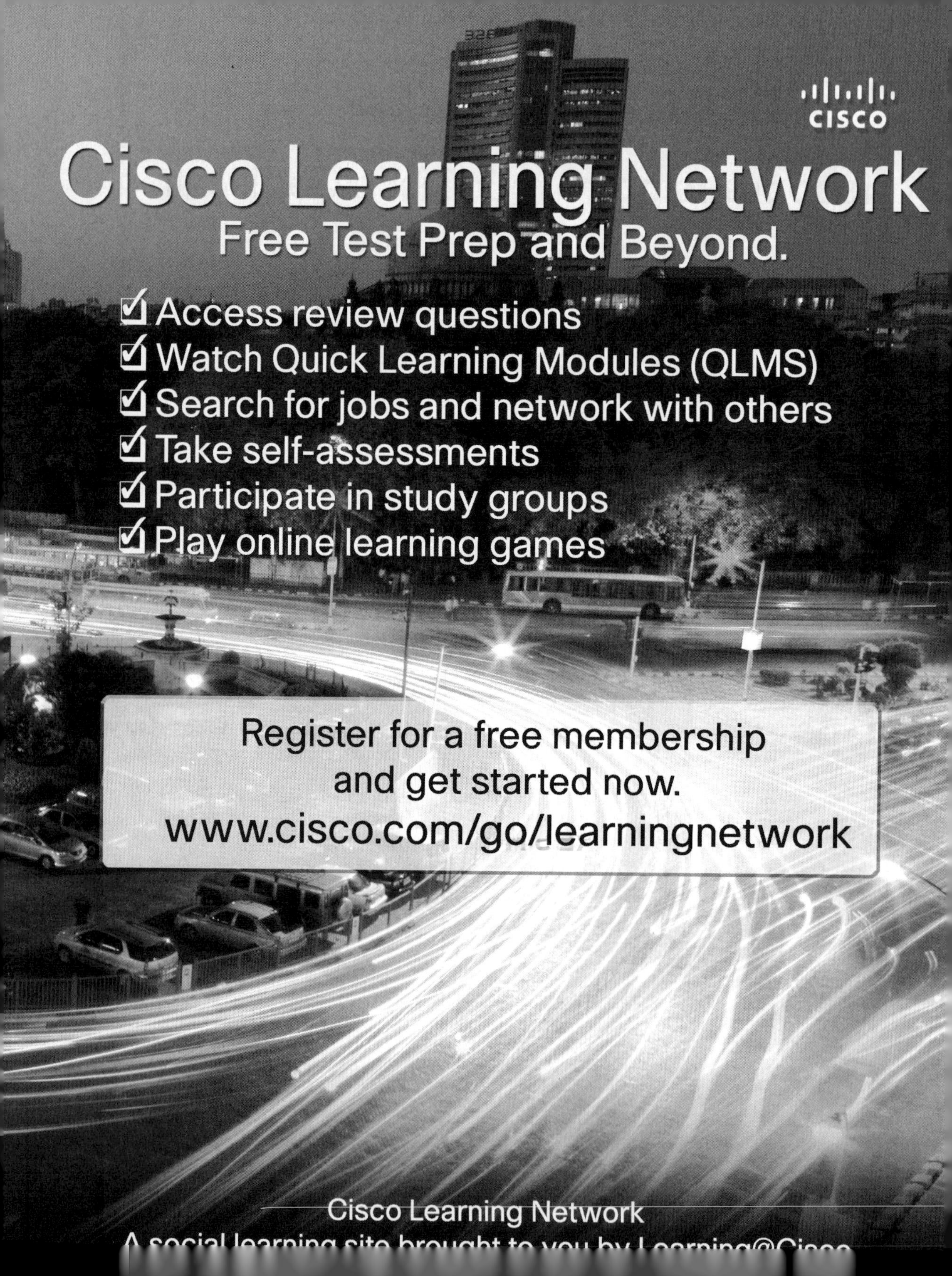
CISCO
Cisco Learning Network
Free Test Prep and Beyond.
☑ Access review questions
☑ Watch Quick Learning Modules (QLMS)
☑ Search for jobs and network with others
☑ Take self-assessments
☑ Participate in study groups
☑ Play online learning games
Register for a free membership
and get started now.
www.cisco.com/go/learningnetwork
Cisco Learning Network

 FREE Online Edition

Your purchase of **Controller-Based Wireless LAN Fundamentals** includes access to a free online edition for 45 days through the Safari Books Online subscription service. Nearly every Cisco Press book is available online through Safari Books Online, along with more than 5,000 other technical books and videos from publishers such as Addison-Wesley Professional, Exam Cram, IBM Press, O'Reilly, Prentice Hall, Que, and Sams.

SAFARI BOOKS ONLINE allows you to search for a specific answer, cut and paste code, download chapters, and stay current with emerging technologies.

Activate your FREE Online Edition at
www.informit.com/safarifree

R.C.L.

AVR. 2011

G

> **STEP 1:** Enter the coupon code ▓▓▓▓▓▓

> **STEP 2:** New Safari users, complete the brief registration form.
> Safari subscribers, just log in.

If you have difficulty registering on Safari or accessing the online edition, please e-mail customer-service@safaribooksonline.com

  Addison Wesley Adobe Press   ALPHA Cisco Press   Press IBM Press   lynda.com Microsoft Press New Riders

O'REILLY   Peachpit Press   PRENTICE HALL que   Redbooks sAMS SAS Publishing   Sun microsystems   WILEY